# Unheeded Hinterland

This book presents a comprehensive account of the debates on sovereignty, self-determination and nationalist upsurges in India's Northeast, especially Assam. At a deeper level, it analyses how multi-ethnic societies engage with the nation-state. Based on the framework of international relations and regional geo-politics, the volume locates internal tensions and contradictions among different ethnic groups, alongside the complex interrelationships between the Centre and the region. It also proposes a new structure of 'Common Ethnic House' to resolve persistent inter-ethnic tensions among different communities and the impasse between the Northeast and the Centre.

This book will interest scholars and researchers of politics and international relations, sociology and social anthropology, area studies, peace and conflict studies, especially those concerned with South Asia and Northeast India.

**Dilip Gogoi** is Assistant Professor at the Department of Political Science and teaches International Politics and Human Rights at Cotton College, Cotton College State University, Guwahati, Assam, India. An alumnus of Jawaharlal Nehru University, New Delhi, Gogoi has edited *Beyond Borders: Look East Policy and Northeast India* (2010), co-edited *Shifting Terrain: Conflict Dynamics in Northeast India* (2012) and *Marginal Frontier: Select Essays on Northeast India* (2012). His research interests span Northeast India and transnational relations.

# Unheeded Hinterland
Identity and sovereignty
in Northeast India

Edited by Dilip Gogoi

NEW DELHI LONDON NEW YORK

First published 2016
by Routledge
2 Park Square, Milton Park, Abingdon, Oxon OX14 4RN

and by Routledge
711 Third Avenue, New York, NY 10017

*Routledge is an imprint of the Taylor & Francis Group, an informa business*

© 2016 Dilip Gogoi

The right of Dilip Gogoi to be identified as the author of the editorial material, and of the authors for their individual chapters, has been asserted in accordance with sections 77 and 78 of the Copyright, Designs and Patents Act 1988.

All rights reserved. No part of this book may be reprinted or reproduced or utilised in any form or by any electronic, mechanical, or other means, now known or hereafter invented, including photocopying and recording, or in any information storage or retrieval system, without permission in writing from the publishers.

*Trademark notice*: Product or corporate names may be trademarks or registered trademarks, and are used only for identification and explanation without intent to infringe.

*British Library Cataloguing-in-Publication Data*
A catalogue record for this book is available from the British Library.

*Library of Congress Cataloging-in-Publication Data*
A catalog record has been requested for this book.

ISBN: 978-1-138-10009-1 (hbk)
ISBN: 978-1-315-65782-0 (ebk)

Typeset in Galliard
by Apex CoVantage, LLC

In memory of innocent civilians who lost their lives in atrocities in the turbulent days of Northeast India

# Contents

| | |
|---|---|
| *Contributors* | x |
| *Acknowledgements* | xi |
| *List of abbreviations* | xii |

**PART I**
**Locating the problem** — 1

**1 Sovereignty and national identity: the troubled trajectory in Northeast India** — 3
DILIP GOGOI

**PART II**
**Situating the debate: interface of sovereignty and self-determination** — 15

**2 Sovereignty at the frontiers: contests and contradictions** — 17
ÅSHILD KOLÅS

**3 Self-determination, multi-ethnic state and quest for Assamese nationhood** — 30
RUBUL PATGIRI

**4 *Sarbabhoumo Asom*: three public discourses** — 49
UDDIPAN DUTTA

viii  *Contents*

5  *Swadhin Asom*: contesting territories and linkages 70
SHUBHRAJEET KONWER

PART III
Migration, contested citizenship and the identity 87

6  Immigration, indigeneity and identity: the
Bangladeshi immigration question in Assam 89
CHANDAN KUMAR SHARMA

7  The state and the migrants: contextualising
the citizenship debate in Assam 114
RUMI ROY

PART IV
National consciousness: the role of students
and literary bodies 131

8  Identity consciousness and students'
movement: the role of AASU 133
PROTIM SHARMA

9  Assamese identity and the ethnic dissent:
*Asom Sahitya Sabha* at the crossroads 144
IVY DHAR

PART V
Civil society, Indian state and conflict resolution 163

10  Between state and the insurgents: violation
of human rights in Assam 165
DILIP GOGOI AND UDDIPAN DUTTA

11  The ULFA and Indian state: role of
civil society in conflict resolution 186
AKHIL RANJAN DUTTA

*Contents* ix

**12 Accommodating differences: the Indian democracy and Assamese nationalism** 209

RUBI DEVI

**13 Postscript: ending the impasse and reintegrating Northeast India** 227

DILIP GOGOI

*Glossary* 245
*Index* 247

# Contributors

**Rubi Devi** is Research Scholar at the Department of Political Science, International Development & International Affairs, University of Southern Mississippi, USA.

**Ivy Dhar** is Assistant Professor at the School of Development Studies, Ambedkar University Delhi, India.

**Akhil Ranjan Dutta** is Professor of Political Science at Gauhati University, Guwahati, Assam, India.

**Uddipan Dutta** is Research Associate at OKD Institute of Social Change and Development, Guwahati, Assam, India.

**Dilip Gogoi** is Assistant Professor at the Department of Political Science and teaches International Politics and Human Rights at Cotton College, Cotton College State University, Guwahati, Assam, India.

**Åshild Kolås** is Research Professor at the Peace Research Institute, Oslo (PRIO), Norway.

**Shubhrajeet Konwer** is Assistant Professor in Political Science at Gauhati University, Guwahati, Assam, India.

**Rubul Patgiri** is Associate Professor in Political Science at Dibrugarh University, Dibrugarh, Assam, India.

**Rumi Roy** is Research Scholar at the Centre for Political Studies, Jawaharlal Nehru University, New Delhi, India.

**Chandan Kumar Sharma** is Professor of Sociology at Tezpur University, Tezpur, Assam, India.

**Protim Sharma** is Associate Professor in English at Dikhowmukh College, Sivasagar, Assam, India.

# Acknowledgements

In bringing out this work I sincerely express my gratitude and appreciation to all the contributors for their well-researched papers which have made this volume possible. I would like to thank Shoma Choudhury for taking interest to publish the book on behalf of Routledge and providing critical boost to the volume with important inputs as per the review reports of the draft manuscript. I express my sincere thanks to the Routledge team, especially Rimina Mohapatra and Denise File, for bringing out the volume. I also wish to acknowledge Nilanjan Sarkar with whom the idea of this project was initiated. My heartfelt thanks go to Jaideep Saikia, security analyst, Guwahati, Professor Niru Hazarika, Professor Nani Gopal Mahanta, Gauhati University and Dr Pahi Saikia, IIT, Guwahati, for their valuable suggestions on the issues of nationality and question of sovereignty in Assam. I am grateful to my colleagues at the Department of Political Science, Cotton College, for their constant support and encouragement. I take this opportunity to record my appreciation and gratitude to my family members for being the constant support in my endeavours. Finally I thank my friend and colleague Dr Sanghamitra Sadhu for her critical insights and suggestions in the making of this volume.

# Abbreviations

| | |
|---|---|
| AAGSP | All Assam Gana Sangram Parishad |
| AAMSU | All Assam Minority Students' Union |
| AASU | All Assam Students' Union |
| ABSU | All Bodo Students' Union |
| ADF | Arunachal Dragon Force |
| AFSPA | Armed Forces Special Powers Act |
| AGP | Asom Gana Parishad |
| AIUDF | All India United Democratic Front |
| AJYCP | Asom Jatiyatabadi Yuba Chatra Parishad |
| APHLC | All Party Hill Leaders Conference |
| ASDC | Autonomous State Demand Committee |
| ASS | Assam Sahitya Sabha |
| ASTC | Assam State Transport Corporation |
| BJP | Bharatiya Janata Party |
| BLT | Bodoland Liberation Tigers |
| BRO | Border Roads Organisation |
| BSS | Bodo Sahitya Sabha |
| BTAD | Bodoland Territorial Area District |
| CRPF | Central Reserve Police Force |
| DGFI | Directorate General of Forces Intelligence |
| DHD | Dima Halim Daoga |
| EC | Election Commission |
| GOA | Government of Assam |
| GoI | Government of India |
| HC | High Court |
| IM(DT) | Illegal Migrants (Determination by Tribunals) Act |
| INC | Indian National Congress |
| INGOs | international non-governmental organisations |
| ISI | Inter-Services Intelligence |
| KIA | Kachin Independence Army |

*Abbreviations*   xiii

| | |
|---|---|
| KLNLF | Karbi Longri North Cachar Hills Liberation Front |
| KLO | Kamatapur Liberation Organization |
| NCERT | National Council of Educational Research and Training |
| NDA | National Democratic Alliance |
| NDFB | National Democratic Front of Bodoland |
| NEFA | North East Frontier Agency |
| NNC | Naga National Council |
| NRC | National Register of Citizens |
| NSA | National Security Act |
| NSCN(I-M) | National Socialist Council of Nagaland(Isak-Muivah) |
| NSCN(K) | National Socialist Council of Nagaland(Khaplang) |
| ONGC | Oil and Natural Gas Corporation Limited |
| PCG | People's Consultative Group |
| PIP | Prevention of infiltration into India of Pakistani Nationals |
| PLA | People's Liberation Army |
| PSU | public sector undertakings |
| RAW | Research and Analysis Wing |
| RPF | Revolutionary People's Front |
| SCI | Supreme Court of India |
| SJA | Sanmilita Jatiya Abhibartan |
| SULFA | Surrendered United Liberation Front of Assam |
| TADA | Terrorist and Disruptive Activities (Prevention) Act |
| ULFA | United Liberation Front of Assam |
| UN | United Nations |
| UNLF | United National Liberation Front |
| UNPFII | United Nations Permanent Forum on Indigenous Issues |
| UPDS | United People's Democratic Solidarity |
| URMCA | United Revolutionary Movement Council of Assam |

# Part I
# Locating the problem

# 1 Sovereignty and national identity

## The troubled trajectory in Northeast India

*Dilip Gogoi*

The post-colonial Northeast India represents a land of *claimed* multiple sovereignties. With fractured histories, multiplicity of ethnicities and peculiar geographical location, the region has been grappling with multiple political crises – from ethno-nationalism to the demand for territorial sovereign homeland. The protracted history of exploitation, denial of rights of self-determination and systemic discrimination against the ethnic communities living in the region by both the British India and the postcolonial state, coupled with a primordial ethnic consciousness, have encouraged separatist sentiments and movements, leading to variety of violent radical liberation movements headed by groups like National Socialist Council of Nagaland (NSCN) for independent 'Nagalim', United Liberation Front of Assam (ULFA) for 'sovereign Assam', National Democratic Front of Bodoland (NDFB) for 'independent Bodoland' and others in India's Northeast.[1] This development exposes that there is a disengagement between the Indian nation-state and ethnic people living in the peripheral borderlands. This dichotomy has brought severe disenchantment among the people of periphery, thereby subsequently giving birth to several independent armed groups as well as popular protest movements directed against the Centre. The radical groups are extremely uncomfortable with the idea of India as the nation-state and are constantly resisting the Indian civic nationalism[2] by espousing ethnic nationalism.[3] In fact they believe that India is a multinational state and every nationality has the right to decide their own destiny through exercising the principle of self-determination. This contradiction between Indian civic nationalism (political nationalism) and ethnic nationalism remains perennially unresolved in the region with ample scope for the rise of sovereignty-based ethno-nationalists' armed movements. Notably, the sovereignty-based armed movements across the world witness some disturbing trends: the past evidence suggests that conflicts are exceedingly difficult to resolve, second, these types of conflict frequently give rise to terrorism; third, they often involve massive

4   *Dilip Gogoi*

human rights violations and finally, the existing international legal norms and principles are often practically less relevant for resolving these conflicts (Williams and Pecci 2004:1–3). These trends are equally reflected in the ethno-political crises afflicting the present Northeast India.

*Unheeded Hinterland* tries to reflect on the interconnectivity of national identity and sovereignty with a historical perspective and its subsequent implications for modern nation-state, especially in the context of post-colonial states to understand the present problem of sovereign ethnic homeland question, particularly in the backdrop of the ULFA's radical armed movement for 'sovereign Assam'.

## Sovereignty and national identity

Sovereignty – *the supreme authority within a territory* – which is a common notion of political authority in modern times has been inherited from the Treaty of Westphalia in 1648 which concluded among the European powers to end the Thirty Years' War (1618–48). Under the Westphalian system, an ultimate authority was established within the territorial limits of the state and sovereign authority was exercised by an absolute monarch with divine rights to rule its subjects rather than political community within the state. In Westphalian sense, the citizenship fundamentally consisted of subjecthood, defined by the territory of the state. Under the divine rule, the monarch was empowered to exercise its authority within the territory by confirming his religion as the religion of the state. Thus, Westphalian peace treaty had brought substantial changes in the political system and provided the ground for emergence of the territorial states in Europe. In fact the national identity had no space to express its collective will and was subservient to the state and to the monarch who ruled on the basis of divine rights. However, the rise of nationalism in the West along with the American and French Revolutions in late eighteenth century had galvanised the national consciousness which subsequently redefined the relationship between nationalism and the absolutist state[4] drastically. It also signified the end of the feudal absolutist state and rise of modern European nation-state through the articulation and exercise of popular sovereignty[5] by the respective national groups. Consequently, the authority of the state radically shifted from the single absolutist monarch to the collective will of the people. Earlier the sovereignty of the state was inherently linked with the monarch with the territory being under his control. Under the absolute state system, people within the territory were treated as subjects, subservient to the monarch. With the emergence of the nation-state, people and territory were increasingly linked with the nation in Europe. Hobsbawm, who defines nationalism as 'invention of tradition', observes, 'Each people

*Sovereignty and national identity* 5

is independent and sovereign, whatever the number of individuals who compose it and the extent of the territory it occupies. This sovereignty is inalienable', and 'the equation nation-state-people, and especially sovereign people, undoubtedly linked nation to territory, since the structure and definition of states were now essentially territorial' (Hobsbawm 1990:19). Thus, nationalism binds the people, territory and sovereignty of state together by national identity within the framework of nation-state. Therefore, the creation of national identity was vital to realise popular sovereignty, belonging to all and exercised by the citizens within the collectivity. As popular democracy became the ultimate form of governance, national identity through the idea of nation assumed more significant role in European nation-state system in collectivising sovereign will and upholding the rights of the national people. As a result, feudal Europe was disintegrated completely and replaced by modern nation-states with 'national' idioms and symbols such as national flag, national army, national borders, national currency etc. The national identity and nationalism gave a degree of permanence to the European nation-state system. However, this experiment did not succeed outside Europe especially in the eighteenth- and nineteenth-century colonial world, although European colonial powers introduced an expanded definition of 'national identity' to include their colonies through the imperialist agenda by maintaining loyalty and allegiance from the occupied colonies. On the other hand, colonies had also developed a sense of unified identity despite the deep-rooted racial, linguistic, cultural, religious, ethnic differences to stage a freedom struggle under the common nationalist leadership against the rule of colonial powers. The unified identity assumed significance as national identity in course of the independence struggle as the nationalist leaders successfully established a link between the territory and sovereign right of the oppressed people through the 'imagined' (Anderson 1983) or 'invented' (Gellner 1983) nation. In fact, the very concept of nation-state, which primarily originated from the Europe, came to occupy the imagination of the colonial world in the form of 'derivative discourse' (Chatterjee 1986). Partha Chatterjee in his *Nation and Its Fragments* further observes two aspects of nationalism which shaped nationalist discourse, i.e. material (which replicates the statecraft, economy and technology of the West) and spiritual (which espouses the inner sphere as bearer of cultural identity) in the context of anti-colonial nationalism with reference to Asia and Africa. This was a significant development in the world of sovereign nation-state system in the non-Western world. But the problem remains once the post-colonial nation-states increasingly decided to pursue the nation-building process through constructing single national identity with majoritarian principle with the over-centralisation of the bureaucracy and monopolisation of the national resources. This affected the rights of the minorities of ethnic and other cultural groups causing

## 6 *Dilip Gogoi*

widespread dissatisfactions among the intelligentsia of victim nationalities with an upsurge of a host of sovereignty-based self-determination movements in the line of renewed national identities across the post-colonial world. Thus, the practice of the European nation-state system, which was highly successful in relatively homogenous societies, has been challenged by most of the post-colonial heterogeneous societies, questioning its relevance and sustainability in the non-Western world. The armed insurrections for sovereign homeland in Northeast India, especially in the present-day Assam, could be seen through this inimitable prism of thought and realism.

### The unheeded hinterland and the essays

The *Unheeded Hinterland* is an attempt to explore many hidden issues grappling Northeast India with the prime focus on the present state of Assam and the Assamese nationality since its assertion as a distinct national identity. The book attempts to analyse the complexities engulfing the Assamese nationality from a theoretical and an empirical perspective. The ULFA's endeavour to establish a sovereign Assam, or *Swadhin Asom*, has not only led it to wage war against the Indian nation-state but also brought to the fore the question of sovereignty as an issue being projected as a binary concept: either one is for sovereignty or against it. However, apart from a few stray, isolated attempts, the question of sovereignty and self-determination – as envisaged by the ULFA – has not been elevated to the status of an academic debate.[6] To that end, questions arise such as: How has Assamese national identity and nationalism originated? Why does it contest with Indian nationalism? Has the idea of *Swadhin Asom* emerged out of such contestation? What is the basis of such claim and implications for a multi-ethnic state like Assam? Is such claim legitimate as per the principle of self-determination and also relevant in the changing context of sovereignty? How are public discourses on sovereignty formed? What are the geo-political realities of such claims? What are the implications and possible conflict resolution of such demands, especially in the context of a nation-state such as India?

However, the interest to bring together a group of scholars to examine the issues of national identity, self-determination and question of sovereignty in Northeast India with a special focus on Assam arose in my mind for a variety of reasons, some of which emerged as a result of my personal observations, some as a result of a continual academic interaction with the realisation that the hinterland in which we live and work is an unheeded constituency. But, has the Indian nation-state heeded the cry of her hinterland? This question is subjected to the deeper scrutiny. The volume argues that challenges to the Indian nation-state from Assam and the Northeast primarily came out of the continuation of the same colonial

*Sovereignty and national identity* 7

legacies, a form of 'colonial constitutionalism' (Baruah 2010) maintained by the Centre. The question of sovereignty and the upsurge of nationalist movement which has characterised the situation in Assam are a direct result of exploitation and domination of colonial in form and nature. Unless properly addressed, under such circumstances, identity politics and multiple nationalisms are more likely to be manifested in the region with proliferation of newer challenges. As ethnic identity is a collective cultural identity, it has the potential to take the shape of political nationalism. As Plamenatz argues, nationalism is primarily a cultural phenomenon, which often takes a political form (Plamenatz 1976). In this context, it has to be reckoned how ethnic identity transforms into a violent nationalist upsurge in Assam. These crucial and contentious questions are analysed to understand the ongoing complexities of Assam. It is pertinent to note that historically Assamese nationalism, which is primarily an ethnic nationalism, bonded by common language and common inheritance, predates to the Indian civic nationalism (formed after the formation of independent India as territorial political community). However, the Assamese nationalism has never been evoked so strongly during the time of India's Independence as it happened in the 1980s. It cannot be denied that the armed organisations like the ULFA in Assam and others in the rest of the north-eastern states have been able to highlight the fault lines of Indian nation-state in ways more than one.

The *Unheeded Hinterland* focuses on the emerging state–society conflict dynamics primarily concerning Assam in the north-eastern region of India with a conceptual view point on the issue of nationality and sovereignty that grapples the region over the decades in the introductory part of the volume. In the second part of the book, *Situating the Debate: Interface of Sovereignty and Self-determination*, Åshild Kolås explains the changing contours of sovereignty and contemporary practices from the perspective of theoretical traditions. She argues that the sovereign state is increasingly being challenged by the non-state actors vying for secession, autonomy or self-government. At the same time, the notion of sovereignty has been undergoing a major transformation at the aegis of globalisation. Drawing inference from case studies in other parts of the world, she argues, the old notion of sovereign state and practice of sovereignty is slowly getting disengaged and this development is equally reflective in the context of the sovereignty debate in Northeast India as the claimants and stakeholders have begun to look for alternatives to secession, including frameworks for non-territorial forms of self-rule. Reflecting the changing circumstances, Rubul Patgiri examines the contradictions and contestations revolving around the application of the principle of self-determination in a multi-ethnic state. He highlights the contradiction that while there has been increasing demands

## 8 Dilip Gogoi

for territorial form of sovereign rights and self-determination by social groups within state, on the other hand there has been equally strong resistance on the part of states and international community for such demands. Considering the changing realities and practices, the author tries to assess the legality and justifiability of self-determination claim for the people of Assam. He further observes that notwithstanding the various objections against the self-determination movement for Assam, any genuine attempt to resolve the current problem must address the outstanding grievances of people of Assam. Pushing the debate further, Uddipan Dutta elaborates on how public discourses play a very important role in shaping the nationalist upsurge in vernacular narratives. Earlier, the idea of independent India was crystallised with similar discourses with pan-Indian nationalism as the narrative of popular national consciousness. Serious challenges, however, came to this pan-Indian nationalist discourse in a form of armed insurrections from the Nagas, the Manipuris, the Mizos, the Sikhs, Kashmiris and of late a segment of the Assamese with an ideological mooring for a 'sovereign Assam'. Even though there are rich bodies of writings on the issue, the author has chosen three published texts in Assamese to represent the three distinct discourses on the issue of 'sovereign Assam'. The legitimacy of the issue of the sovereignty raised by ULFA is central to the radical nationalist discourse advocated by Parag Kumar Das through his writing *Swadhinatar Prastab*. Kanaksen Deka represents the constitutional status-quoist discourse, legitimises the rule of the Indian state and invalidates the claim of a sovereign Assam through his writing *ULFAr Swadhin Asom*. The discourse of radical federalist, initiated by Devabrata Sharma through his writing *Sarbabhoumo Asom Aru Anyanya Prasanga: Raktakta Der Dashakar Dalil*, questions the legitimacy of the Indian state as well as the claim of ULFA with a possible answer in the federal restructuring of India; however, the idea of a 'sovereign Assam' has not been discarded altogether. These viewpoints have quite often been debated in the public space of Assam, both oral and written, for resolving the nationality problem in Assam. Interrogating the basis of ULFA's claims for sovereign Assam, Shubhrajeet Konwer raises territorial dissonance of the ULFA's sovereign Assam and invalidates the idea as it is not feasible in a multi-ethnic Northeast India in the light of overlapping territorial claims and counterclaims by leading contending groups such as NSCN and NDFB in the region. He also emphasises the role of the extra-regional forces in destabilising the region which can further complicate the fragile peace process in the state.

Part three of the book explains the complexities arising out of immigration and its subsequent impact on identity consciousness and nationalist upsurge among the indigenous people of Assam under *Migration, Contested Citizenship and the Assamese Identity*. It questions the ambivalent

*Sovereignty and national identity* 9

role of the Indian state which is often held responsible for the crisis of Assamese nationality. The part comprising two chapters highlights the fallout of immigration in specific ways. Chandan Kumar Sharma traces the root causes of immigration from colonial East Bengal to present Bangladesh in post-colonial times and its consequences upon the indigenous identities. He stresses that despite available legal and constitutional instruments for solution, insincerity on the part of Indian state towards regulating the continuous influx of immigrants further complicates the problem affecting rights of the citizens, identity of the indigenous communities and sovereignty of the state. In consonance with the immigrant-induced complexities, Rumi Roy brings a new citizenship debate by highlighting the emerging politically contested notion of citizenship and practices in the state at the backdrop of controversial IM(DT) Act, 1983, introduced by the central government, made exclusively applicable only to Assam. She further explains that the state witnesses a new electoral politics revolving around the issue of citizenship in spite of the Supreme Court verdict scrapping the controversial act.

The fourth part of the book, *National Consciousness: The Role of Students and Literary Bodies*, traces a few aspects of regional histories to get an overview of the root of the nationalist consciousness under the aegis of the All Assam Students' Union (AASU) and the subsequent contestations with ethnic dissents, despite the *Asom Sahitya Sabha*'s effort to maintain composite Assamese identity. Protim Sharma gives an historical account by tracing the growth of Assamese nationalism and how national consciousness takes its root in the Assamese psyche in the later part of the nineteenth century under the leadership of emerging educated Assamese middle class in a background of an introduction of Bengali language over Assamese in the state by the British. The student community asserted against the move and tried to unite the people through espousing Assamese linguistic nationalism. Subsequently, the official language movement in 1960 and the medium of instruction movement in 1972 led by the students in later period saw the continuation of same nationalistic mindset. Large-scale migration in both pre- and post-independence India has also galvanised the Assamese nationalistic sentiment, which culminated in a six-year-long (1979 to 1985) anti-foreigners movement under the leadership of the AASU. In the second chapter of this part, Ivy Dhar reflects the Assamese identity assertion through the language politics of the *Asom Sahitya Sabha*, largely in post-independence period by highlighting how the dominance of the Sabha is threatened by the emerging divergent ethnic identities of Assam. It focuses on both the influence of the Sabha on the people and the State and the challenges that reduces its ambit of influence in recent times.

10   *Dilip Gogoi*

The final part of the book, *Civil Society, Indian State and Conflict Resolution*, goes back to the present problem of armed movement and explores how common people have become victims of an armed struggle, subjected to the gross violation of human rights at the hands of both state and non-state actors, and how civil society of Assam has reacted against the ongoing problem with its subsequent role as facilitator in the peace process between the Government of India and the ULFA. It also addresses the question whether Indian democracy can accommodate Assamese nationalism within a broader perspective of democracy. Dilip Gogoi and Uddipan Dutta trace the nature and intensity of human rights abuses by both the state actor and the non-state actors in the context of armed conflict between the state and the ULFA. The chapter questions the Indian state's role in counter-insurgency operations which can be held largely responsible for the extra-judicial killings, custodial and encounter deaths and other worst form of human rights abuses popularly known as secret killings. These violations are inflicted upon its own citizens, further alienating people of Assam from the mainstream. By imposing the coercive laws such as the Armed Forces Special Powers Act (AFSPA), the National Security Act and TADA in the name of national security and counter-insurgency operations, the Indian state has violated not only domestic constitutional rights but also international human rights norms. The chapter also highlights the various forms of human rights abuses by the insurgents and observes that the state can't abdicate its responsibility to protect the rights of the people in any circumstances. The primary responsibility of the state is to protect the people from any form of human rights abuses which has not been realised in insurgency-affected Northeast. Reflecting the importance of the civil society in resolving armed conflict, Ahkil Ranjan Dutta traces the evolution of the civil society in the context of Assam and highlights its subsequent role towards conflict resolution. Dutta argues that ethnically divided Assam has both ethnically defined civil societies and a trans-ethnic civil society. Historically, the civil societies in Assam evolved in the domain of literature and education, and not in the economic domain to counterpose the state as is the case with the Western countries. The civil society in Assam at most instances has been overtaken by collective passion, and therefore, it has not been a domain of free exchange of ideas and critical thinking at many instances. However, Dutta states that in the last three decades, the civil society in Assam has undergone different experiences and has actively engaged as a broker of peace between insurgent groups and Government of India in various phases of peacemaking and peace-building efforts in Assam. Keeping in mind the possibility of accommodating Assamese nationalism within the broader framework of Indian democracy, Rubi Devi draws theoretical understanding of developing democracy and ethnic nationalism in her

*Sovereignty and national identity* 11

chapter to find a logical path towards resolving the ongoing multiple crises in Assam – a state where Assamese identity has been disintegrating on the basis of ethnic divisions and loyalties with more violent inter-group competitions for exclusive ethnic territory and even sovereign homeland demands. On such reflections the concluding chapter of the volume, authored by Dilip Gogoi, offers an alternative model of governance for the Northeast region through Common Ethnic House – a proposed inclusive institution organised on the principle of equal recognition of ethnic communities with a non-territorial arrangement within the broad framework of consociational democracy.[7] The chapter argues that group-specific piecemeal approach of the Indian state towards the crisis-ridden Northeast may engineer more conflicts instead of resolving the present crises. The primary reason of such apprehension is that the Northeast is ethnically divided and territorially contested society, yet in a reasonable way the Northeast qualifies to be a distinct region with regional identities not only in historical and geographical sense but also in ethno-political sense. Although the ethnic territories and histories are often overlapping and are subjected to contestation, the chapter argues that it has a logic for creating a trans-ethnic federating unit – a form of 'Common Ethnic House' – with a common objective for promoting collective interests of cohabited communities. Selective policy intervention in case of Assam may invite further complexities in the face of the present problem. The need of the hour is to look an inclusive alternative model for better governance of the Northeast and meet the aspirations of struggling ethnic people. The chapter argues that the proposed model must recognise non-territorial basis of political arrangement and guarantee group autonomy and scope for sharing power among the communities. This may give more democratic space for dialogue and autonomy by ruling out the probability of dominance by one upon others. If the present state of dismal situation in the Northeast is socially engineered and politically constructed, then the possibility of reversal of the situation is also equally a greater possibility, as the chapter argues, under the consociational democratic arrangement by incorporating all ethnic groups and democratising their aspirations along with group autonomy.

The scholar-contributors, who I was able to draw together for this volume, have put their diverse views forward with a unique understanding of the region's multiple problems. Indeed, the spectrum is so large that at times it was felt that a compendium of this kind of volume might not be possible. However, in the course of many debates and discussions, agreements and disagreements, a meeting ground was perceived. Finally, the process brought forth clarity over the complex issues of Assam and way forward to conflict resolution. In this respect, I believe, the present book is a deliberation of the Assam problem with a difference.

## 12   *Dilip Gogoi*

## Notes

1  NSCN is now divided into NSCN(I-M) and NSCN(K); ULFA divided into ULFA(Pro Talk) and ULFA(I); NDFB divided into NDFB(P), NDFB(R) and NDFB(S).

2  Civic nationalism means political allegiance based on a vision of a community of equal citizens, allowing respect for ethnic and cultural diversity that does not challenge core civic values.

3  Sanjib Baruah termed it as 'sub-nationalism' and elaborated in chapter 4 in detail in his book *India Against Itself*, 1999. Ethnic nationalism is an exclusive form of idea which seeks the organic and usually ethnic unity of the nation and tries to protect and promote national identity on cultural sameness. For details on civic nationalism and ethnic nationalism see Smith, Anthony D. 1991, *National Identity*, London: Penguin pp. 19–41, 116–22.

4  French theorist Jean Bodin (On Sovereignty, 1592) thought that sovereignty must reside in a single individual and sovereign is the supreme authority. English philosopher Thomas Hobbes (Leviathan 1651) agreed to it and advocated absolute state, putting the sovereign above the laws.

5  For instance, Rousseau contra Bodin and Hobbes saw the collective people within a state as the sovereign, ruling through their general will (*The Social Contract*, 1762). In constitutional government, it is the people ruling through a body of law that is usually known as popular sovereignty.

6  The issue of sovereignty and self-determination, which needs an intensive academic assessment, is missing in the existing literatures of India's Northeast. To enumerate the books available from the early years to the present, books like Sanjib Baruah's *India Against Itself*, 1999, analyse the nationality question of Assam in the context of sub-nationalism, while Udayon Misra's *The Periphery Strikes Back*, 2000, highlights the challenges to the India's nation-building with reference to Assam and Nagaland. Nani Gopal Mahanta's *Confronting the State*, 2013, highlights the genesis of conflict between the Indian state and the insurgent group ULFA through the help of local narratives but does not theoretically scrutinise the question of sovereignty and self-determination.

7  Implies participation of communities in political decision making along with the right of group autonomy. See Lijphart, *Democracy in Plural Societies*, 1977.

## References

Anderson, Benedict. 1983. *Imagined Communities: Reflections on the Origin and Spread of Nationalism*. London: Verso.

Baruah, Sanjib. 1999. *India Against Itself: Assam and the Politics of Nationality*. New Delhi: Oxford University Press.

Baruah, Sanjib. 2010. 'AFSPA: Legacy of Colonial Constitutionalism'. *Seminar* No. 615: 7–14.

Chatterjee, Partha. 1986. *Nationalist Thought and the Colonial World: A Derivative Discourse*. London: Zed.

Chatterjee, Partha. 1993. *Nation and its Fragments: Colonial and Post Colonial Histories*. Princeton, NJ: Princeton University Press.

## Sovereignty and national identity 13

Gellner, Ernest. 1983. *Nations and Nationalism*. Oxford: Blackwell Publishing Ltd.

Hobsbawm, Eric J. 1990. *National and Nationalism Since 1780*. Cambridge: Cambridge University Press.

Lijphart, Arend. 1977. *Democracy in Plural Societies*. New Haven: Yale University Press.

Mahanta, Nani Gopal. 2013. *Confronting the State: ULFA's Quest for Sovereignty*. New Delhi: Sage Publications.

Misra, Udayon. 2000. *The Periphery Strikes Back: Challenges to the Nation-State in Assam and Nagaland*. Shimla: Indian Institute of Advanced Study.

Osinder, Andreas. 2001. 'Sovreignty, International Relations, and the Westphalian Myth', *International Organisation*, 55(2):251–287.

Plamentaz, John. 1976. 'Two Types of Nationalism'. In *Eugene Kamenka* (ed.), Nationalism: The Nature and Evolution of an Idea. London: Edward Arnold.

Rudolph, Christopher. 2005. 'Sovereignty and Territorial Borders in a Global Age', *International Studies Review*, 7(1):1–20.

Smith, Anthony D. 1991. *National Identity*. London: Penguin.

Williams, Paul R. and Pecci, Francesca J. 2004. 'Earned Sovereignty: Bridging the Gap Between Sovereignty and Self-Determination', *Stanford Journal of International Law*, 40(1): 1–40.

# Part II

# Situating the debate

Interface of sovereignty and self-determination

# 2 Sovereignty at the frontiers

## Contests and contradictions

*Åshild Kolås*

Sovereignty is commonly understood as the absolute authority a state holds over a territory and its people (Weber 1995:1). Regardless of its 'mythical' origins in the 1648 Treaty of Westphalia (Osiander 2001), it was only with the advent of the United Nations after World War II that the nation-state was universally recognised as the sole legitimate vehicle of sovereignty. At the same time, the club of states agreed that nations or peoples held the right to self-determination.

Post-colonial studies have shown how the 'Westphalian' notion of sovereignty was executed in the colonies (Hansen and Stepputat 2005; Sidaway 2003). The state was conceived as the only legitimate form of sovereign rule within clearly demarcated colonial territories, with stringently defined peoples under its sway. The results are still to be found today. They appear in continuous disputes over once arbitrarily drawn-up borders, struggles over ethnic designations and ongoing identity contestations (Comaroff and Comaroff 2009; Mamdani 1996; Rajasingham-Senanayake 2002). Most accounts of political conflict in Northeast India similarly set out from a description of the region's tremendous ethnic diversity and complex history (Biswas and Suklabaidya 2008). In fact, the contemporary ethnic map of Northeast India is based on the colonial pursuit of ethnic classification and its construction of distinct peoples and races, deeply intertwined with nationalist ideology.

Reflecting the hegemony of the nation-state ideal, ethno-nationalist movements across the colonial world have demanded independence or ethnic homelands backed by discourses of ethnic purity and homogeneous identity, representations of historical 'facts' and 'scientific' ethnographic data (Anderson 1983; Bhabha 1990). Language and literary traditions have been key issues in many such movements. In Assam, popular associations such as the literary society (*Asom Sahitya Sabha*) and All Assam Students' Union (AASU) were focal points of Assamese nationalism, inspired by the same ideologies as the Indian freedom struggle. Demands for an

18  *Åshild Kolås*

independent Assam followed, turning militant in the 1980s with the rise of the United Liberation Front of Assam (ULFA).

As described by Sanjib Baruah (1994:653): 'the modern nation state seeks a monopoly of the collectivist imagination of all its citizens; it would like the national political community to be the sole repository of the poetics of a homeland and of a chosen people'. However, as the literature on nationalism and identity politics has amply illustrated, there has never been such a thing as a 'pure' nation. Nation-building is inherently difficult, and often challenged by groups that emphasise their uniqueness and difference from the national mainstream. Ironically, however, separatist movements engaging in micro-nationalist politics invariably reiterate the ideology of nation statehood as they replicate or mimic the nation-building project of the state. While rejecting assimilation or integration into the state, nationalists accept the basic premises of state sovereignty and reiterate dominant discourses on the nation-state, thereby strengthening the idea of the state as the vehicle of sovereignty (Englebert 2009).

People inhabiting frontiers and borderlands often present particular challenges to the state, especially when they are labelled as racially or culturally 'other'. This is evident from the history of colonial Assam and the north-eastern Frontier areas, where measures to 'protect' hill people were enshrined in the Government of India Act, 1935, and its special provisions for Excluded Areas and Partially Excluded Areas. Allegedly offering autonomy as well as protection, the hill areas continued to be treated as exceptions in independent India with the adoption of the Sixth Schedule of the Constitution and the continuation of the Inner Line. As reflected in the Inner Line regulations, hill people were regarded as incapable of taking care of their own interests, and in need of protection from those more civilised. In the Constituent Assembly debate on the Sixth Schedule, issues such as headhunting and 'Naked Nagas' (a monograph by the Austrian anthropologist Fürer-Haimendorf) were brought up. The assembly concluded that administration of such people required a unique governance structure, different from the rest of India (Kolås 2012).

Despite the efforts of the Union Government to incorporate the Naga Hills into the Union, the Naga National Council (NNC) eventually asserted the sovereignty of Nagaland. In 1956, NNC declared the founding of a Naga Federal Government and Naga Federal Army, after carrying out a plebiscite on independence. This provoked the Union Government to launch military operations to take direct control of the Naga Hills (Franke 2006:78). To accomplish this mission, colonial legislation was revived with the Armed Forces Special Powers Act, 1958 (AFSPA), allowing security forces to enter, search and arrest without a warrant, and to fire on suspects 'even to the causing of death' in the region's 'disturbed areas'. Armed

*Sovereignty at the frontiers* 19

conflict soon spread into neighbouring districts of Assam and Manipur, all designated as 'disturbed areas'.

Studies of governance and politics shed light on how statehood is contested on the ground, and particularly the role of institutions for such contestation. Returning to the drafting of the Indian Constitution, proponents of the Sixth Schedule maintained that it was a temporary measure that would help unify India rather than set up the north-eastern hills as 'forever apart'. After six decades of conflict, however, new areas such as Bodoland have been brought under the Sixth Schedule, and even more autonomy is allegedly offered in recently created 'territorial councils'. It seems that what was once meant to be temporary has not only survived, but also is gaining ground (Kolås 2012). A brief summary of events is needed here, in order to recapitulate this history.

After a period of heavy militarisation in the 1950s, the state of Nagaland was formed in 1963 in an attempt to reach a peaceful settlement of Naga demands for sovereignty. However, the success of the Nagas in achieving their own state set a powerful example, motivating other groups to make their own territorial demands. After the state of Meghalaya was formed in 1972, several new administrative units were set up as a result of negotiations with armed groups, including the state of Mizoram in 1987 in agreement with the Mizo National Front, and the Bodoland Territorial Council in 2003 in agreement with the Bodo Liberation Tigers. In neighbouring West Bengal, the Darjeeling Gorkha Hill Council was established in 1988 based on an agreement between the government and the Gorkha National Liberation Front (Lacina 2009).

Despite a long history of settlements, militancy has continued throughout many parts of Northeast India, with new groups or factions often emerging as spoilers. In negotiations with the most powerful Naga militants, the National Socialist Council of Nagaland (Isak-Muivah) (NSCN-I-M) led by Muivah and Swu – the government even offered Nagaland a 'special federal relationship' with India. However, the talks remain deadlocked over the NSCN(I-M)'s demand for a sovereign 'Greater Nagaland' including hill areas in neighbouring Manipur and Assam.

As noted by Robert Jackson (2007:xi): 'Sovereignty is not originally or primarily an abstract idea fashioned by philosophers and other theoreticians and then applied in practice. [. . .] The political arrangements and legal practices of sovereignty came first, the academic theories later'. Departing from philosophical and normative perspectives on sovereignty as ideology, a body of recent work emphasises how sovereignty is constructed and practiced in daily life, as a key site of political contestation over authority and power (Biersteker and Weber 1996; Brace and Hoffman 1997; Duara 2003; Howland and White 2009; Kapferer and Bertelsen 2009; Liu 2003).

20   *Åshild Kolås*

While this has provided useful conceptual tools and theories for reinvestigating sovereignty, there is still a lacuna between the dynamic and continuously evolving sovereignty practices around the world, and the often abstract and theoretical literature seeking to explain these practices. This should be addressed through grounded empirical research that explores new political arrangements, changing governance practices and emerging debates in sovereignty contestations. While investigating the discrepancies between theory and practice, we need to take into account both local shifts in the ground realities, and the changing global environment, which will be reviewed in the following sections.

## Frontiers of globalisation

The nature of sovereignty is in fact fiercely contested in the contemporary world, as evidenced by numerous cases of conflict and political protest, ranging from multiple insurgencies affecting the Great Lakes region and the Horn of Africa, to the mass mobilisations of the 'Colour Revolutions', the 'Arab Spring' and the 'Occupy' movement in the United States. The characteristics of sovereignty are also changing with the development of new institutions such as the Northern Ireland Assembly, the self-government authorities in Greenland and even the Arctic Council (Kolås 2013). Obviously, the role of the state as the key vehicle of the 'will of the people' can no longer be taken for granted, nor can we safely leave the meaning of sovereignty unquestioned. In order to understand these developments, we need to look at the frontiers of globalisation, where transnational legal and political mechanisms, new governance techniques and global interconnectedness are changing the sites and means by which sovereignty is exercised and negotiated (Agnew 2009; Sassen 2006; Shinoda 2000).

A range of global phenomena pose challenges to the idea of the sovereign state. These include the seemingly limitless reach of multinational business, trade agreements and financial interdependence which have forced into obscurity the former goals of many states to retain a minimum of self-reliance, whether in terms of energy supplies, vital raw materials and resources or food items of critical importance for national security and survival. Add to this the worldwide interconnectedness of civil societies, the borderless nature of political activism via digital networks, the increasing importance of international non-governmental organisations (INGOs) and the ever-expanding mandates of multilateral humanitarian agencies and supranational bodies. Add also the pervasiveness of 'twilight institutions' (Lund 2006) on the margins of many so-called fragile states in particular, but also relevant to emerging economies such as India. Another global trend is the turn towards privatisation of 'security', which many

*Sovereignty at the frontiers* 21

commentators have seen as a challenge to the state monopoly of the legitimate use of violence. In countries affected by asymmetrical warfare, civilians are increasingly threatened by the new face (or facelessness) of modern warfare or counter-terrorism in which the superpower has the benefit of high-tech satellite imagery and sophisticated unmanned drones that can be directed to targets virtually anywhere on the planet. Consider also the increasing reliance of states on computerised data systems as tools for electronic governance coupled with biometrics for identification, as in India's unique identification system (*Aadhar*). The flipside of the coin is not only an increased threat of cybercrime, but also the risks related to diffusion of the boundary between state and subject, and a potential clash between state sovereignty and individual privacy concerns. The brave new world of biopolitics lies just round the corner.

The outer reaches of the nation – such as immigrants, tribals, indigenous peoples and religious minorities – have often been subjected to heightened social control and scrutiny, just as state borders can be spaces of assiduous surveillance. This is where the all-too sovereign state is most often challenged. In the era of globalisation, however, the spaces and conditions for exercising sovereignty are changing as a result of tremendous technological, demographic and cultural transformations. When studying contestations over sovereignty, we should recognise that we live in an increasingly interconnected and ideationally borderless world, where anything and everything held to be 'true' is subject to critical interrogation. On the other hand, the notions we hold about sovereignty and legitimate rule continue to form a part of the cultural and ideational foundation from which we act in the world and interact with each other. As a key social construct, we should study the contestation of sovereignty as both context-dependent and historically contingent (Evans 1997; Everard 1999).

In studying the changing nature of sovereignty, it is important to address impacts of both tangible and intangible or discursive forms of globalisation on sovereignty debates. We can take as an example how self-determination is debated in the context of indigenous movements, in the United Nations Permanent Forum on Indigenous Issues (UNPFII), and among INGOs working for the rights of indigenous people and minorities. Organisations such as these have brought the right to self-determination to the centre stage of debates on fundamental human rights. This highlights how sovereignty as a concept, and its relationship to statehood, are no longer within the precinct of state agents, but must be renegotiated multilaterally, in non-governmental (civil society) as well as governmental fora.

Contemporary contestations over sovereignty are invariably influenced by globalisation, whether in the form of transnational judicial and legal mechanisms, new technologies of governance, communication and

## 22   *Åshild Kolås*

surveillance, changing customs and mobility regimes, global movements to promote human rights or the related discourses of stakeholders. Just as sovereignty practices affect the course of conflict, they should also be expected to impact on negotiations between conflict parties to end conflict. In fact, issues of sovereignty, territoriality and citizenship are at the core of most peace processes.

Sovereignty is not merely an issue of relevance to the bygone era of decolonisation in the so-called Third World. Sovereignty competitions continue today in a range of different settings and places, from the relatively peaceful and 'developed' Australia, where Aboriginal people contest the ownership of mineral resources as well as sacred sites, to war-torn Sudan, where the southern part of the country has finally seceded to form the new state of South Sudan. This illustrates that state sovereignty is still very much 'in the making'. Sovereignty remains contested not only on the European margins, as in Greenland and Northern Scandinavia (home of indigenous peoples such as the Inuit and Sami), but even in the European heartland, as in Belgium, the United Kingdom (Northern Ireland, Scotland and Wales), and the Basque Country (spanning the border between Spain and France).

Globalisation significantly impacts the way sovereignty claims are debated by opening up new avenues for communication and exchange. This also harbours potential for cross-border alliances between groups with converging interests and sovereignty demands. Changing practices of governance and new means of contestation affect claims made by state agents as well as their non-state contenders. The evolving global or transnational order is reflected in everyday contestations and struggles over sovereignty, changing the parameters of negotiations over sovereignty and self-governance on the ground. The 'hinterlands' of Northeast India are no exception.

## The hinterlands

Northeast India is a good place to explore parapolitics, or 'criminals behaving as sovereigns and sovereigns behaving as criminals in a systematic way' (Cribb 2009:8). In fact, there is probably no better way of describing the sovereignty contestations of the region, with its lucrative shadow economies and transnational underground networks implicating numerous state and non-state actors, securitised by multiple and often competing intelligence agencies, and hosting a diverse range of gun-wielding 'security' forces. The Armed Forces Special Powers Act, 1958 (AFSPA) is central to the regional (in)security complex. Commonly referred to as a 'draconian law', AFSPA not only confers 'special powers' over life and death to security forces operating in areas defined as 'disturbed', but it also protects persons acting under it against persecution, suit or other legal proceeding. AFSPA

*Sovereignty at the frontiers*   23

thereby provides immunity to security forces involved in otherwise criminal activities such as arbitrary searches and detention, custodial torture, rape, extrajudicial killings and 'fake encounters' (South Asia Human Rights Documentation Centre 1995). In recent years civil society organisations have repeatedly called for a repeal of AFSPA, and there has been widespread protest against the Act. The UN Human Rights Committee has questioned the Act's justification, and AFSPA has also been challenged numerous times in Indian courts. Those who argue for a repeal see the Act as unconstitutional and a threat to human rights, maintaining 'disturbed areas' as warzones where ordinary citizens are caught in the crossfire between security forces and militants. As Ananya Vajpeyi (2009:38) points out, 'after being applied for half a century and with an ever-expanding scope, [AFSPA] has only confirmed the rupture between what is and what is not India'.

When 'disturbed areas' under AFSPA are set legally apart from the rest of India and essentially kept under a perpetual state of emergency, this obviously creates a significant legitimacy problem for the government. It is against this backdrop that state agents and 'parastate' actors (Wilson 2009) compete for the role as providers of justice and security. Drawing on Ola Tunander's distinction between the 'democratic state' and the 'security state' (2009:57), political legitimacy can be seen as negotiated not only on the basis of legality, as in 'normal' (democratic) political contestations where the legitimacy of the sovereign ruler is grounded in the law and the sovereign 'will of the people', but, equally importantly, in the 'exception' and the parapolitical, where legitimacy is negotiated on the basis of the very different logics of security and monopoly of the legitimate use of violence. Despite (or due to) heavy militarisation, security forces in Northeast India frequently fail to offer protection or provide security to ordinary citizens. This provides an opportunity for rivalling parastate actors to compete with state actors in offering security or protection to the local community, simultaneously threatening those who fail to support their 'cause'. The competitions are related to two basic dimensions of sovereign statehood, namely political representation and monopoly of the legitimate use of violence. As will be shown, state and parastate actors implicitly use shared logics, while the mimicking of the state by parastate actors is important in both dimensions.

As regards political representation, mechanisms to exclude and 'protect' hill areas, first enacted in 1935, were continued in independent India with the adoption of the Sixth Schedule of the Constitution. Separate states and autonomous district councils were later on established in response to ethno-nationalist claims. Newly formed 'ethnic' elites subsequently took control of legislation and justice, collection of revenue and taxes, issuance of leases for mineral extraction and many other subjects. This triggered further demands for 'ethnic' homelands. The legitimacy of both militants and

24  *Åshild Kolås*

politicians has now come to rest on their ability to represent the demands of their own 'ethnic' group. This is one pillar of sovereignty contestation in Northeast India.

As regards the monopoly of legitimate use of violence, parastate actors have consciously constructed their 'armies' to both mirror and contest state forces as they justify their use of violence. Importantly, authorities also treat parastate armies as 'exceptional' militaries, thereby reinforcing their legitimacy. When an armed group enters into a ceasefire with the government, the group is hence allowed to build designated camps where militants can continue to train in uniform, and perform annual 'Raising Day' ceremonies and other functions in their efforts to reproduce the legitimacy as well as the external forms of the military. Both militant and non-violent organisations have demanded 'sovereignty', whether in the form of an independent country or a separate state within the Union. However, the government implicitly accepts the militants' assertion that they are engaged in 'armed resistance', and negotiates only with armed groups, not with non-violent civil society actors.

Is there such a thing as legitimate violence? A vast philosophical literature on theories of 'just war' and a substantial body of work in political theory on sovereignty and the legality of warfare suggests that there is. On the other hand, the premises and definitions of such legitimacy are situational, as what is (and is not) legitimate is 'continuously (re-)established through conflict and negotiation' (Lund 2006:693; Kelly 2006). As described by Charles Tilly (1985:169), war making and state making are 'quintessential protection rackets with the advantage of legitimacy'. This begs the question of whose legitimacy, or who can legitimately define not only the state of emergency or exception, but the law itself, if the boundary between the state and the non-state is no longer taken for granted analytically as a distinction between the legitimate and the illegitimate. One could even argue that the militant logic follows Carl Schmitt's famous dictum 'sovereign is he who decides on the exception' (Tilly 1985:5).

While the government continues to portray its peacemaking efforts as successful, *bandhs*, riots, communal violence, kidnapping and extortion prevail. In some areas, people are still forced to pay 'tax' to multiple armed groups as well as the state. Members of security forces have been caught operating extortion rackets of their own. In one such case, angry villagers attacked soldiers of the Assam Rifles who were posing as militants and trying to extort money from them at gunpoint. Whereas militants emulate state security forces, Indian armed forces also copy their non-state counterparts, albeit not for the same reasons. More importantly, since the enactment of AFSPA, security forces have left local communities with a legacy of abuse, including organised attacks on villages in which houses have been

*Sovereignty at the frontiers* 25

torched by units of special commando forces, state police and paramilitaries. It is this legacy that makes the legitimacy claims of non-state (or parastate) actors understandable as they compete with and mimic the state in its role as protector and law enforcer. When the state is perceived as unable to protect people against encroachment, or even as a security threat rather than a protector, a space is opened up for armed groups to act as security providers within the legitimacy deficit created by the state.

## Rethinking sovereignty: contests and contradictions

Sovereignty contestations in Northeast India can be viewed as disputes along two parallel dimensions: political representation and the monopoly of legitimate violence or 'security'. Whether contenders in Northeast India are state agents or parastate actors, their claims draw on different premises as related to two different dimensions (or 'pastoral functions') of government or domains of sovereignty: protection and wealth (Chatterjee 2005:222). The legitimacy of (armed) violence is concerned with protection, and follows a different logic than the legitimacy of 'normal' (democratic) politics, concerned with wealth. The latter depends on legality, 'fairness' of political representation and elections, and the classical 'will of the people'. The former regards security, and is a matter of life and death.

Whereas old-school nationalism and the nation-state obviously persist, the relationship between statehood and sovereignty can no longer be taken for granted. This is apparent in the nature of politics and activism around the world, from the rise of multilateral institutions to the mass demonstrations of the 'Arab Spring'. This is also reflected in recent research that questions the sovereignty-state equation. In India, the Union Government is still talking with ULFA, and explicitly or not, sovereignty is on the negotiating table. Despite the positive side to negotiations, the government's conflict management efforts are facing major challenges. Various 'peace talks' have been carried out with little or no transparency or inclusiveness, and many of the militants at the negotiating tables are factions and groups with histories of violent rivalry. Several of the negotiating groups and factions are also raising competing territorial demands, all vying for some kind of sovereign territory in a region where ethnic groups live in scattered, non-contiguous communities.

According to the Indian government, the granting of statehood and autonomous status is a means to devolve decision making and maintain the 'demographic uniqueness' of Northeast India. In effect this provides ethnic 'homelands' to certain groups (Baruah 2003, 2005; Vandekerckhove 2013). The Sixth Schedule now gives autonomous councils extensive powers of legislation and administration of justice, as well as powers to assess

## 26 *Åshild Kolås*

and collect land revenue and impose taxes, issue leases for prospecting for or extracting minerals and make regulations for the control of moneylending and trading by non-tribals. However, with development schemes and public works weakly monitored and funds poorly accounted for, power over these councils and the funds that go with them have become stakes in 'homeland politics'. Moreover, the government's policy of signing settlements with militant groups rather than non-violent civil society actors has invariably given credence to armed groups as political actors who can legitimately represent their 'tribe' or ethnic group in their quest for independence, statehood or self-government (Kolås 2011). Even more unfortunately, whereas settlements may serve to pacify contestants, they do not solve deep-rooted governance problems or address highly unequal power relations.

Stakeholders in peace processes commonly investigate institutional frameworks for autonomy and self-governance. However, institutional frameworks, theories and terminologies are slow to develop, while governance practices are changing rapidly. A more nuanced understanding of such practices and thinking 'out of the box' on autonomy and self-determination are potential keys to successful negotiations in conflicts where territory and group rights are crucial issues. The kind of grounded and critical work on sovereignty contestations presented in this book is therefore highly relevant to peace processes in which sovereignty is at stake, and especially to ongoing dialogues between the Indian government and armed groups in Northeast India.

Contemporary debates among stakeholders in Northeast India's sovereignty contestations have slowly shifted towards focusing on alternatives to secession, including frameworks that would allow non-territorial forms of self-government. Current debates are inspired, among other, by increasing exposure to global movements in support of indigenous rights, and through participation in UN institutions such as the Working Group on Indigenous Populations. In a region where claims of indigeneity have figured prominently in demands for ethnic homelands, new debates on indigenous rights are leading to further strife over the implications of indigeneity. At the same time, global debates on indigenous rights are starting to inform new attempts to rethink the relationship between identity, citizenship and territoriality. Within this context, notions of the state and sovereignty are slowly beginning to be disengaged.

## References

Agnew, John. 2009. *Globalisation and Sovereignty.* Lanham: Rowman and Littlefield Publishers.

Anderson, Benedict. 1983. *Imagined Communities.* London, New York: Verso.

*Sovereignty at the frontiers*   27

Baruah, Sanjib. 1994. ' "Ethnic" Conflict as State-Society Struggle: The Poetics and Politics of Assamese Micro-Nationalism', *Modern Asian Studies*, 28(3): 649–71.

Baruah, Sanjib. 2003. 'Citizens and Denizens: Ethnicity, Homelands, and the Crisis of Displacement in Northeast India', *Journal of Refugee Studies*, 16(1): 44–66.

Baruah, Sanjib. 2005. *Durable Disorder: Understanding the Politics of Northeast India*. New Delhi: Oxford University Press.

Bhabha, Homi K., ed. 1990. *Nation and Narration*. London; New York: Routledge.

Biersteker, Thomas J. and Cynthia Weber, eds. 1996. *State Sovereignty as Social Construct*. Cambridge Studies in International Relations. Cambridge: Cambridge University Press.

Biswas, Prasenjit and Chandan Suklabaidya. 2008. *Ethnic Life-Worlds in Northeast India. An Analysis*. New Delhi: Sage Publications.

Brace, Laura and John Hoffman, eds. 1997. *Reclaiming Sovereignty*. London and Washington: Pinter.

Chatterjee, P. 2005. 'Sovereign Violence and the Domain of the Political'. In *Sovereign Bodies: Citizens, Migrants and States in the Postcolonial World*, ed. T. B. Hansen and F. Stepputat. Princeton, NJ: Princeton University Press.

Comaroff, John L. and Jean Comaroff. 2009. *Ethnicity, Inc.* Chicago: University of Chicago Press.

Cribb, Robert. 2009. 'Introduction: Parapolitics, Shadow Governance and Criminal Sovereignty'. In *Government of the Shadows. Parapolitics and Criminal Sovereignty*, ed. Eric Wilson. New York, NY: Pluto Press.

Duara, Prasenjit. 2003. *Sovereignty and Authenticity: Manchukuo and the East Asian Modern*. Lanham: Rowman and Littlefield Publishers.

Englebert, Pierre. 2009. *Africa: Unity, Sovereignty, and Sorrow*. Boulder, CO: Lynne Rienner.

Evans, Peter. 1997. 'The Eclipse of the State?' *World Politics*, 50: 62–87.

Everard, Jerry. 1999. *Virtual States: Globalisation, Inequality and the Internet*. London and New York: Routledge.

Franke, Marcus. 2006. 'Wars without End: The Case of the Naga Hills', *Diogenes*, 212: 69–84.

Hansen, Thomas B. and Finn Stepputat, eds. 2005. *Sovereign Bodies: Citizens, Migrants, and States in the Postcolonial World*. Princeton, NJ: Princeton University Press.

Howland, Douglas and Luise White, eds. 2009. *The State of Sovereignty: Territories, Laws, Populations*. Bloomington: Indiana University Press.

Jackson, Robert. 2007. *Sovereignty: Evolution of an Idea*. Cambridge: Polity Press.

Kapferer, Bruce and Bjørn E. Bertelsen, eds. 2009. *Crisis of the State: War and Social Upheaval*. Oxford: Berghahn.

Kelly, Tobias. 2006. *Law, Violence, and Sovereignty among West Bank Palestinians*. Cambridge: Cambridge University Press.

## 28  *Åshild Kolås*

Kolås, Åshild. 2011. 'Naga Militancy and Violent Politics in the Shadow of Ceasefire', *Journal of Peace Research*, 48(6): 781–92.

Kolås, Åshild. 2012. 'What's Up with the Territorial Council?' *Seminar*, 640 (December 2012), Special Issue on Assam: Unstable Peace: 2–7.

Kolås, Åshild. 2013. 'Indigenous Rights, Sovereignty and Resource Governance in the Arctic', *Strategic Analysis*, 37(4): 499–504.

Lacina, Bethany. 2009. 'The Problem of Political Stability in Northeast India: Local Ethnic Autocracy and the Rule of Law', *Asian Survey*, 49(6): 998–1020.

Liu, Lydia H. 2003. 'Desire and Sovereign Thinking'. In *Grounds of Comparison around the Work of Benedict Anderson*, ed. J. Culler and P. Cheah. London and New York: Routledge.

Lund, Christian. 2006. 'Twilight Institutions: Public Authority and Local Politics in Africa', *Development and Change*, 37(4): 685–705.

Mamdani, Mahmood. 1996. *Citizen and Subject: Contemporary Africa and the Legacy of Late Colonialism.* Princeton, NJ: Princeton University Press.

Osiander, Andreas. 2001. 'Sovereignty, International Relations, and the Westphalian Myth', *International Organization*, 5(2): 251–87.

Rajasingham-Senanayake, Darini. 2002. 'Identity on the Borderline: The Colonial Census, New Ethnicities, and the Unmaking of Multiculturalism in Ethnic Violence', *Identity, Culture and Politics*, 3(2): 1–26.

Sassen, Saskia. 2006. *Territory, Authority, Rights: From Medieval to Global Assemblages.* Princeton, NJ: Princeton University Press.

Schmitt, Carl. 1963/2004. *The Theory of the Partisan: A Commentary/Remark on the Concept of the Political.* Berlin: Duncker&Humblot, 1963. English translation: Michigan State University Press, 2004.

Sidaway, James. 2003. 'Sovereign Excesses? Portraying Postcolonial Sovereignty Scapes', *Political Geography*, 22(2): 157–78.

Shinoda, Hideaki. 2000. *Re-examining Sovereignty. From Classical Theory to the Global Age.* New York: St. Martin's.

South Asia Human Rights Documentation Centre. 1995. *Armed Forces Special Powers Act: A Study in National Security Tyranny*, http://www.hrdc.net/sahrdc/resources/armed_forces.htm.

Tilly, Charles. 1985. 'War Making and State Making as Organized Crime'. In *Bringing the State Back In*, ed. Peter B. Evans. Cambridge: Cambridge University Press.

Tunander, Ola. 2009. 'Democratic State vs. Deep State: Approaching the Dual State of the West'. In *Government of the Shadows. Parapolitics and Criminal Sovereignty*, ed. Eric Wilson. New York, NY: Pluto Press.

Vajpeyi, Ananya. 2009. 'Resenting the Indian State. For a New Political Practice in the Northeast'. In *Beyond Counter-Insurgency. Breaking the Impasse in Northeast India*, ed. Sanjib Baruah. Oxford: Oxford University Press.

Vandekerckhove, Nel. 2013. 'Democracy through the Gun: Challenges of Post-Conflict Reconstruction in War-Torn Assam, India'. In *Routes and*

*Sovereignty at the frontiers* 29

*Roots of Democracy in the Himalayas*, ed. V. Arora and N. Jayaram. London: Routledge.

Weber, Cynthia. 1995. *Simulating Sovereignty: Intervention, the State, and Symbolic Exchange*. Cambridge: Cambridge University Press.

Wilson, Eric. 2009. *Government of the Shadows. Parapolitics and Criminal Sovereignty*. New York, NY: Pluto Press.

# 3 Self-determination, multi-ethnic state and quest for Assamese nationhood

*Rubul Patgiri*

The concept of national self-determination has been a matter of intense controversy, and, behind this controversy, lays the dichotomy that surrounds it. On the one hand, there has been growing proliferation on the demand for national self-determination and, on the other hand, there is an equally strong resistance to it. In this sense, the challenge before the concept is to find ways and means to solve this contradiction. The notion of self-determination interpreted as a means to secure sovereign statehood for every national group has surely reached a dead end. Self-determination, in this sense, no longer remains an exercisable principle, and there are serious objections to such interpretation of self-determination. However, such a tendency of judging every case against some common standard or criterion is of not much use as such an approach may fail to acknowledge the legitimate aspirations and grievances of the people behind those demands. Instead of such a liberal approach, people have now come to favour some sort of communitarian approach which would judge each case on its merits. More importantly, there has been a growing recognition of the need to examine the ethics or morality of such claim in the context of the specific situation in which such demands come up.

Against this background, the examination of justification of demand for self-determination of Assam makes an interesting study. In contrast to the strong conviction of proponents of self-determination of Assam about the legality and justifiability of their demands, the overwhelming mood of the majority of people of Assam is to dismiss such an idea and see themselves as an integral part of India. However, despite their strong affiliation to the idea of being Indian, a sizeable section of the Assamese people also evince some grievances because of their belief about some injustice that the Assamese nation historically has been subject to. This probably explains the complexity of the Assamese attitude towards the demand for a sovereign, independent Assam which oscillates between total disapproval to sympathy for such voice which is sometimes seen as assertion of Assamese

*Self-determination, multi-ethnic state* 31

right. Against this background, this chapter first seeks to highlight the main objection against the secessionist self-determination demand, and then, against these objections, attempts to examine the justification of claim for Assam's sovereignty. The chapter then goes on to examine the morality of the demand for self-determination of Assam in the context of the evolving theories to analyse the morality of such claims. The chapter argues that notwithstanding the problems and inconsistency regarding the demand for self-determination for Assam, there is a sentiment behind this, and hence, recognition of this fact would be useful for developing an effective approach to deal with the issue. The concluding section questions the rationality of the present territorial form of expression of self-determination, particularly, in the context of a multi-ethnic society of the Third World, and insists on the need to move away from territorial form of self-determination to other form of self-determination. It is in this context that the solution to the problem of self-determination for Assam should be negotiated within the federal structure of India.

# I

Self-determination has been an accepted principle of international law and state practices. Over the years, there has been recognition and materialisation of a number of self-determination demands, thereby making it a basis for dissolution of older states, and formation of new states. For instance, during the decolonisation period, a number of territorial political units have been granted independence on the basis of this principle. However, soon afterwards, the world has witnessed an increasing reluctance on the part of the states to recognise the claim for self-determination, particularly in its ethno-national version. In order to understand the change in the attitude towards the principle of self-determination, one must understand the context in which such cynicism crept in. As the decolonisation process was closing in, people were writing epitaph about self-determination under the impression that with decolonisation, the days of self-determination is over. Contrary to the general expectation, the post-colonial phase witnessed growing proliferation of self-determination claims, and this time, the flag-bearers of these demands were not the people of accepted political unit but the different ethno-national groups of established states. These changed nature of claimant groups created serious difficulties for acceptance and recognition of self-determination demand in this version. The difficulties were attributed to two important facts – first, the multi-ethnic character of most of the post-colonial states, and second, the fluid and flexible character of ethnic identity. In such a scenario, the fusion of self-determination and malleable ethnic identity has changed the character of the principle

## 32    *Rubul Patgiri*

of self-determination, which has, for quite a long period of time, been a source of liberation for oppressed nationalities who have become a potentially destabilising force now threatening the stability of those very states that once owed their origin to this very principle. Against this background, it would be pertinent now to look at some of the major objections that are made against the demand of self-determination in its ethno-national version today.

The first major objection against national self-determination comes from the problem of indeterminacy. While the principle insists on the right of people, there is no clear-cut definition to decide on the people who are legitimately entitled to this right. The principle insists on group right without defining the group, the people who are legitimately entitled to this right. Referring about this problem, Ivor Jennings once observed: 'Nearly 40 years ago, a professor of political science, who was also the president of the United States, President Wilson, enunciated a doctrine which was ridiculous but was widely accepted as a sensible proposition, the doctrine of self-determination. On the surface, it seemed reasonable. Let the people decide. It was, in fact, ridiculous because the people cannot decide until somebody decides who the people are' (Jennings 1956:55). All the texts, including International Bill of Human Rights 1966, Declaration on Friendly Relations 1970, have reposted the right on 'the people', but none of them elaborates the meaning of people. As a result, the meaning of the 'self' of self-determination has remained contested concepts, and so far has eluded any consensus. In fact, the term has assumed different meaning at different times. So far, one can observe two distinct concepts of the people. While the first concept defines it in ethnic term, the second concept has a civic connotation. Under the first definition, all the ethnic and national groups of the world have the right to self-determination. This interpretation of 'self' of self-determination remained dominant up to the First World War. Such an idea was also at the core of the Wilsonian notion of self-determination and formed the basis of the redrawing of European boundaries after the First World War. It is interesting to note here that even during the period when the term 'people' was conceived in ethnic lines, it had European ethnocentric bias implying ethnic and national groups of Europe only. And, it was put into practice in an even more restricted manner, to secure liberation only for East European nationalities. However, the world could not continue for long with this interpretation of the term, and the changing scenario of the world, precipitated by the decolonisation process, warranted some modification in the meaning of the term. By this time, the colonial liberation movement was under way. During the period of the freedom struggle, the people of colonies fought collectively for the independence of the political and administrative unit under which

*Self-determination, multi-ethnic state* 33

they were living. So, the liberation of colonial world meant independent statehood for those political-administrative units which were constructed by the colonial masters. This had a serious implication on the meaning of the 'self' of self-determination. As the colonial powers drew the boundaries of the territory under their occupation simply for their administrative convenience without any regard for cultural distribution of the people, when they retreated, these territories emerged as independent countries with heterogeneous people and overlapping cultural and political boundaries. Moreover, immediately after Independence, these post-colonial states have undertaken homogenisation projects as a part of their state-building process under which they have tried to forge national identity among its citizens irrespective of their cultural differences. In such a scenario, continuation with the ethnic interpretation of the 'subjects' of this right would have spelt disaster for the legitimacy and state-building process of these infant states. After the decolonisation, it became almost impossible, in view of the emerging post-colonial reality, to sustain with the ethnic connotation of the term, and soon, in accordance with the post-colonial reality, there was a shift from ethnic to civic interpretation of the term. Now, the 'people' in question was reinterpreted not as ethnic or national groups, but, rather, as multi-ethnic people under colonial rule. Self-determination has been conceived in international law as the 'right of the majority within an accepted political unit to exercise power', and boundaries have been without regard for the linguistic or cultural composition of the state (Emerson 1971:464).

The second major criticism against the principle of self-determination is its demonstration effect. The general apprehension is that the acknowledgement of this principle may encourage similar demands on the part of others also and, thus, jeopardise the stability of the state system. Thus, the concern about the principle is that this could license a secessionist free-for-all, and lead to the break-up of most of the world's states. Ernest Gellner, echoing this view, argues that the principle of national self-determination is impractical because there are many potential nations but only room for a small number of political units (Gellner 1983). He has talked about two distinct types of demonstration effect. One type has been in relation to the impact that the self-determination of one colony had on the other colonies, particularly during the decolonisation period. The other type is regarding minorities within the secessionist regions. Here, the self-determination of one group is viewed as compromising the self-determination of another group in the same territory. In this case, the minority within the seceding region demands self-determination on the ground that they are 'self, or a nation, similar to the nation that has achieved, or is striving to achieve self-determination for itself' (Moore 1998:4). With the completion of the

## 34   *Rubul Patgiri*

decolonisation process, the demonstration effect in the first sense has lost its relevance, and in the present context, the second form of demonstration which remains a valid concern. In order to appreciate this concern, one should keep in mind the nature of the societies which are facing these demands. Barring some exception, most of the region with the claims for self-determination, because of their multi-ethnic nature, contains minorities. In such a situation, the exercise of right to self-determination, in its secessionist form, would result in trapped minorities. The minority groups in those cases, taking encouragement from the national group which has successfully exercised the right, may also come out with a similar demand. In this regard, it is also important to keep in mind the fact that majority of such claims are coming out of states which are still in the midst of a nation-building or a state-building process. As most of these states are of recent origin, they still have not completed their state-building process in terms of territorial satiation, social cohesion and political stability (Ayoob 1997:136). Because of this fact, the dangers of demonstration effect in these countries are much more serious. This probably also explains the security approach that these states have adopted while dealing with such claims as they view such demand as security threat to them.

The third major objection against the principle of self-determination relates to the problem of overlapping nationalities. This, of course, is a problem typical of multinational societies. Multinational societies can be defined as those societies which are with a group of people having historical claim to the territory they live in. The exercise of self-determination in the ethno-national form is most problematic in these societies. The problem pertains to two issues – first, regarding the territory over which such a right can be exercised, and second, how to ensure similar rights for those national groups which occupy the same territory but do not share the claim of the claimant group. Regarding the first issue, if the territory is determined on the basis of the people, then, this would mean encroachment on the similar rights of others in such a situation where members of the claimant groups are not territorially concentrated. And, pertaining to the second issue, the right to self-determination cannot be exercised in favour of any group in those cases where people of different nationalities intermingled without denying the same for others unless they do not object to such claim by any of that group. If each nation has the right to self-determination, then it cannot be at the cost of the other. Therefore, the exercise of self-determination can be non-problematic only in those situations where the aspiring nations are territorially concentrated. But, in reality, this has rarely been the case. And, in most instances, the claimant group shares territory with the other national groups. In other words, in those multinational societies where different national groups have equal historical claim to the same

*Self-determination, multi-ethnic state* 35

territory, right to self-determination cannot be exercised in favour of any group without denying the same for the other groups.

Against the objections discussed earlier, the legality of self-determination demand for Assam can be examined. It is interesting to note that the demand for self-determination of Assam invites all the criticism on which the existing objection against the national self-determination movements rest. The self-determination demand for Assam has been conceived as a quest for self-determination status for the Assamese nation. In other words, the demand for self-determination status for Assam is an ethnonational claim. And, precisely, this kind of self-determination demand the existing legal regimes and state practices do not encourage. The self-determination demand for Assam is anchored on the assumption that the Assamese, because of their distinct history, language and culture, constitute a distinct nation and, therefore, is entitled to a separate independent status. Under such interpretation, the subject of the right to self-determination is the Assamese nation. This becomes clear when we examine the arguments put forward by the supporter of this demand. The history of origin of such sentiment also proves this point as the idea of self-determination for Assam could be fairly seen as an offshoot of the growth of Assamese nationalism. In fact the desire for independent political status emerged in the early twentieth century with the consolidation of Assamese nationalism. From this period onwards Assamese nationalism grew in competition with pan-Indian nationalism. While under the influence of pan-Indian nationalism people of Assam joined the all India freedom struggle, proponents of Assamese nationalism tried to secure the political, cultural and economic interests of Assamese nation, and for this purpose, the more radical section of Assamese nationalist even imagined a free and independent Assam outside India. For instance Kamalakanta Bhattacharjya urged for an independent self-reliant Assamese nation and a similar desire were expressed in number of writings published in *Jonaki* (Misra 1999:80). Similarly Ambikagiri Roychoudhury conceived Assamese as one among many such nations that make the Assamese nation. He therefore referred to India as a *mahajati* and Assamese as a *jati* (Baruah 1991:57). According to him Assam's position as a nation could be ensured only in a federation of equal nationalities that independent India would be. This kind of nationalist sentiment both in moderate and radical version continued to exist and laid down the foundation for growth of different demands, including the demand for independent Assam to protect the interest of Assamese nation. However, this kind of reasoning has serious problems in terms of securing legal sanction. Interestingly, the proponents of self-determination for Assam cite the endorsement of right of all people for self-determination in the Charter of the United Nations (UN) and Universal Declaration of Human Rights,

## 36  Rubul Patgiri

1948, in support of their claim. This was clearly reflected in the memorandum submitted by the United Liberation Front of Assam (ULFA) to the Secretary General of the United Nations (UN), which was published in *Budhbar*, on 26 November 1990.

But such an argument is based on the misreading of those texts as a number of subsequent texts have made it clear that the right of all people for self-determination does not imply the rights of all ethnic and national groups but only of a majority people of an accepted political unit. In this sense, only the majority people of India are legally entitled to the right of self-determination, and not any other ethnic and national groups.

However, even if the legitimacy of the right to self-determination in its ethno-national form is accepted, the problem for the claim of self-determination may not be over. This is in view of the fact that the idea of an Assamese nation itself has come under scrutiny. In this regard, the question is not about the existence of the Assamese nation but about the political and cultural boundaries of Assamese nation or who the people that constitute Assamese nation are. So far the dominant approach in this regard has been to define Assamese nation in terms of Assamese language and culture of Assamese-speaking people. The idea of Assamese nation defined on the basis of Assamese language and culture is considered to be exclusive in nature given the fact that many groups of people living in Assam have their own language and culture different from that of Assamese-speaking people and thus leave a lot of people of Assam, including different ethnic groups, outside the purview of Assamese nation. Such formulation of Assamese nation, however, prompted some section of Assamese nationalist leaders to impose Assamese language and culture on the different ethnic groups of Assam as a means to create a culturally homogeneous Assamese nation structured around the language and culture of Assamese-speaking people. For instance, in 1960 the Assam Legislative Assembly passed the State Official Language Act, which made Assamese the sole official language of Assam. The different ethnic groups of Assam have resented against such nationalist project of Assamese-speaking people. For instance, the *Mikir* and *North Cachar Hills Leaders' Conference* alleged that Assamese junta are determined to *Assamise* the linguistic minorities by forcing Assamese language and culture upon them and wiping out their own language and culture which they too cherish to develop. This was evident from the Memorandum submitted to the Prime Minister of India demanding a separate state comprising the Mikir Hills, North Cachar Hills and the contiguous Tribal Areas in Assam on behalf of the Mikir and North Cachar Hills Leaders' Conference, Assam on 9 June 1973. Therefore a generally accepted and inclusive definition of Assamese nation that will include all sections of people is yet to be decided. More importantly the very idea of

*Self-determination, multi-ethnic state* 37

Assamese nation consisting of different ethno-cultural groups of Assam is being questioned today. Some of these groups like Bodo and Koch have distanced themselves from the larger Assamese nation and asserted themselves as distinct and separate nation. Here it should be remembered that cultural and territorial boundary of Assamese nation has never been settled one. A group of people once viewed as Assamese have already moved away from Assam and today constitute different national group with their own separate provinces, and such process is still on. The self-determination demand for Assam in the form of a sovereign, independent Assam is also susceptible to the problem of demonstration effect. The recognition of independent status claim for Assam may have serious demonstration effect particularly due to the prevailing situation in Assam and India as well. The demonstration effect may take place in two ways. First, it will legitimise similar existing secessionist demands that India is facing today, and may encourage rise of similar demands outside. In such a scenario, the recognition of the self-determination claim would not only mean loss of territory for India but the demonstration effect of this will lead to the challenge of very survival of India. As mentioned earlier, it is extremely difficult for those states which are still in the middle of their state making process to recognise separatist claim as they are vulnerable to such demands. The same can be said about India also. India, since Independence, has been engaged in the nation-building process and, in this process, it has occasionally encountered secessionist demand. But, India has never succumbed to such demands as it would derail the nation-building process of India. This is why one can clearly observe a security-based approach on the part of India while dealing with separatist movements under which the Indian state has tried to stifle such voice through military means instead of showing any accommodation. The second, which seem more serious given the situation in Assam, will have serious repercussions on that section of people of Assam who do not share such demand for self-determination of Assam. This will have an impact again in two ways – it will intensify or embolden existing self-determination claims such as self-determination demand for Bodos, and will generate a similar demand on the part of those who are till now without such a demand. This will happen because, as we have discussed earlier, the exercise of self-determination for Assam would be seen by those who do not associate themselves with that claim as dilution of their right to self-determination, and raise or intensify similar claim on the ground that they are 'self', or nation, similar to that has achieved or striving to achieve, self-determination for themselves.

The third objection against self-determination that emanates from the problem of overlapping nationalities is also applicable to the self-determination case of Assam. In this regard, the crucial question is whether

## 38   *Rubul Patgiri*

we can consider the Assamese society as a multinational society or not. The categorisation of Assam as a multinational society may be contested. For example, the proponents of Assam's self-determination would consider Assam as a multi-ethnic state but not as a multinational state. For them, Assam constitutes a single nation, and the different ethnic groups of Assam are a part of the greater Assamese nation. On the other hand, the realities of Assam seem to indicate the opposite of the thesis. There are groups in Assam which do not subscribe to the view that the people of Assam constitute a single nation. Instead, they consider themselves as a distinct nation different from the Assamese nation. Even those ethnic groups who so far considered themselves as only ethnic group are acquiring political aspirations and thereby fast turning into nations. Given this fact, it would be difficult to materialise the self-determination claim, in its territorial form, for Assam or to determine the territorial unit in which such a right should be exercised. Already, some ethno-national groups, aspiring for self-determination status, are coming out with contesting territorial claim. The conflict over territorial claim is not just between self-determination status aspiring groups in Assam but self-determination demand present in other parts of the Northeast are also having territorial designs which would conflict with the territorial limit of the self-determination claim for Assam. For example, the demand of Naga people for Nagalim includes a significant amount of territory of Assam. It is interesting to note here that proponents of self-determination demands for Assam still has not come out with the territorial map of the proposed independent Assam. This issue of cartographic dissonance among conflicting self-determination claims would remain a serious hurdle for the exercise of self-determination right for Assam.

## II

So far, the discussion has been on the legality of self-determination for Assam in terms of existing international norms and practices, but it has not examined the justifiability or morality of the case. This is important because the two may not always coincide. The international legal norms and practices governing the recognition of self-determination claims so far are state-centric, and have been developed keeping in mind the interests of states and state system. The assumption behind these norms and practices is that territorial integrity of states is inviolable, and stability of the state system should be preserved at all cost. While territorial integrity of states and stability of state systems are important values, rigid adherence to them may result in the neglect of legitimate aspirations and demands of some groups of people. Thus, the liberal approach of framing general standards and judging every case against these general standards may not

*Self-determination, multi-ethnic state* 39

always be helpful. Instead, a communitarian approach which would see such demands in their specific contexts and ready to show more flexibility in addressing such claims seems to be more effective. Recognising this reality, the world is already moving in this direction and the post–Cold War period has witnessed fresh attempts to formulate new standards and norms which are more flexible and accommodative.

More importantly, there seems to be a shift in focus from legality to justifiability. People are now focusing on the morality and ethics of self-determination claims, and are trying to develop arguments from this perspective to examine the morality of these claims. We can broadly classify these arguments that have so far been developed into three categories – national self-determination theories, choice theories and just cause theories (Norman 1998).

According to the national self-determination theory, the entire mankind is divided into different nations, and each nation is entitled to a self-determination right. The theory insists that political and cultural boundaries must, as a matter of right, coincide (Moore 1998:7). Here, self-determination is seen as a political expression of cultural identity. The political expression of nationalistic sentiments is seen as crucial on two accounts – it has its own intrinsic ethical significance, and it is seen as having instrumentalist utility as a means to achieve other means. The extreme version of the national self-determination theory argues that each nation has a right to self-determination, including a right to state in which the members of the nation form a majority. For minority nations in a multinational state, this implies a right to secede and form their own state. The moderate version of this theory, however, does not recognise a right of secession for such groups but insists on some form of political autonomy as a means to protect their distinct language and culture. The underlying assumption for denial of right of secession is that such kind of political autonomy can be accommodated within a federal structure, and secession can be exercised only when such federal accommodation is not available (Norman 1998).

On the other hand, the choice theory emphasises that if a majority of people in a region express their desire for self-determination, which includes right to self-determination, and hence, the right to secede, they should be granted with the right. According to choice theory, the demand for self-determination in order to be legitimate, even in its secessionist form, does not have to prove that the people in question is a distinct nation or they have been victims of injustice or they have a special claim to the territory they intend to take away. The expression of mere choice is sufficient to have such a right. The supporters of such theory base their claim on principles of individual autonomy and democracy. The logic of individual autonomy and democracy automatically qualifies a group for such a right (Philpott 1995).

## 40   Rubul Patgiri

The third theory, the just cause theory, in contrast to the other two theories, sees the right to self-determination not as a general right but as a remedial right to be exercised as a means to end injustice. According to this theory, a group can exercise this right only in a situation where the subject group is victim of injustice like illegal occupation of territory, gross human rights violations and exploitation, and the situation is unlikely to change without the exercise of such a right. In this sense, the right to self-determination is like the right to revolt (Buchanan 1991).

All these theories discussed earlier have their own limitations and are not without critiques. For example, the nationalist theory, in its extreme version, is dangerous as it may lead to proliferation of self-determination demands. And, more importantly, this theory either by grounding the right to self-determination on inscriptive criterion or by associating the national community with certain territory neglects the importance of national and cultural identity of the members of the minority community residing in the same territory (Moore 1998). Similarly, the just cause theory fails to acknowledge the fact that self-determination movements are not all about justice and, hence, ignore the dynamics that are behind the origin of such claims (Moore 1998). The choice theory, of all these, seems to be most handicapped. The choice theory ground the right to self-determination on the choice of people but, without discussing the reasons like national sentiment or sense injustice which, at the first place, will lead to formation of such a choice. In other words, the choice theory is a simplified version of the other two theories but without the explanation of the two. The only thing it does best is to relieve the claimant group of the burden of establishing the claim.

Thus, the arguments contained in these theories are not conclusive and cannot be mechanically applied to examine the morality of each self-determination claims. Nevertheless, it gives us a new perspective for looking at these demands. And, it is in this context, these theories, particularly the nationalist theory and just cause theory, hold some interesting insight regarding what explains the demand for sovereign Assam and, hence, what standard one should adopt to judge this claim.

One way to see the self-determination claim for Assam is by viewing it as an expression of the Assamese nationalism, a perspective which is close to the nationalist self-determination theory. Such interpretation sees this as a manifestation of the nationalist urge of the Assamese people. The Assamese people are viewed as a distinct nation with distinct culture, history, language, and, therefore, as the national self-determination theory emphasises, are entitled for self-determination right, including a right for independent statehood. The history of origin of self-determination demand for Assam would lend strength to this view. The demand for self-determination for

*Self-determination, multi-ethnic state*   41

Assam came with the growth of heightened awareness about the Assamese nation as back as late nineteenth century. The last part of the nineteenth century witnessed the growth of the Assamese national consciousness and, in the subsequent times, under some historical conditions, having undergone the process of nationalist mobilisation, led to the demand for self-determination of Assam. From this perspective, the demand of Assam for a sovereign status is a national claim, and legitimacy of this demand would depend on the ability to establish Assamese as a nation.

A detailed analysis of the authenticity of the idea of an Assamese nation is beyond the scope of this chapter, but a few points can be made. Of late, the whole idea of an Assamese nation has come under scrutiny, and the Assamese nation has come to be seen as a 'discourse community'. This is, of course, in line with the recent theories on nation which sees nation as constructed or imagined community (Anderson 1991). Having conceded the fact that this kind of interpretation can offer useful insight into the study of the Assamese nation-making process, it would be wrong to dismiss the notion of the Assamese nation as merely an imagination without any real basis. There is no doubt about the fact that nations are the functions of modern conditions, but what remains contested is whether the roots of a nation can be traced back to the earlier times or whether the Assamese nation has an ethnic core (Day and Thompson 2004:9). Similarly, the idea of an Assamese nation, against the claim of being 5,000 years old, is a modern concept which was consciously developed under new conditions. But it would be simplicity of history if we see the Assamese nation merely as a human artefact without any cultural basis. The cultural element of the Assamese nation was available for a long time but, it was only in recent period, that out of these cultural elements, the Assamese nation has been formed.

However, the existence of a distinct Assamese nation would ensure a separate state for the Assamese nation only in extreme version of the nationalist theory. But the acknowledgement of the existence of an Assamese nation indicates some right for the nation, and the importance of acknowledging the nationalistic sentiment of the Assamese nation. The more moderate version of the nationalist self-determination theory insists on some sort of political autonomy in this regard. The linguistic reorganisation of provinces within the Indian federal structure, to a large extent, accommodates this kind of right. While the degree of autonomy available for provinces has remained an issue of contention between the provinces and the Union Government, the provision of such a federal structure has so far successfully absorbed a number of self-determination demands.

The insistence on a distinct Assamese nation should not lead us to overlook the fact that the members belonging to the Assamese nation also equally share the idea of belonging to the Indian nations. The Assamese

## 42   *Rubul Patgiri*

people take pride in being a part of the Indian nation. The Assamese, despite their cultural, racial and ethnic differences that majority of Assamese people have with the rest of India, share a lot of cultural and emotional ties with India. This is probably the result of a cultural integration process that has been at work for centuries. In fact, the cultural base of the Assamese nation was provided by the people of Aryan origin who migrated from north India to Assam at a very early stage of Assam history. As back as in the fifteenth century, Sankardeva, the great religious and social reformer of Assam, boasted himself for being born in the land called Bharatbarsha. Even during the pre-Independence period, when the demand for self-determination was initially surfacing, the proponents of such demands like Ambikagiri Roychoudhury also acknowledged this fact when he described the Indian nation as a *mahajati*, and the Assamese nation as a *jati* (Misra 1999:85). Initially, therefore, the demand was not for complete severance of Assam from India but for some sort of autonomous status which would be sufficient to protect and promote the Assamese culture. And this process of cultural integration is still on by means of constant interaction through multiple channels of communication.

Thus, the nationalist thesis cannot explain wholly the insistence on the sovereign independent status for Assam by some as the appropriate form for exercising the right to self-determination. And, it is in this context, the relevance of the just cause theory, which seeks to examine the legitimacy of self-determination claims in the context of grievances of the claimant group, comes into picture. The people of Assam have historically had some grievances against some injustice that have been meted out to them. The sense of being victim of some injustice is very deep-seated in the minds of the Assamese people. A quick look at the historical context of the demand will bear this point. Recapturing of the historical developments is not within the scope of this chapter, but some points can be safely made. First, the legitimacy of the incorporation of Assam into India has remained disputed. Before the advent of the British, Assam had politically never been a part of India, and had always been an independent state. Assam was annexed into British India in 1826 through the Treaty of Yandabo whose legitimacy remains contested. Therefore, the incorporation of Assam into India is seen by some as illegal occupation of Assam.

Second, the people of Assam had to confront with certain political, cultural and economic challenges with the establishment of British rule in Assam. From the middle of the nineteenth century outsiders started pouring in to Assam with serious implication for socio-cultural, political and economic life of Assam. The colonial requirements of the British rule and the prevailing conditions of Assam contributed to such migration from the rest of India. From 1830 onwards the British capitalists started

## Self-determination, multi-ethnic state  43

establishing tea gardens in Assam and the absence of workforce compelled the British to import labourers from other part of India like Orissa, Jharkhand, Tamil Nadu, West Bengal, Kerala etc. And as the tea industry in Assam expanded the numbers of people imported to act as workers in tea gardens also went up (Hussain 1993:44). They were followed by the Western-educated Bengali people who were brought by the British to carry out different colonial administrative functions. This group of people, though numerically not very significant, came to enjoy significant political clout by virtue of their control over the government jobs (Phukon 1984:12). Another section of people who migrated to Assam was the Nepalese who came to Assam as cattle growers, dairy farmers, chowkidars, farmers etc. The integration of Assam with the British India also facilitated the coming of Marwaris and Biharis to Assam. Out of all these people, the immigration of Bengali peasants from East Bengal had been most serious and numerous. The British government in order to raise land revenue encouraged large-scale migration from overpopulated East Bengal to Assam which was at that time having surplus of land due to very low population. As a result from the beginning of the twentieth century the land and oppressed people of overpopulated East Bengal under direct official patronage started moving to Assam in lakhs and thousands in search of lands (Guha 2006:166). Such demographic invasion generated serious resentment among the Assamese people as such large-scale immigration was seen as threat to the existence and survival of Assamese as a distinct nation. It was feared that if the migration remained unchecked, Assamese would be reduced to minority in their homeland. As a result of steady inflow of outsiders, Assam witnessed sharp increase in the number of Muslim and Bengali-speaking population during the first half of the twentieth century. Such demographic changes also threatened the Assamese culture defined primarily in terms of Assamese language and Hindu religion. Moreover from the beginning of British rule, economy and resources of Assam had been subject to systematic exploitation by the outsiders. After coming to Assam they established complete domination over the economy of Assam and turned it into colonial economy. In the process Assamese lost their land, resources, business and other economic benefits initiated by the colonial rule.

In the post-independence period also, the situation did not improve for Assam. Assam continued to bear the burden of accommodating people coming from outside. The immediate aftermath of partition witnessed large-scale Hindu refugees from East Pakistan entering Assam for shelter. It was estimated that during 1947 to 1950 around three lakh Hindu Bengalis crossed the Assam border. The number of Hindu refugees in the state increased up to six lakh and twenty-eight thousand in 1961 (Misra

44   *Rubul Patgiri*

1999:111). Further, the flow of people from East Bengal did not stop. The census reports showed that during 1941–51, 1951–61 and 1961–71 the population growth rates of Assam were 20.1 per cent, 35.0 per cent and 34.7 per cent, respectively, against all-India rates of 13.3 per cent, 21.6 per cent and 24.6 per cent, respectively (Baruah 1980:544). Again, during 1971 to 1991 the rate of increase of Hindu population in Assam was 41.9 per cent, while during the same time Muslim population increased by 77.4 per cent. In 1991–2001, the growth rate of Hindu population was 15 per cent, whereas the corresponding figure for Muslim during the same period was 31 per cent (*Census Reports of India*, 1971, 1991, 2001). Such abnormal high growth rate of Muslim population indicates the continuous migration of Muslim people initially from East Pakistan and now from Bangladesh.

As a result of unabated and unchecked migration of Bengali-speaking Muslim population from East Pakistan and then from Bangladesh into Assam, the fear of Assamese culture being swamped by alien culture remains alive in post-independence period also. It is important to note here that in the post-independence period the number of Assamese-speaking people has increased from 36 per cent in 1931 to 61 per cent in 1971. At the same time the share of Bengali-speaking population of Assam declined from 30 per cent in 1931 to 21 per cent in 1951 and 20 per cent in 1971 (Guha 2006:94). These statistical figures indicating the increase of Assamese-speaking people, however, conceal more than they reveal. This is because first, the decline in the number of Bengali-speaking people is primarily due to the partition of Sylhet district and not because of decline in the migration of people to Assam and second, the rise in the number of Assamese-speaking people is the result of linguistic conversion of immigrant communities instead of rise of indigenous Assamese-speaking people. In the economic front too, the post-independence period has failed to bring any relief for the Assamese people, and in fact, there has been a clear sign of decline of Assamese economy after Independence. The poor economic condition of Assam has come to be conceived by the Assamese people as the result of domination and exploitation of Assam's economic resources by the outsiders. It is against this background that the thesis of Assam, being the internal colony of India, came up. It has been argued that the resources of Assam like oil, tea etc. have been siphoned out of Assam by the Centre without giving anything substantive in return. For instances, the royalty that was given to Assam for its oil was significantly low compared to the rate given to the other oil-producing regions of India. The revenue from tea was also not available to Assam as the tea auction centre was located in West Bengal. Despite producing the bulk of oil, Assam was not granted with a refinery, and only after the intense refinery agitation Assam

*Self-determination, multi-ethnic state* 45

got a refinery of nominal capacity. The Northeast, including Assam, has always been neglected in the matter of setting up of industries, institutions etc. There has been, it is maintained, inadequate representation of locals in the central institutions, offices and public sector undertakings (PSUs) situated in Assam. More importantly, the condition of the economy of this region remains poor in terms of infrastructural facilities, and it has remained outside the economic map of India because of lack of roads, infrastructure etc. (Misra 1980; 1999; Phukon 1984).

Fifth, the bitter experience of Assam about the grouping provision also deserves special mention. When, under the grouping provisions, Assam was clubbed with Group C provinces, Assam vehemently protested. But the Indian National Congress (INC) was unsympathetic to this genuine demand of Assam on the basis of their belief that the interest of India could not be hostage to the problem of Assam. This unsympathetic attitude of the INC towards such a crucial issue regarding the future of the Assamese left a deep scar on the minds of the Assamese people. Sixth, the Partition, which accompanied the Indian Independence, put Assam in a geographically disadvantageous position. Assam found itself geographically on the periphery without any access to the rest of India, and joined together only by a narrow stretch of 22 km, better known as Chicken's Neck. From this perspective, the demand for sovereign Assam can be seen as remedial right to these injustices.

Thus, the demand for self-determination for Assam can be seen as a result of the sense of belonging to the distinct Assamese nation, and existence of some threats, real or perceived, to the Assamese nation. The demand derives much of its support and legitimacy from these facts. Geographical insularity, lack of visibility in the mainstream national discourse and absence of effective communication between them have further increased the gulf. The net result of all these was the formation of a complex peripheral mentality on the part of a section of the Assamese people, and it is in this mentality that the roots of separatist tendencies among a section of Assamese people should be found.

## III

The idea of national self-determination was initially developed in Europe in response to the socio-political realities of Europe. In Europe it served important purposes, including the liberation of a number of subjugated nations. The principle of national self-determination is based on the belief that there should be congruence between cultural and political boundaries. In Europe the implementation of this principle was relatively easy because of the homogeneous character of their society. In subsequent time this idea of

## 46 *Rubul Patgiri*

self-determination travelled across to reach the Asian and African states and inspired the national liberation movements there. The appeal of the principle of national self-determination, however, did not disappear in this part of the world even after the completion of decolonisation process. Instead in the post-colonial period more and more ethno-national groups belonging to these newly independent states of Asia and Africa started defining their national aspiration in terms of the principle of national self-determination.

The blind emulation of this principle of national self-determination, particularly in its territorial version by the different ethno-national groups of the post-colonial states, has raised serious problems given the multi-ethnic character of their societies. The problem associated with the implementation of this principle, however, should not lead to the disapproval of this principle altogether as this principle may help the different ethno-national groups of the multi-ethnic states to realise their political and cultural aspirations. The acknowledgement of both the value and difficulty associated with the exercise of the principle of national self-determination calls for reformulation in the existing form of expression of this principle. If the principle of self-determination implies political and cultural right of people, then there is certainly space for some other form of expression of this right. Any such form of manifestation of self-determination, true to its meaning, must be able to ensure these cultural and political spaces of the aspiring group of people. Iris Marion Young has talked about non-domination as such a possible alternative form of expression of self-determination. She has argued that the existing interpretation of self-determination as sovereign independent state or non-interference as neither essential nor sufficient and instead offers an alternative interpretation of self-determination as non-domination which will ensure political, cultural and economic space for a group of people in the context of their mutual relation through some institutional arrangement (Young 2004:176–98).

The demand for self-determination of Assam in the form of a sovereign independent state cannot be supported in view of the situation of (in) Assam. Without going into the controversy, for a moment if we accept the genuineness of the grievances of the people of Assam and agree to see the demand for independent Assam as an expression of this feeling, does that automatically imply independent state as the appropriate solution? Such solution does not seem to be tenable both on account of the nature of the Assamese (people's) relation with India, and of the relation among the different groups of people within Assam. Like other groups of people, the Assamese also possess multiple and overlapping identity. The Assamese (community) by and large, besides their identity as Assamese, also share a strong sense of Indianness. Similarly, people belonging to different ethnic communities of Assam also carry a sub-identity in terms of their ethnic

*Self-determination, multi-ethnic state* 47

affiliation. Given this fact, the granting of an independent state to Assam would mean prioritising one identity over other identities. Moreover, the sense of dissatisfaction prevalent in Assam is not only in relation to Assam and the rest of India but also in relation among different groups of people living within Assam. As Assam blames India for its woes, so do the different ethnic groups of Assam who blame the dominant section of Assam for their backwardness. So, any solution to the problem of self-determination of Assam must address these two aspects – the relation between Assam and India, and the relation among the different groups of people within Assam. In these circumstances, the recognition of a sovereign independent status for Assam will not be of much help. Instead, some other alternative mechanism must be evolved which will take into account the legitimate demands of the people and would ensure the non-domination of people in their mutual relations. Such a mechanism can be negotiated within the federal structure of India.

## References

Anderson, Benedict. 1991. *Imagined Community*, 2nd edition. London: Verso.
Ayoob, Mohammed. 1997. 'Defining Security: A Subaltern Realist Perspective'. In K. Krause and M. Williams (eds), *Critical Security Studies*. Minneapolis: University of Minnesota Press.
Baruah, Apurba K. 1991. *Social Tension in Assam: Middle Class Politics*. Guwahati: Purbanchal Prakash.
Baruah, Sanjib. 1980. 'Assam Cudgel of Chauvinism or Tangled Nationality Question?', *Economic and Political Weekly*, 15(11): 543–45.
Buchanan, A. 1991. *The Morality of Political Divorce from Fort Sumter to Lithuania and Quebec*. Boulder, CO: Westview Press.
Census Reports of India, 1971, 1991, 2001.
Day, Graham and Andrew Thompson. 2004. *Theorizing Nationalism*. Palgrave: Macmillan Press.
Emerson, Rupert. 1971. 'Self-determination', *The American Journal of International Law*, 65: 459–75.
Gellner, Earnest. 1983. *Nation and Nationalism*. Oxford: Basil Blackwell.
Guha, Amalendu. 2006a. 'Little Nationalism Turned Chauvinist: Assam's Anti-Foreigner Upsurge, 1979–80'. In A. N. S. Ahmed (ed.), *Nationality Question in Assam: The EPW 1980–81 Debate*. New Delhi: Akansha Publishing House.
Guha, Amalendu. 2006b. *Planter Raj to Swaraj: Freedom Struggle & Electoral Politics in Assam 1826–1947*. New Delhi: Tulika Books.
Hussain, Monirul. 1993. *The Assam Movement-Class, Ideology and Identity*. New Delhi: Manak Publishers.
Jennings, Ivor. 1956. 'The Approach to Self-Government' cited in Michla Pomerance, 'The United States and Self-Determination: Perspective on

48   *Rubul Patgiri*

Wilsonian Conception', *The American Journal of International Law*, 70(1976): 16.

Memorandum submitted to the Prime Minister of India demanding a separate state comprising the Mikir Hills, North Cachar Hills and the contiguous Tribal Areas in Assam on behalf of the Mikir and North Cachar Hills Leaders' Conference, Assam, 9 June 1973.

Misra, Udayan. 1999. *Periphery Strikes Back: Challenges to the Nation-State in Assam and Nagaland.* Shimla: Indian Institute of Advanced Study.

Misra, Tilottomma. 1980. 'Assam: A Colonial Hinterland', *Economic and Political Weekly*, 15(32): 1357–59, 1361–64.

Moore, Margaret (ed.). 1998a. *National Self-Determination and Secession.* Oxford: Oxford University Press.

Moore, Margaret (ed.). 1998b. *The Self-Determination Principle and the Ethics of Secession: National Self-Determination and Secession.* New York: Oxford University Press.

Norman, Wayne. 1998. 'The Ethics of Secession as the Regulation of Secessionist Politics'. In Margaret Moore (ed.), *The Self-Determination Principle and the Ethics of Secession: National Self-Determination and Secession*, pp. 34–61. New York: Oxford University Press.

Philpott, D. 1995. 'In Defense of Self-Determination', *Ethics*, 105: 352–85.

Phukon, Girin. 1984. *Assam's Attitude to Federalism.* New Delhi: Sterling Publishers.

Pomerance, Michla. 1976. 'The United States and Self-Determination: Perspective on Wilsonian Conception', *The American Journal of International Law*, 70(1): 1–27.

The Memorandum submitted by the United Liberation Front of Asom (ULFA) to the Secretary General of the United Nations (UN), published in Budhbar, 26 November 1990.

Young, Iris M. 2004. 'Two Concepts of Self-Determination'. In Stephen May, Tariq Modood and Judith Squires (eds), *Ethnicity, Nationalism and Minority Rights.* Cambridge: Cambridge University Press.

# 4 *Sarbabhoumo Asom*
## Three public discourses

*Uddipan Dutta*

The idea of *Swadhin Asom* (independent Assam) is not entirely a new concept in the public discourse of Assam. But, the notion had assumed a greater importance after the emergence of the United Liberation Front of Assam (ULFA) as a distinct political force with the ideology of establishing a 'sovereign, independent Assam based on scientific socialism' (Hazarika 1989). The writings of Ambikagiri Roychoudhury and Jnananath Bora are often invoked in this connection. Ambikagiri Roychoudhury, an iconic figure in Assam, well known for his radical voice, had raised consistently the issue of danger to the Assamese identity in the face of state-sponsored migration during the colonial period and afterwards. He was one of the earliest Assamese thinkers to come up with a clearly distinct idea of Assamese nationalism with reference to its relationship with pan-Indian nationalism way back in 1920 in a well-articulated editorial 'Bharatiyar Swaraj Aru Asamiyar Swaraj' in *Chetana*, the magazine published and edited by him.

When he referred to India as a *mahajati* and the Assamese as a *jati*, he tried to work out the position of Assamese in a federal state. Despite deeply being involved in Congress politics, Roychoudhury not only maintained this federalist position throughout his political career, but also shifted closer to the notion of an independent Assam towards the end of his trajectory. The idea of *Swadhin Asom* was posed even more radically by Jnananath Bora, a leading intellectual of Assam, during the 1930s in articles published in *Awahon*, the journal acclaimed for heralding a new age in Assamese literary and intellectual world, and in *Dainik Batori*, considered as the first daily newspaper in Assamese with similar headings and concerns. The call for an independent Assam was not only an expression of emotion and pride – it had its basis in problems such as the British-sponsored migration,[1] annexation of Assam with Bengal in the beginning of the British rule,[2] later amalgamation of historically unattached Sylhet district in Assam Province,[3] introduction of Bengali as the medium of instruction,[4] tension over the policy on opening up of reserve land for immigrant cultivators

50   *Uddipan Dutta*

since 1930s, Jinnah's bid for inclusion of Assam in Pakistan which posed constant threat to the Assamese identity during the colonial period. The peculiarity of Assam's situation assumed so much of significance that it almost bottlenecked the national-level negotiations with the Cabinet Mission.[5] Against this backdrop, the proposition of independent Assam gained currency during the gestation period before the birth of the Union, among a wide range of political groups, such as the All Assam Ahom Association (AAAA), Communist Party of India (CPI), a group within Pradesh Congress, and the likes. However, the pre-independence demand for a *Swadhin Asom* died down once the Muslim majority of Sylhet voted for Pakistan[6] and the threat to Assam and Assamese identity temporally receded.

Although the 'step-motherly treatment of centre towards Assam'[7] was a dominant theme in the public discourse of Assam after Independence, the discussion on a separate independent, sovereign Assam was a strict no till the emergence of ULFA in the political arena of Assam. The military infrastructure it has developed, the foreign links it has established, the mass base it has created and, most importantly, the terror tactics it has adopted make the organisation's claim a much more serious political issue for the Indian state as well as for the people of Assam. For the last three decades, the state is in a state of conflict and uncertainty, revolved around the concept of 'independent Assam'. It has witnessed the growth of ULFA, its popularity, fear psychosis, euphoria, subsequent crackdown of it by the Indian state, human rights abuse by both state forces and ULFA, surrender of a section of ULFA militants, internecine violence leading to bloodbath of the surrendered and non-surrendered groups, secret killings of the relatives of ULFA members with active support from the state machinery, peace process started by the Union Government with a section of the ULFA leaders led by its chairman amidst hope and disappointment, the total terror tactics adopted by ULFA like bomb blasts in public places and numerous other acts of violence. It is natural that the issue of *swadhin sarbobhoumo Asom* (sovereign, independent Assam) got its way into the public sphere and a rich body of texts around this issue written in both English and Assamese are now available. In one extreme end, the texts took its position for an overall support to the notion of *Swadhin Asom*, and on the other side of it, viewpoints rejecting it completely.

Even though a very rich body of writings on the issue exists, scattered across the pages of both local and national print media, only three written texts in Assamese that got published as books are chosen for the purpose of this chapter, and, wherever necessary, the method of translation is used extensively to understand the texts. It is just a modest attempt to see some of the important points made on this discourse by analysing these important texts written by three important persons known for their distinct public opinions regarding the issue of 'sovereignty of Assam'. The first two texts *Swadhinatar Prastab* (The Proposal for Independence) (Das 1993) and *ULFAr Swadhin Asom* (Independent Assam of ULFA) (Deka 1994) deal exclusively on the issue of sovereignty of Assam. The third text, *Sarbabhoumo Asom Aru Anyanya Prasanga: Raktakta Der Dashakar Dalil* (Sovereign Assam and Other Issues: Document of a Blood Stained One and Half Decade) (Sharma 1993), is a collection of essays in the form of a book based on a few articles published in various contemporary newspapers and magazines on different burning problems of the state. Since only two of these essays deal exclusively with the demand of sovereignty raised by ULFA and the activities of the organisation, the discussion would remain confined to only with these two essays – *Ulfai Pokkhyo Posondo Korok!* (ULFA Must Choose Its Side!) and *Sarbabhoumo Asom Abhimukhe* (Towards Sovereign Assam).

It must be mentioned in this context that these three texts are chosen very carefully as representatives of three distinct views on the issue of sovereignty of Assam. It would not be an exaggeration to categorise the position of Parag Kumar Das the author of *Swadhinatar Prastab* as a radical nationalist favouring an independent Assam and that of Kanaksen Deka, the author of *ULFAr Swadhin Asom*, as a constitutional status quoist. The position of Devabrata Sharma, the writer of *Sarbabhoumo Asom Aru Anyanya Prasanga: Raktakta Der Dashakar Dalil*, on the other hand should be classified as a radical federalist inclined towards a poly-ethnic federal arrangement. Within these three broader ideological classifications, one can put many other texts dealing with the issue of the sovereignty of Assam raised by the ULFA, and these three distinct positions of the authors are used as examples of three distinct patterns representing a wide array of writings on this issue. A look at these three texts individually to see how the 'facts' got represented is required to elicit how arguments got built up and inferences were drawn in accordance with respective ideological moorings of the authors.

*Swadhinatar Prastab*, written by the late Parag Kumar Das, was first published in November 1993, and was proscribed by the state government after few months of its publication. The verbatim translation of the title – 'The Proposal for Independence' – bears the testimony of its advocacy for a 'free sovereign Assam'. Clearly, Parag Kumar Das wrote the book for the masses and with the agenda of validating the argument for a free sovereign Assam by showing the distinctness of Assam from India. In his advocacy-discourse, he selectively picks up the examples from the various fields of knowledge like geography, anthropology, history, economics etc. The narrative starts rather dramatically, the first chapter telling the story of the 'heroic' birth of ULFA. In the second chapter, the author

## 52 *Uddipan Dutta*

tries to validate the demand for an independent sovereign Assam by looking at the various resolutions passed in the two international forums – the League of Nations (LN) and the United Nations (UN) – on the criteria for becoming a nation-state. One of the principal arguments of the book stems from the definition of non-self-governing territory adopted by the Resolution 1541(XV) of UN General Assembly in 1960 which according to him is that 'a territory is *prima facie* non-self-governing if it is both geographically separate and ethnically distinct from the country administering it'. He cites it and builds up his discourse in validating this point. According to him, India had argued for the independence of Bangladesh on the floor of the UN on the ground of this resolution, and so, he argues that the Indian state should not hesitate to look into the acceptability of the demand for a 'sovereign Assam'. Then he focuses his argument on showing how Assam is different geographically and ethnically from 'Indian mainland'.

In almost all militant nationalist discourses, we find the argument that Assam is connected to the 'mainland India' by a very narrow corridor, often called the Chicken's Neck, to show the geographical isolation of the region. Parag Kumar Das is also not an exception, and he emphasises this point in his discourse. Selectively picking up data from physical anthropology, he then goes on to build up his argument that the Assamese people are different from the people of the rest of India. According to him, whereas the Caucasian group of people who had migrated from the northwestern side of India now constitutes the main inhabitants of India, the Mongoloid group of people who had migrated through the north-eastern side of Assam constitutes the major populace of Assam. Although he does not deny the existence of the people with the Caucasian root in Assam, he claims that these people have long ago lost their original cultural and linguistic traits due to the process of assimilation. He goes even further and picks up a hypothesis drawn by A. H. Keane (*Man: Past and Present*, 1920), and some other anthropologists, and argues that even Caucasians had migrated to Assam through the north-eastern routes. According to this theory, one branch of the Caucasians had migrated to the eastern side and reached China and Japan, and later on, a smaller group from that branch of people entered Assam through the north-eastern side. He identifies physical traits like yellowish colour, short nose, flat face, scattered beard etc. as representative features of Assamese people. The most glaring example of the selective representation of this scientific fact is found in his claim that the anthropologists have discovered haemoglobin E in the blood samples of the native communities of Assam which is absent in the blood samples of other communities in India, and that it was found in a survey that the earwax of the indigenous communities of Assam is dry while the earwax of

*Sarbabhoumo Asom* 53

the people from the other parts of the country is tacky. So, he berates those people of Assam who are trying to hide their unique anthropological characteristics in order to get assimilated into the Indian mainstream.

Das then brings examples from cultural anthropology and avers that the Assamese way of life is completely different from the Indian way of life. First, he takes the example of the food habit, and argues that it is marked by an overwhelming non-vegetarianism. To prove his point, he argues that in Assam the people of the upper castes are non-vegetarians to the core while the upper castes of India are strong vegetarians. According to him, for that reason only, even Sankardeva[8] had established his *satras*[9] where fish was abundant and there is a description at *Katha Guru Carit*[10] how he had relished different fish cuisines. *Kumol chawal,*[11] boiled rice and alkali made of banana peels used in place of salt are some of the unique characteristics of Assamese food as argued by the author. In his view, the traditional house building technique of Assamese people with bamboo and hay is also quite unique. In the same way, the rigid caste system and the custom of taking dowry from the bride's family – the two defining features of Indian tradition – are absent in Assamese tradition, according to the author. He endorses his argument by the following examples: there is no inhibition in Assam for a Brahmin to work in the field, there is no weaving community in the state and that the Assamese women of each family weave clothes necessary for their own use, whereas making of musical instruments with animal skin is regarded as a profession of the lower birth in Indian society – it is not so in Assam, and there is the mention of Sankardeva himself making *khol*[12] using animal skin, and contrary to the Indian tradition, there is still a tradition of taking customary gifts from the groom's family as a bride price instead of taking dowry from the bride's family among some traditional communities of Assam. He also mentions that the Tibeto-Burman influence is very evident in the music and musical instruments of Assam. He even goes further and opines that whereas the Indian languages are part of the Indo-European linguistic family, the native languages of Assam are part of the Tibeto-Burman language family. He complains that there is a constant effort at eliding these unique characteristics of the Assamese people by the Indian state machinery. Thus, Parag Kumar Das makes an attempt to distinguish the 'Assamese people' from the 'people of India' ethnically and culturally, overlooking the age-old cultural-linguistic ties with the other parts of India. He makes a serious faux pas by putting all the languages of Assam in the Tibeto-Burman language family. Ironically enough Assamese, the language in which he is writing, is, in fact, an Indo-Aryan language. It is also a fallacious argument that the caste system does not prevail in Assam. Although it is not as severe and rigid as that of North India, it still exists and is rooted deeply in Assam.

## 54    *Uddipan Dutta*

In the making of a nationalist discourse of uniqueness, history plays a very important role; some events are often invoked, while some others get excluded. *Swadhinatar Prastab* too reads and interprets history selectively to suit its set agenda of demonstrating the separate past of Assam from that of India. Interestingly, however, Das selects those examples which suit his argument and skilfully discards the others that seem contrary to his contention.

Parag Kumar Das starts with *Ramayana and Mahabharata* and shows how the people of the region (now called Assam, were described derogatorily in these texts as asura,[13] *danaba*[14] *or dustatma*.[15] According to him, the examples he cites is enough to show that the Aryan people of India always had a condescending attitude towards the Mongoloid people of Assam and also that racially the people of these two regions were quite different. He goes further and says that even 'Mahatma'[16] Gandhi had described Assam as the country of *thugs* and *pindaris* during the beginning of the twentieth century without mentioning, however, the fact that Gandhi had apologised immediately for such a comment due to his ignorance. Then he goes on to show that Assam had never been a part of any of the empires that were built up in the Indian subcontinent. The territory of Emperor Ashoka extended only to North Bengal. Although there is mention of Kamarupa[17] in one of the inscriptions of the Allahabad stone pillar, in his opinion it is highly improbable that Kamarupa was ever under the Gupta Empire as such important information is not to be found in any other historical documents. Das, however, ignores the very fact that the ancient Assamese art and architecture had largely been influenced by the Indian art, particularly the Gandhara art and Gupta art. According to him, there is evidence that the pre-medieval kings of Kamarupa had taken the title of *Maharajadhiraj*, the traditional title of the sovereign kings skilfully evading the fact that taking such a title was an all-India fashion, and it does not necessarily mean any separate identity. According to him, Hiuen Tsiang[18] who had visited Kamarupa, described it as a sovereign country ascribing its people with different anthropological characteristics. He also claims that ancient Kamarupa had never been subjugated, even after its fragmentation into smaller states. Then he goes on to show how the Ahoms, who had consolidated their reign in the region during the thirteenth century, had maintained its sovereignty in the face of repeated Muslim invasion.

As Parag Kumar Das puts it, Kanai Baroxi Stone of North Guwahati bears testimony of the unsuccessful expedition of Mohammad Ibn Bakhtiar in 1205. That was the beginning. In 1257, Ikhitiyar Uddin Yuzbek Tughril Khan got defeated in his expedition of Kamrup. In the same manner, Alauddin Hussain Shah's expedition was repelled by the Ahoms taking advantage of the rainy season. In the seventeenth century, there was a series

## Sarbabhoumo Asom 55

of Moghul expeditions in Assam. In 1661, Aurangzeb sent his powerful lieutenant Mirzumla to invade Assam. Although he was successful in bringing Gargaon, the capital city of the Ahoms, into his possession, his success was short-lived; within six months the Ahoms defeated the Moghuls and reclaimed their territories.

He concludes how Assam maintained its sovereignty in the face of repeated Muslim attacks during the medieval period, quoting it from Sir Edward Gait's *A History of Assam*, which reads as 'Assam was one of the few countries in India whose inhabitants beat back the tide of Moghul conquest and maintained their independence in the face of repeated attempts to subvert it'. He also quotes Shihab al-Din Talish,[19] the famous chronicler accompanying Mirzumla, for recognising the uniqueness of Assam and the Assamese people.

Most ironically, Parag Kumar Das invokes Bipan Chandra to reinstate his argument. According to him, Bipan Chandra's *Modern India*, published by National Council of Educational Research and Training (NCERT), does not mention Assam in the chapter dealing with the states of India during the eighteenth century. Rather, Assam appears in the chapter dealing with the neighbouring states of India. And from it Parag Kumar Das draws the conclusion that Assam was never ever a part of India, before its 'illegal' occupation by the British.

In the chapter *Paradhinotar Duhswapna* (The Nightmare of Subjugation), Das traces the history of Assamese resistance to the British rule. According to him, although the middle class extended its support to the British rule, the resistance was mounted on by the peasants. He ends up that part of the history of Assam by quoting a portion of the article of Jnananath Bora who raised the issue of independence. In the chapter titled *Kshyamota Hostantoror Tikto Odhyay* (The Bitter Chapter of the Transfer of Power), he avers that the leadership of the Indian National Congress used Assam as a pawn in the gamble of transfer of power from the British to Indian hands. In March 1946, the Cabinet Mission came to India to discuss the matter of transfer of power. The Mission put forward the proposal of grouping, and without any hesitation the Indian National Congress leadership agreed to the proposal of inclusion of Assam in Group C. As soon as the White Paper of the Cabinet Mission was released, Assam lodged its opposition to the proposal. But the central leadership was not ready to listen to the protest lodged by the Assamese leadership, and had decided to go ahead with its proposal. According to him, Jawaharlal Nehru even scolded the Assamese leadership as 'India cannot wait for Assam'. But, the Mission Plan was thwarted by the Assamese leadership with the active support of Mahatma Gandhi. Then he casts his attention upon Gopinath Bordoloi. According to him, although Bordoloi's political

## 56  Uddipan Dutta

ideology was shaped by the Congress politics of that period, he never hesitated to recognise Assam as a unique political entity. He credits Gopinath Bordoloi of making a plan for a sovereign Assam in the prospect of Azad Hind Fauj occupying Assam. Citing Md. Tayabulla,[20] he recounts how Bordoloi had convened a secret meeting in the jail, where he was lodged with his colleagues, to shape Assam's destiny independent of India, during the precarious period of the Second World War. The author also states that Bordoloi had proposed an American-style constitution in his meeting with the Cabinet Mission, in which the provincial units would get the highest power. Not only that, according to him, during the height of the anti-grouping movement, Bordoloi had passed a resolution in the Assembly that the people's representatives would draft their own constitution, and that they would not accept a constitution given from the top. In his account of Assam's resistance to British, he selectively brings in the example of staunch Assamese nationalists like Jnananath Bora, Ambikagiri Roychoudhury and Nilomoni Phukan, and glorifies their vision and contribution without mentioning the selfless contributions and martyrdom of the many other Congress workers of that period.

The history of the transfer of power from the British to the Indian hand is reinvented and recreated by Parag Kumar Das. He brings into the light a rather unknown aspect of the transfer of power. According to him, the British agreed to the transfer of power on the basis of a secret pact with the Indian leadership during the period, and one of the conditions was the protection of the 'Sterling Capital' that was invested in India at that time. The leadership from the Hindi belt had nothing to worry as there was no investment of 'Sterling Capital' in North India, but that secret agreement was quite dangerous for Assam, as all the tea gardens were under the control of the Sterling Capital. Still, these dangerous conditions were not reported to the people of Assam, and thus the so-called independence spawns in the soil of Assam an enclave-economy, on which the people of Assam has no right as interpreted by the author. Every year, crores of rupees are taken away by the multinational companies on the basis of that secret pact, and the gardens get sold in the international market in hundreds of crores of rupees. To prove this point, he provides an instance how the tea gardens of Assam are bought and sold in the international market, the deals over which not only the people of Assam but also Indian state has no right – in 1991, a company called *Inscap* had sold 12 tea gardens of Assam to another company of Uganda at the price of Rs 110 crore. So, he maintains that the people of Assam must claim their right in their own land. Like the previous occasions, here also Das does not provide the source of his information, and there is no way to refute or endorse his claim on the secret pact and transaction of tea gardens.

Like history and anthropology, Parag Kumar Das makes use of economics, as well, in his argument for a 'sovereign, independent Assam'. To break the myth that Assam would not be able to survive without the Centre's financial aid, he calculates in terms of international market how much Assam would have earned from the crude oil extracted from the region, and the tea produced. According to him, from 1947 to 1962, Assam would have earned US$24 million, from the 1.6 million tons of crude oil extracted with the average of US$15 per ton, and from 1963 to 1970, in eight years, 28 million tons of crude oil was robbed from Assam, and the price would have been US$616 million with an estimated average price of US$22 per ton. In the same way, with the increasing prices of the crude oil in the international market, he estimates that Assam had lost US$5,500 million during the period 1971–80 and US$12,740 million in the period 1981–93. According to Das, these figures are much higher than the allotted central funds to Assam in those years.

He goes on further and surmises that had Assam developed its own petro-chemical industries, the international market price of the products would have been thousands of crores. Then he takes the example of tea, and tries to calculate the international price of the tea extracted from the tea gardens of Assam. He divides the post-independence period into three phases, takes the average price of the tea in the international market and then calculates the value. According to him, during 1947–61, Assam had produced 2,625 million kg of tea, and fixing the price at US$2 per kg, he calculates the international price of extracted tea as US$5,250 million during that period. With the increasing production of tea, and its price, the author puts the international price of the tea produced in the tea gardens of Assam as US$9,375 million during 1962–76, and US$13,500 million during 1977–92. Thus, he tries to show how the resources of Assam are getting plundered, and also the potentiality of using these resources in making a very prosperous Assam. The possibility of using bamboo-based industry is also mentioned by the author. He does not forget to refer to the discovery of microphone quartz in Karbi Hills, zircon sands at Subansiri Valley and granite stone found in the Khasi Hills (interestingly, he includes Khasi Hills in the industrial possibility of a sovereign Assam). Thus, Das argues that the economic prospect of sovereign Assam should be considered only from the perspective of the international market of the natural resources of Assam.

Parag Kumar Das gives a description of the state-terror on the innocent people, and mentions the degeneration of a section of ULFA after their surrender. He concludes his discourse with the proposal of recognising the right to self-determination and the right to secession from the Indian state. According to him, this is the last proposal to the Indian state, meaning that after this, direct actions would be undertaken by the people of Assam.

## 58  *Uddipan Dutta*

Quite opposite to the argumentation of Parag Kumar Das, we get the discourse of Kanaksen Deka, a well-known critic of ULFA and its set objective of a sovereign, independent Assam. In his book *ULFAr Swadhin Asom*, he rejects straightforwardly the principle of self-determination as unrealistic, shows Assam's historical and cultural ties with mainland India, puts absolute faith in the existing system of governance in India and identifies inferiority complex as the source of the separatist trend among a section of the youth of Assam. The author expresses his view that ULFA's demand for a sovereign, independent Assam is based upon the principle of self-determination. But he warns that the model of self-determination adopted and implemented in Europe cannot be adopted and implemented in India, because for thousands of years the people belonging to the different communities, religion and language have been living in India sharing the same cultural and linguistic traits. According to him, the division of a country does not solve the problems but rather multiplies, and makes them more complicated. He then discusses the political debate on the issue of self-determination, and quotes selective excerpts from the political thinkers like Professor Hayes, J. S. Mill, Professor Maclver, Burns, Lord Action, Bertrand Russell, Karl Marx, Joad, Hegel, Dr Garner and Harold J. Laski to draw his inference that the nation-state is indispensable to the human existence. He blames the various self-determination movements for blocking the development of the state. In his opinion, a huge amount of money gets spent on defence, and keeping law and order, which could have been spent otherwise in various development schemes. He draws the conclusion that although it may sound ideal to provide exclusive administration to each ethnic, religious and linguistic group, it is not realistic.

To show how unrealistic the demand of the sovereignty of Assam on the principle of the right to self-determination is, he argues that there will be more than 20 sovereign states alone in Assam if that principle is to be followed in the truest sense of the term. To reinforce his view that the nation-state represents its citizens, and that it is the best existing organised system, he orchestrates the welfare schemes undertaken by the Indian state, particularly in sectors like public health and education. According to him, in 1952, the average age of Indian people was just 32 years, and there was a time when epidemics like malaria and black fever had threatened to wipe out the entire population of Assam, but it is due to the effort of the Indian state that the average age of the Indian people has soared up to more than 60 years, and these two epidemics have almost been eradicated. Deka also reminds the readers that till 1947 there was not a single university in Assam, but it now has five universities and a large number of colleges, higher secondary schools and high schools. He also praises the Indian state for the uplift of the conditions of the backward communities

## Sarbabhoumo Asom 59

by providing reservation in jobs and education. The betterment of the conditions of women is also put forward by the author to praise the Indian state. He also castigates the people who criticise the state machinery for every evil in the society. According to him, every citizen is a shareholder and architect of this machinery. He emphasises the indispensability of the state machinery, and affirms that even if a separate independent Assam is achieved, it must be administered by the state machinery only. He also nullifies the assumption that the government is run with the blessings of the capitalist forces, by citing the example of the successful victory of Asom Gana Parishad (AGP) in the 1985 election, which it fought with people's power. According to him, the characteristics of the people get reflected in the characteristics of the government.

After rejecting the principle of self-determination as unrealistic in the contemporary world, and putting his absolute faith upon the institution of the nation-state, he goes on to discuss specifically the issue of sovereignty of Assam raised by ULFA. The unresolved issue of the Assamese identity along with the changing map of Assam is brought by the author to show the weakness in the claim of ULFA. According to him, the term as well as the notion of Assamese identity was not extant a few hundred years back, and the boundary of the Ahom kingdom was never stable. In his view, Assamese nationality has come to existence by the process of assimilation of the various communities with distinct cultural, linguistic and religious heritage. He warns that if that process gets thwarted as a result of the growth of a separatist mindset, the result would be quite catastrophic to the Assamese nationality. Taking a cue from the writings of Jyoti Prasad, he calls upon the people of Assam to become a world-citizen, and an Indian-citizen in order to become an Assamese citizen. In his view, Swami Vivekananda and Rabindranath Tagore were worthy Bengalis because they were great Indians as well. He reiterates his position that in this age of co-existence, Assamese tradition would not survive if it attempts to deny the influence of the traditions like Hindustani, Islamic and Mongoloid on it.

He goes on to counter the propaganda that the Assamese people would become minority in their own place in the coming years. According to him, this fear of being outnumbered in Assam has caused irreparable loss to the Assamese society. With statistical data and historical account, he then tries to demystify this assumption and calls upon the people who are orchestrating such slogans to work towards the growth of the Assamese language. In his opinion, Assamese language requires a total reform, so that groups like Tai-Ahoms, Bodos, Karbis etc. could discover themselves in Assamese language. He also emphasises the need to upgrade the standard of the Assamese-medium schools. He quotes the *Manorama Yearbook*, 1994, to show that the position of Assamese among the languages of the world in

60    *Uddipan Dutta*

terms of its user is 36, and avers that the attitude of the speakers of a language only determines its fate; if the speakers of Assamese maintain a progressive and accommodative attitude, no external force can wipe out the Assamese language.

The exploitation of the resources of Assam by the Indian Union is an oft-used argument in favour of the sovereignty of Assam, and quite predictably, Kanaksen Deka argues that there is no such exploitation and puts his statistics in favour of his argument. He takes the hint for his argumentation from the statement of a CPI leader that every year the central government takes away petroleum worth Rs 2,000 crore annually from Assam. Deka rues the fact that it was not mentioned by the CPI leader that more than Rs 1,000 crore gets spent in the process of the extraction, and Assam gets a royalty of Rs 528 crore every year in lieu of the petroleum. Deka concludes that the Union Government gets only Rs 472 crore from the petroleum extracted in Assam. In the same vein, he argues that it is a myth that the central government takes away Rs 2,000 crore annually from the tea produced in Assam. According to him, the central government received only Rs 78 crore, whereas Assam had received Rs 150 crore as tax from the tea industry of Assam in the year 1993. However, Deka concedes that the profit goes into the coffers of the owners of the tea gardens. He calculates the amount and finds that the central government receives only Rs 550 crore as tax from the resources of Assam, but excluding the expenditure on defence and internal security, Assam receives Rs 2,500 crore as grant from the central government. Thus, with these figures, he attempts to prove that the central government is not to be blamed for the lack of development in Assam. He claims that the central government judiciously distributes the money among all the states of the country.

Nor does he subscribe to the view that the unemployment among the youths is the cause of the rise of separatist insurgency in the state. According to him, the situation of unemployment is graver in states like West Bengal, Bihar, Madhya Pradesh etc. but, unlike the youths of Assam, the youths of these states have neither set up camps in Bangladesh nor taken up the suicidal path. Deka rather identifies the distorted representation of the history of Assam as the primary reason for the emergence of a separatist mindset. He recounts the history of Assam with an emphasis on its historical ties with mainland India, and shows that the demand of a sovereign independent Assam is not valid historically. In this context, he also makes the distinction between the demand of sovereignty raised by the Nagas and the same demand raised by the Assamese youths. According to him, the relationship of Assam-Kamarupa-Pragjyotish with the Indian mainland is 5,000 years, and there is no need to elaborate over the cordial relationship maintained by Bhaskarvarman and other kings of the region during the

*Sarbabhoumo Asom* 61

pre-Ahom period. But his main emphasis is on the relationship that the Ahoms had established with Hindustan. In his view, it is quite significant that the Ahoms had used languages like Tai, Sanskrit and Parsi in their coins.

Through selective reading of history, he also shatters the argument often put forward by the proponents of *Swadhin Asom* that the Treaty of Yandabo (1826), which brought Assam into British India, is unacceptable as it was signed between two foreign powers, the British and the Burmese, without the consent of the Assamese people. According to him, this is a fallacious reasoning as the Treaty was welcomed by the people of Assam as well as the exiled Ahom monarchy during the period. He goes further and argues that *Swargadeu* Purandar Singha[21] was the representative of the Ahom monarchy, and the people of the Ahom kingdom during the period, and it was he who was entitled to lodge complaint against the Treaty, but, instead of lodging any complaint, Purandar Singha had welcomed it. The author then cites martyrs like Maniram Dewan,[22] Kushal Konwar[23] and Kanaklata[24] to drive home the point that these martyrs were part of the all-India struggle against the British. Then he argues that the Assam Association[25] which was formed in 1903 with the objective of liberating Assam from the British, had merged with the INC in the year 1921. In his opinion, had the people of Assam wanted a sovereign country, the Assam Association would never have merged with the INC. The refusal of the Assamese leadership to join hands with Phizo, the legendary Naga rebel, is also put forward by the author as the proof of the emotional oneness of the Assamese people with mainland India.

Throughout the discourse, Kanaksen Deka mentions the lack of self-confidence and a growing inferiority complex among the present generation of Assamese people as the cause of the present pitiable state of Assam. According to him, due to the lack of self-confidence, Assamese people are suffering from a fear psychosis, and due to the fear psychosis, we do not find any original technical book in Assamese. But, in his view, earlier the people of Assam were confident and brave, and to prove his point he traces that part of the glorious history when the Ahoms had defeated the Moghuls in the Battle of Saraighat.[26] He argues that the lack of self-confidence among the Assamese people is best exemplified in the failure of the Assam Movement. Elaborating his point, he blames the Assam Movement for the sorry state of affairs in the state, and the chasm dividing the society. According to him, this period has witnessed the worst form of moral decadence, and everybody in Assam is bearing the brunt of the Assam Movement. The reason he identifies for the growth of ULFA is also the inferiority complex among the present generation of Assamese people. As a salvage of his contention, the author puts the demand of All Assam Students' Union

## 62   *Uddipan Dutta*

(AASU), and the Asom Jatiyatabadi Yuba Chatra Parishad (AJYCP) for the special protection of the natives of Assam. According to him, the protection and reservation are sought only by weaklings. It is quite interesting to note that AASU and AJYCP, the two student bodies, are identified by the author as supporters of ULFA.

He ends his discourse with an elaborate discussion on the terrorism across the world. He tries to find out the definition of terrorism, the modus operandi of the terrorists and the measures taken by the states to curb the menace of terrorism. Needless to say that he classifies ULFA as a terrorist organisation and asks its cadres to shun the path of violence and join the mainstream. A calendar of the major events of violence related to ULFA from 1979 to 1994 is also appended with the book.

As has already been stated earlier, *Sarbabhoumo Asom Aru Anyanya Prasanga: Raktakta Der Dashakar Dalil* is a collection of essays by Devabrata Sharma where he discusses the different aspects of the politics of Assam; however, only two of these essays deal exclusively with the demand of sovereignty raised by ULFA, and the activities of the organisation. So, an attempt is made here to read through these two articles to understand some of the points the author tries to make in his discourse. The article titled *ULFAi Pakkhyo Posondo Korok!* (ULFA must choose its side!) originally got published in *Sutradhar*, March 1990. In this essay, he had criticised ULFA on strategic and theoretical ground. The author had to face bullet attacks from the ULFA cadres for opposing the activities of the organisation. The edited version of the original article is reproduced in this collection, and it must be understood in the context of 1990 when ULFA was virtually running a parallel administration, and there was no state resistance to it.

The context of this essay is derived from the call given by ULFA at that time to stop Hindi expansionism perpetrated by the Indian bourgeoisie. According to the author, he would have also welcomed that call of ULFA had it originated from a healthy aspiration to strengthen the local capital, instead of an unproductive jealousy of the Assamese middle class. To describe the prevailing situation of that period, he brings in the simile of a rail engine moving ahead without the coaches, and making a record in terms of its speed. He points out to the fact that the Assamese media at that time was mesmerised by the bravado of the petit-bourgeois young revolutionaries who had kept the peasant-labourer proletariats away from their struggle. So, the author proposes to bring some aspects of the uncomfortable facts regarding the strategy of ULFA. According to him, the formation of capital in Assam should involve rapid industrialisation, and equal redistribution of land. He reminds the reader that although the people of Assam were aware of the exploitation of the north Indian capitalist force during the Assam Movement, the leadership adopted the shallow programme of *swabalambita* (self-help) which got evaporated no sooner than it was launched. The leaders of the Assam Movement who had assumed power after the historic Assam Accord draws his censure for involving themselves in the corruption of permit, dealership and brokerage instead of a whole-hearted effort to strengthen the local capital. From the experience of the Assam Movement, the author expresses his doubt whether the same non-productive mindset is at work behind the insurgency started by ULFA. He criticises ULFA for its daydream of making an end of the exploitation of the Hindi-Hindu lobby by way of coercion and gun. In his opinion, there cannot be an end to the cultural expansionism of the Hindi lobby unless the economic and political hegemony of that lobby is brought to an end. He acknowledges that India is ruled by a circle of north Indian caste Hindu capitalists and landlords. The struggle against this dominant class can be successful only through a united struggle of the Assamese people. According to him, the Assamese caste Hindu-petty-bourgeois class has long been queering the pitch of such a struggle. So, in his views, one of the important preconditions of this struggle is to remove this class from the leadership. But, to his utter astonishment, he finds ULFA maintaining a silence on this issue. So, in his opinion, ULFA should first decide upon its leader-ship in its war against the Hindi-Hindu expansionism, and then only the common people would jump into its bandwagon to lay their lives for its cause. He also warns ULFA not to be trapped by the caste Hindu mind-set of the Assam Movement leadership. According to him, ULFA, which is so accustomed to using Marxist phrases, must understand that in the nationalist struggle of independence, the leadership has to come from the Assamese proletariat, not from the bourgeois. So, he questions the ULFA as to whom have they assigned the task of the nationalist struggle: the proto bourgeois which has not fully developed in Assam or the Assamese petit-bourgeois. Then, he goes on to define and analyse the proletariat class in Assam. In his view, the Jharkhandi tea garden labourer with a 50-lakh population constitutes the largest section of the labour-proletariat class in Assam. He regrets the fact that the tea garden labourers are even denied the Scheduled Tribe (ST) status in Assam, although they enjoy this status in other states of India. Sharma brings a very important point regarding the attitude of ULFA towards these labourers. According to him, the mini-mum wage of the tea garden labourers in other states of India is Rs 25 per day, but in Assam they are not paid even half of that standard wage. So, he urges ULFA to take up this issue in its revolutionary programme instead of its populist programmes like putting a blanket ban on poaching, drinking, eve-teasing etc. He also makes a fervent appeal to the leadership of ULFA to involve the downtrodden religious minorities living in the *char* (which

## 64  *Uddipan Dutta*

means riverine) areas in their struggle. In his opinion, ULFA should not even imagine of winning the battle against the Hindi-Hindu-Hindustani power lobby by keeping aside these two downtrodden communities which constitute almost half of the population of Assam.

Devabrata Sharma then raises the question of the right to self-determination of the indigenous communities like the Tai-Ahoms, the Moran-Muttoks, the Chutiyas and the Koch-Rajbanshis who are the indispensable part of Assamese social life. He cautions that the mere change of the seat of power from Delhi to Dispur would not solve the problem, and that ULFA cannot keep this issue aside casually by simply branding the movements of self-determination spearheaded by these communities as conspiracies hatched by the anti-Assamese lobby.

Towards the end of the essay, the author cautions ULFA that the support of the caste Hindu Assamese middle class to it is guaranteed only till the blessings of the AGP government along with the police inertia extended by it. But, as soon as the state starts its repressive measures, the author prognosticates that this class would take away its support from ULFA, as indeed has been the case. So, he urges ULFA to involve the downtrodden communities and lower class in its struggle against the Hindi expansionism, and avers that victory is assured only this way.

In his second article, *Sarbabhoumo Asom Abhimukhe* (Towards Sovereign Assam), the author seeks solution of the nationality problem in India in a broader federalist structure. In the first part of the article, he gives a vignette of the progress of the federalist movement in India. According to him, the movement for a federalist restructuring of India gained momentum only after the famous *Anandpur Sahib Resolution*[27] had been adopted by the Akali Dal in 1978. As the Resolution goes, the central government would only look after the departments like Defence, Transport, External Affairs and Currency; the rest would be in the hands of the state government. In 1991, a new front called Federal Front for a New India consisting of 50 organisations had been formed which proposed that India would be a voluntary union of states, where the constituent states might delegate some power to the Centre. According to the author, the phrasing of 'voluntary union' signifies that the states would have the 'right to secede', and the 'states may delegate some power to the centre' indicates that the states will have the option of delegating power to the Centre.

He identifies the group of north Indian capitalists, feudal lords and bureaucrats as the main enemy of this struggle, as this group has been maintaining its hegemony in India with the principle of India for Hindi-Hindu-Hindustani. Then he goes on to classify the different political groups in accordance with their attitude towards federalism. He criticises the two nationalist parties, the Congress and the BJP, for opposing the

*Sarbabhoumo Asom* 65

idea of federalism, and dubs them as the protectors of the interest of the Hindi-Hindu-Hindustani power lobby. He reports that the other groups like Communist Party of India (Marxist) CPI (M), Telugu Desam Party (TDP), Janata Dal (JD) in Bihar and Orissa, AGP, Natun Asom Gana Parishad (NAGP), AASU and Autonomous State Demand Committee (ASDC) favour federal restructuring of the country; but their notion of decentralisation is limited to the devolution of more power to the states, and they are either mute or unenthusiastic about decentralisation of power to the lower levels. He criticises these groups for not favouring a multi-layered system of autonomy. In the same vein, he discusses ULFA which has raised the issue of self-determination, and the right to secession, and dared to question the Hindi-Hindu hegemonic rule. So, next he discusses the inherent contradictions in the demand of ULFA.

First, he criticises ULFA for not waging a unified battle along with the other forces opposing Delhi. He emphasises the need to wage a united battle to defeat a giant like India. He also berates ULFA for wrongly characterising India as colonial state. According to him, socialism has taught that the highest development of capitalism is imperialism, and India is just in the state of a 'semi-colony'. He urges the organisation to establish internal democracy among the various communities living in Assam. The non-homogeneity of Assamese nationality is also brought to the focus of the discussion by the author. He raises the question of the non-assimilation of various communities living in Assam like the different tribal groups, the immigrant Muslims, the tea garden labourers, the ex-tea garden labourers, the Bengalis and the Nepalis. According to him, the process of the formation of a composite Assamese identity is still going on, and the positions of these communities within this identity are going to be very crucial in the struggle against New Delhi. ULFA draws his censure for floating the idea of 'denationalisation' of these communities, and jeopardising the problem further. Thus, he exposes the apparent contradictions in the ideology of ULFA: the organisation raises the issue of right to self-determination for the Assamese community, but, at the same time, it preaches denationalisation for the smaller ethnic communities of Assam. He cautions ULFA not to vitiate the atmosphere with Assamese ultra-nationalist jingoism as this might help the Indian state to use the different alienated communities against the struggle waged by ULFA.

Interestingly, certain preconditions are laid down by the author for the victory of ULFA. First, he emphasises on a united struggle, and calls upon ULFA to tie up with other struggles of the downtrodden people of India. Second, ULFA should stand for the decentralisation of power to the village and community level. He provides a formula for this multi-layered autonomous rule. He emphasises that the communities with a homogeneous

## 66    *Uddipan Dutta*

population, and majority in a particular area, must be given autonomy, and those communities without a homogeneous population should be provided with reservation and other facilities. According to him, a definitive proposal like this can only assure guarantee to the ultimate victory of the struggle of sovereignty of Assam.

He ends his essay with a fervent appeal to the reader to become a partner in the struggle for the reconstruction of India in a federal structure where the sovereignty of the constituent states is assured. In these three write-ups, we see three distinct views on the issue of sovereignty of Assam. While the radical nationalist discourse of Parag Kumar Das advocates a sovereign, independent Assam, and puts forward his argument in favour of it, the discourse of Kanaksen Deka favouring the maintenance of status quo rejects this concept completely, and argues that this demand would put Assam on the back foot, and traces its origin in the inferiority complex among a section of the youths in the present generation of Assam. He puts his maximum trust on the existing structure of Indian nation-state. Between these two extreme polarities, we can view the federalist discourse of Devabrata Sharma as an alternative, although his argument is more tilted towards the ideology of Parag Kumar Das. Like Parag Kumar Das, he also identifies the exploitation of the Hindi-Hindu-Hindustani power lobby as the main reason of the underdevelopment of Assam. But, unlike Das, he is in favour of a complete restructuring of the Indian Union in a federalist line which provides maximum autonomy to the constituent states, including the right to secession.

Kanaksen Deka is completely against any form of self-determination, and denounces the various self-determination movements for causing loss to the public exchequer. Parag Kumar Das stands for the secession of Assam, but he does not talk about the devolution of power to the smaller ethnic communities within Assam, and his *sarbhoumotto* (sovereignty) stands for the transfer of power to Assam. Devabrata Sharma advocates the devolution of power to the lowest level of the administrative hierarchy. In his opinion, every community must get the benefit of restructuring of the administration, and *sarbhoumotto*, in his opinion, means the devolution of power to the lowest level of our society. It is quite interesting to note how the arguments got built up by the authors in favour or against the concept of *sarbhoumotto*. Both Parag Kumar Das and Kanaksen Deka refer to the history and anthropological features of the Assamese people, but draw completely different inferences. While Parag Kumar Das invokes history and anthropology, he does so to show the separateness of Assamese people from the rest of India. Kanaksen Deka does it to show the strong pan-Indian influence in Assam. For example, the defeat of the Moghul army by the Ahoms is the reference point for both Parag Kumar Das and Kanaksen Deka. Parag

Kumar Das invokes this event to show the invincibility of the Assamese will to draw inspiration in the present times, while Kanaksen Deka uses this event to censure the Assamese youths, who, according to him, are suffering from the lack of self-confidence. He also argues that as the Moghuls now cannot claim India by invoking history, so also the Assamese people cannot question the merger of Assam with British India in 1826, and its subsequent transfer into the Indian Union after independence.

The statistics from economics is manipulated by both the authors: Parag Kumar Das and Kanaksen Deka. The former shows how the resources of Assam get extracted by the Indian state, extrapolates the price of the two commodities – tea and petroleum – in the international market in retrospect and characterises this extraction as a case of colonial exploitation. The latter, on the other hand, shows with statistics and extrapolation that while the central government provides fund to Assam quite liberally, in return, it earns only a paltry sum as royalties from tea and petroleum.

Parag Kumar Das characterises the Indian state as a terrorist state taking away the freedom of Assam illegally. Kanaksen Deka, on the other hand, brands ULFA as a terrorist outfit and compares it with other terrorist organisations of the world. Devabrata Sharma, again, looks at ULFA through the prism of its attitude towards federalism, and criticises it for floating dangerous notions like 'denationalisation' for the minorities, and the smaller ethnic communities of Assam.

These three important writings have raised some of the fundamental points on the subject of sovereignty of Assam. And these points have quite often been referred to in the public discourse of Assam, both oral and written. The authenticity of the facts or the accuracy of the statistics is outside the purview of this discussion. What stands out as interesting is the ingenious way the facts and the figures got represented in these writings that best suit the ideologies of the respective authors. The legitimacy of the issue of the sovereignty raised by ULFA is central to the radical nationalist discourse of Parag Kumar Das. Kanaksen Deka, the status-quoist, legitimises the rule of the Indian state in the present form, and invalidates the claim of a sovereign Assam. The discourse of Devabrata Sharma questions the legitimacy of the Indian state as well as the claim of ULFA, and finds an answer in the federal restructuring of India though it has not totally discarded the idea of a sovereign Assam.

Thus, along with the grammar of the militarisation of the two warring parties, the ULFA and the Indian state, there flows the poetics of discourse around the issue of sovereignty of Assam. The accounts often turn polemic favouring one of the dominant views on this issue, and an effort is being made here to look at some of the major arguments of the discourse generated in the public sphere of Assam.

# 68   *Uddipan Dutta*

## Notes

1 The British colonial administration was instrumental in two large-scale migrations, the indentured labour migration to work in the tea gardens from Central India and the Muslim peasant migration from East Bengal.
2 After the accession in 1826, the British experimented ruling Assam with Ahom princes but later on amalgamated it with Bengal.
3 Assam was recognised as a separate province in 1874 but with the appendage of the historically unrelated District of Sylhet within it.
4 From 1837 to 1873, Bengali was the language of the courts and government schools of Assam. While it was an administrative decision, it created a situation where Assamese was regarded as a dialect of Bengali.
5 The Cabinet Mission Plan, its threat to Assam and Assamese people and the resistance of Assam Congress against its plan are parts of the independent struggle which are invoked time and again to emphasise upon the indifference of the central leadership towards the people of Assam. According to the Cabinet Mission Plan Assam and Bengal was put under Group C. Had this proposal been mooted, Assamese community would have become a tiny minority community in that group.
6 The Sylhet referendum was held in July 1947. Of the valid votes cast in the referendum, 56.6 per cent were in favour of Sylhet's inclusion in Pakistan and 43.4 per cent for an undivided Assam in India.
7 *Kendrar Mahi aiir sokuresuwa niti*, the Assamese equivalent of it is an oft-used phrase in the public discourse
8 Widely acclaimed as the maker of the Assamese nationality, Sankardeva (1449–1568) was the initiator of Neo-Vaishnavite movement in Assam, which was a part of the larger pan-Indian resurgence of bhakti in medieval India. He was not only a religious teacher but also an intellectual, a brilliant poet, an exceptionally gifted dramatist and a talented musician. His influence is indispensable to the social and cultural life of Assam.
9 Neo-Vaishnavite monasteries. Its influence is very prominent in the socio-cultural life of Assam.
10 The biography of Sankardeva.
11 A variety of rice used as a light meal.
12 An important musical instrument of Assam.
13 Demon.
14 Monster.
15 The evil soul.
16 The author writes Mahatma within inverted commas questioning the very essence attached with the name.
17 According to the historians, a large part of existing Assam was known as Kamarupa during the ancient period.
18 Hiuen Tsiang was a Chinese scholar who had visited Kamarupa during the seventh century AD. He came to India to study Buddhist philosophy at the Nalanda monastery in Magadha.
19 Shihab al-Din *nom de plume* Talish accompanied Mir Jumla, the governor of Bengal under the Moghul Empire, as a news writer during his Assam and Koch Bihar campaign in 1662–63.
20 Md. Tayabulla was a prominent Congress leader of Assam during the freedom struggle.

*Sarbabhoumo Asom* 69

21 Purandar Singha was the last Ahom monarch.
22 Maniram Dewan was hanged by the British on charges of hatching a conspiracy during the Sepoy Mutiny.
23 Kushal Konwar was hanged by the British during the Quit India Movement.
24 Kanaklata was shot dead by the British for trying to hoist the Tricolour at Gohpur Thana during the Quit India Movement.
25 The Assam Association was formed with Raja Prabhat Chandra Baruah, Jagannath Barua and Manik Chandra Barua as president, vice-president and general secretary, respectively, in 1903. The association decided to support the Non-cooperation Movement in its Tezpur session of 1920s, and thus the process of its merger with the Congress was started.
26 In the Battle of Saraighat, the Mughal army was trounced by the Ahom forces.
27 The Anandpur Sahib Resolution was a political statement made by the political party Shiromani Akali Dal in 1973.

## References

Das, Parag K. 1993. *Swadhinatar Prastab.* Guwahati: Published by the author.

Deka, Kanaksen. 1994. *ULFA Swadhin Asom.* Guwahati: Dispur Print House.

Hazarika, Uddipta. 1989. *Bixex Prachar Patrika.* Doi-Kaun-Rang: Published on behalf of ULFA.

Keane, A. H. 1920. *Man: Past and Present.* Cambridge: Cambridge University Press.

Sharma, Devabrata. 1993. *Sarbabhoumo Asom Aru Anyanya Prasanga: Raktakta Der Dashakar Dalil.* Guwahati: Lakhimi Printers and Publishers.

# 5 *Swadhin Asom*
## Contesting territories and linkages

*Shubhrajeet Konwer*

The lush green state of Assam has had its own fair share of problems in the last few decades. Apart from genuinely inter-related problems of floods, economic underdevelopment, unemployment and cross-border illegal migration, finding a peaceful solution to the burning issue of a 'sovereign Assam' (*Swadhin Asom*), as raised by the United Liberation Front of Assam (ULFA), is seen by many as one of the most important challenges for the Indian state. There is an earnest need to quickly resolve the territorial and historical claims and counterclaims as well as demands by numerous non-state actors, subsequently the resolution of which will ensure peace and development in Northeast India in general and Assam in particular. The most curious of these issues is the ULFA demand for 'sovereign Assam', which the organisation sees as the restoration of the historical reality of Assam's sovereign status (Prabhakara 2004).

ULFA, which formally took its birth in April 1979, began to affirm its presence through its initial acts of 'armed propaganda' only after the bloodstained Assembly elections of February 1983, and secured some free space to operate after the first regional party government under the Asom Gana Parishad (AGP), a child of Assam's anti-illegal migrants agitation, assumed office in December 1985 (Hussain 2007). ULFA's transformation to an active insurgent outfit having links with international forces hostile to the Indian state, and prosecuting its stated objective of a 'sovereign Asom' with some vigour, is a post-1990 phenomenon (Prabhakara 2006), has now established trans-border linkages, and the Indian security establishment has been openly talking of the group's alleged patronage by authorities in Bangladesh and Pakistan.

However, the conditions currently prevalent are very different. The ULFA, which came into existence on the anti-infiltration plank, has itself now sought to explain away the problem in a 15-page booklet addressed to 'The people of Assam of East Bengal origin' which makes for an interesting reading as it tries to justify the role of the migrants in the life of the state:

*Swadhin Asom* 71

'When we refer to the Assamese, *instead of meaning the Assamese-speaking people we actually mean the different inter-mixture of tribal nationalities –* those who are committed to working for the good of Assam. *The mixture of nationalities that is the Assamese is, in reality, the result of immigration. We consider the immigrants from East Bengal to be a major part of the national life of the people of Assam. Our freedom struggle can never be successful without these people . . . the masses who earn their living through hard physical labour can never be our enemies. All the labouring masses are our friends and the main motive force of our freedom revolt'* (Misra 2000:141–42).

The chapter highlights the contesting notion of territory in the Northeast. It seeks to examine the overlapping territorial claims and counterclaims for 'sovereign land' by the ULFA and other groups such as the NDFB and NSCN. It also explains the role of extra regional forces in destabilising region. The chapter finally concludes that the lack of consensus amongst the contending parties regarding the claims and counterclaims and failure to arrive at an 'honourable solution' will only further complicate the fragile peace environment in Assam.

# I

Assam, Manipur, Nagaland and Tripura have been in the grip of insurgency for the last few decades. There are at least 18 underground organisations operating in the region. While ULFA has launched an 'armed revolution for an independent Assam', the United National Liberation Front (UNLF) of Manipur and the Revolutionary People's Front (RPF), the political wing of the People's Liberation Army (PLA), are fighting for an 'independent Manipur'. The National Socialist Council of Nagaland (NSCN) fighting for a 'sovereign and independent Nagalim', split in 1988. While the NSCN(I-M) has been active in Nagaland, Manipur and parts of Assam, the NSCN(K), is based in upper Myanmar. It has formed the Indo-Burma Revolutionary Front (IBRF) together with the Manipur-based UNLF (Chaudhury 2000). The NSCN, the All Tripura Tiger Force (ATTF), the National Democratic Front of Bodoland (NDFB) and other groups have sought to wage 'little wars' in order to assert their various identities and protect their community interests (Saikia 2003:1).

Each militant group has its own zone of control of influence which often contradicts and competes with each other. While Assam has been subjected to several consecutive rounds of surgical operations, ULFA is now opposed to any further fragmentation of the state. It takes the territoriality of Assam as it existed on its foundation day (7 April 1979) as both given and unalterable (Das 2002). It considers the question of self-determination of the ethnic

# 72    Shubhrajeet Konwer

communities as only secondary to the question of establishing a *Swadhin Asom* by way of liberating her from 'the colonialism of New Delhi'. ULFA operates effectively in three zones, they are: (i) East Zone – Lakhimpur, Jorhat, Golaghat, Sibsagar, Dibrugarh and Tinsukia districts. (ii) Central Zone – Sonitpur, Darrang, Morigaon, Nagaon, Karbi Anglong and east Kamrup Districts. (iii) West Zone – Barpeta, west Kamrup, Goalpara, Kokrajhar, Bongaigaon and Nalbari districts (Kotwal 2000).

On the other hand, the Bodos claim to be the original inhabitants of Assam and currently maintain their stranglehold over districts of Kokrajhar, Chirang, Baksa and Bongaigaon. The expert committee under Dr Bhupinder Singh in 1991 proposed two autonomous councils north of Brahmaputra. The West-Central Council constituted areas of Dhubri, Kokrajhar, Bongaigaon, Barpeta, Nalbari, Kamrup and Darrang. The Eastern Council constituted the areas of Dhemaji, Lakhimpur and Sonitpur (Chadha 2005:265). While these recommendations were rejected by the Bodos on the ground of non-inclusion of many villages, it does point out that territorial contradictions between a 'sovereign Assam' and 'independent Bodoland' do exist. Speaking on the occasion of the outfit's twenty-first raising day, NDFB chairman Ranjan Daimary said: 'Only independent Bodoland can bring permanent peace. So Bodoland is the component part of peace. Bodoland is an important part of laying the foundation for peace. So let us talk of an independent and sovereign Bodoland' (NL News 2007). In 2012, a four-member delegation of the NDFB(Progressive) submitted a memorandum to Union Home Minister P Chidambaram in New Delhi, in which the outfit reiterated this demand and asked the Centre to create Bodoland by bringing together '32 tribal belts, blocks and tribal sub-plan areas covering 25,478 sq. km on the northern bank of Brahmaputra'. This 25,478 sq. km area spans across from the Sankosh river in the west to Sadiya in the east (*The Times of India*, 4 March 2012). Thus, the demands of 'sovereign Assam' and 'independent Bodoland' territorially overlaps each other, and this further complicates the already fragile peace condition in the state of Assam.

Furthermore, the NSCN(I-M) envisions 'Nagalim' as a Naga homeland comprising the whole of Nagaland and parts of Manipur, Assam and Arunachal Pradesh. Manipur has been the staunchest opponent of this campaign. Nagalim is situated between China, India and Burma. Nagalim occupies a compact area of 120,000 sq. km of the Patkai Range between the longitude 93° east and 97° east, and in between the latitude 22.5° north and 28° north, which lies at the trijunction of China, India and Burma. The part of 'Nagalim' ruled by India consists of territory which today is administered by four different administrative units, the states of Assam, Arunachal Pradesh, Manipur and Nagaland. The purported objective of the

## Swadhin Asom 73

NSCN(I-M) is the establishment of a *Nagalim* (Greater Nagaland), consisting of all the Naga-inhabited areas of neighbouring Assam, Manipur, Arunachal Pradesh and some portions of Myanmar, which it considers to be the rightful homeland of the Nagas. The proposed *Nagalim* spreads over approximately 120,000 sq. km. in contrast to the present state of Nagaland that has an area of 16,527 sq. km. *Nagalim* threatens to include large chunks of territories of three neighbouring states, Assam, Manipur and Arunachal Pradesh, along with some portions of Myanmar. The map of *Nagalim*, released by the NSCN(I-M), claims the Karbi Anglong and North Cachar Hills District of Assam. Besides, the map is also shown to include parts of the districts of Golaghat, Sibsagar, Dibrugarh, Tinsukia and Jorhat. It also includes Dibang Valley, Lohit, Tirap and Changlang districts of Arunachal Pradesh and significant parts of the four of the seven districts of Manipur – Tamenglong, Senapati, Ukhrul and Chandel. Civil society groups in Assam too are strongly opposed to Nagalim. Lachit Bordoloi, a member of the ULFA-constituted People's Consultative Group (PCG) and also the Convenor of the People's Committee for Peace Initiatives in Assam (PCPIA), remarked 'We respect our Naga brothers' right to self-determination but we won't accept any solution that imperils the territorial integrity of Assam. We will be discussing the Nagalim issue and how it can be resolved through intimate dialogue and people-to-people talks' (*The Telegraph*, 29 December 2006).

In November 2007, clashes between the ULFA and NSCN(I-M) came into the open again with the former accusing the latter of killing two of its members. Military spokesman of the ULFA, Raju Baruah, said that 'two ULFA militants were killed and seven others were abducted in the Mon district of Nagaland yesterday by NSCN(I-M)'. Baruah called upon the NSCN(I-M) to release the abducted ULFA members within three days. He also said that the 'ULFA never prevented movement of Naga people through Assam and the NSCN should desist from doing so' (*The Assam Tribune*, 13 November 2007). The ULFA's vision and NSCN(I-M)'s 'greater Nagalim' dream are clearly hurting each other. The four subdivisions – Kohoboto, Niuland, Uriamghat and Hukaiare – are in the disputed zone of the interstate border in Golaghat and Karbi Anglong districts (*The Telegraph*, 26 December 2006) and it is here that these two outfits are regularly crossing each other's way.

Interestingly, alliances among terror outfits are fluid and so is the allegiance. ULFA, which has been a strong ally of the Khaplang faction since a split in the NSCN in 1988, of late has been drifting towards the NSCN(I-M) because of strategic reasons as the NSCN(I-M) has a strong presence in Tirap and Changlang, the twin districts in Arunachal Pradesh from where ULFA's most powerful and active 28th Battalion operates (*The Telegraph*,

## 74    Shubhrajeet Konwer

26 January 2006). The Khaplang faction till recently was waging another turf war against the NSCN(I-M) in Tirap and Changlang from the Tinsukia district of Assam with the help of ULFA.

## II

While 'turf wars' are growing, still a certain degree of 'marriage of cooperation' exists. The ULFA militants are apparently regrouping in Mon district of Nagaland aided by the Khaplang faction of the National Socialist Council of Nagaland. They are chalking out plans for hit-and-run operations to put up a show of strength following the Bhutan offensive. While some of the rebels have taken refuge in Mon district, a stronghold of NSCN(K), many more have fled to NSCN(K) camps in Myanmar (*The Telegraph*, 3 January 2004).

The major militant movements in India have normally enjoyed some foreign support and refuge in safe havens outside the country. Remnants of militant organisations are also able to find shelter in the more accessible terrain within the country, or, to return, temporarily, to normal life among the civilian population at times when the state's operational successes are high. Military operations, consequently, can almost never entirely eliminate terrorist forces (Sahni 2000). Terror network has become transnational.

Since tactical associations, including financial transactions, between militant groups of the Northeast are common, the possibility collaborations between militant groups, irrespective of their goals, are as old as militancy itself (*The Telegraph*, 4 May 2007). Despite counter-insurgency operations by the police, army and central paramilitary forces, new militant outfits are cropping up in Assam with every passing year and what is interesting is that the ULFA and the NSCN are playing the role of 'big brothers' to most of the smaller outfits (*The Assam Tribune*, 3 October 2007). The ULFA has now been divided into two factions with one group playing into the hands of Inter-Services Intelligence (ISI), outgoing AOC-in-C of Eastern Air Command Air Marshal P. K. Barbora said, 'One faction, operating in lower Assam, is playing into the hands of Pakistan's ISI and other fundamentalist forces, while the other operating in Upper Assam has built up nexus with NSCN(K)' (*The Assam Tribune*, 17 December 2007). There is close nexus between the ULFA and smaller outfits. Arabinda Rajkhowa remarked on the occasion of Martyrs Day, 27 July 2001: 'ULFA, NDFB, United People's Democratic Solidarity (UPDS) and Dima Halim Daoga (DHD) have separately run a decade-long armed struggle with immense sacrifices over this period. At this very significant moment, my earnest call to the DHD and UPDS is to practically assist us in this joint political pursuit' (Ramana 2002). The Black Widow group, active in the North Cachar Hills, was considered to be one of the strongest and the terrain in the hill district also put the outfit in a favourable position. The DHD's declared objective is to create a separate state of 'Dimaraji' for the Dimasa ('sons of the great river') tribe, comprising Dimasa-dominated areas of the North Cachar Hills and Karbi Anglong districts of Assam and parts of Dimapur district in Nagaland. The DHD was also reported to have linkages with the National Socialist Council of Nagaland (Isak Muivah) (NSCN(I-M)) and the National Democratic Front of Bodoland (NDFB). DHD also helped the Black Widow group to increase its strength as several members of the DHD switched over to the breakaway faction. Again, the police have pointed out that the ULFA started helping the Karbi Longri North Cachar Hills Liberation Front (KLNLF) to establish bases in the hill district and the mayhem of killing of Hindi-speaking people in Karbi Anglong were mostly joint operations by members of both the outfits.

To strengthen its own position, the NSCN(I-M) also set up an umbrella organisation called the United Liberation Front of Seven Sisters (ULFOSS) comprising the United Liberation Front of Assam (ULFA), Dima Halim Daogah (DHD) of Assam, United People's Democratic Solidarity (UPDS) of Assam, Arunachal Dragon Force (ADF) of Arunachal Pradesh, People's Liberation Army (PLA) of Manipur and the Revolutionary Democratic Front (RDF). At a surrender ceremony at Tamulpur in Nalbari district in 2002, bordering Bhutan, Randeep Kumar Patgiri, one of the NDFB deserters, said the ULFA and Kamatapur Liberation Organisation (KLO) had long been collaborating with the outfit he used to be part of. 'NDFB camps are frequented by ULFA and KLO activists. The arrangement includes sharing of information and collaboration in various activities' (*The Telegraph*, 1 November 2002). The ULFA is using the Garo Hills as a passage to tranship arms from Bangladesh and also as a safe hideout for its cadres (*The Telegraph*, 26 July 2004). The linkages between the larger and the smaller terrorist groups have served two functions. They have provided arms training as well as arms for the smaller of the alliance partners, and they have also provided benefits to the larger group as these smaller groups perform the role of a conduit in reaching arms consignments to the theatre of operation of the larger group. Also, the larger group, in certain instances, have been able to keep its cadres 'busy' by lending its services to the smaller group. This affords dividends to both the groups. These groups have also collaborated in extortion to fill their coffers, with the smaller group providing the 'turf', while the larger group lends its cadre strength. An emerging feature of alliances in India's Northeast is coalition formation for turf control within a theatre (Ramana 2002).

The Director General (DG) of Central Reserve Police Force (CRPF), SIS Ahmed, said that the militancy scenario in the Northeast was compounded

76    *Shubhrajeet Konwer*

by 'external forces' aiding and abetting the insurgent outfits in the region. 'Militancy in the Northeast has been aggravated by external forces aiding the militant outfits in the region' (*The Assam Tribune*, 14 January 2008). Despite claims of an improved internal security situation in the Northeast, the Centre had a tough time answering questions over the existence of rebel camps in Bangladesh and free movement of militants and weapons into the region from the neighbouring countries. Though existence of camps in neighbouring countries was known, a new coordination among the insurgent groups has added a new dimension (*The Assam Tribune*, 7 December 2005). The existence of an elaborate terrorist infrastructure in safe havens across the border, the growth and internationalisation of organised criminal syndicates with powerful political influence and patronage, and a strengthening network of well-funded institutions for the communal mobilisation of the migrants – particularly through a growing complex of *madrassas* (seminaries) – are among the most dangerous trends along the India–Bangladesh border (Lakshman and Jha 2003). A large number of Islamic militants are fleeing Bangladesh and taking refuge in the districts of Assam bordering Bangladesh. The porous international borders have made it quite easy for them, and border districts like Karimganj and Dhubri.

Bhutan's persistent denial of ULFA's resurgence on its territory is being doubted again. Reports suggest that ULFA militants have found their way back into Bhutan. Junior Engineer M. Ganeshan of Border Roads Organisation (BRO), who was kidnapped from Gitibari in Udalguri district on 22 December 2006 by the ULFA and later freed, had been held captive in Bhutan (*The Telegraph*, 2 February 2007). Incidentally, ULFA militants were 'very active' in Udalguri and adjoining Baksa. Both these places are also strongholds of the National Democratic Front of Bodoland. ULFA rebels are supposedly back to extorting money and indulging in subversive activities in Udalguri and Baksa districts and were sneaking back into the jungles of Bhutan after extortion and other such activities in the two districts. The porous border with Bhutan and lack of administrative infrastructure and a proper intelligence network in the Bodoland districts are helping the militants sneak in and out of the Himalayan kingdom (*The Telegraph*, 24 October 2006). For ULFA, a base in the neighbouring country is crucial to the success of any hit-and-run operation in Lower Assam. The 2003 military operation in Bhutan had put a stop to the militant group's subversive activities in this part of the state. The recent burst of militant activity in Lower Assam indicates ULFA's return to the jungles of the neighbouring country (*The Telegraph*, 3 November 2006).

In 1986, ULFA first established contacts with the then unified NSCN and the Kachin Independence Army (KIA). The ULFA has fourteen-odd camps functioning in Bangladesh since 1989 and has since gradually expanded its network there to include operational control of activities and the receipt and shipment of arms in transit before they finally entered India. The leadership is believed to own or have controlling interests in several businesses in Bangladesh, including a tannery, a chain of departmental stores, garment factories, travel agencies, shrimp trawlers and transport and investment companies (*Frontline*, 16 January 2004). Apart from running several training camps, the ULFA has launched several income-generating projects in Bangladesh. It is believed to have set up media consultancies and soft drink manufacturing units. It is also reported to own three hotels, a medical clinic and two motor driving schools in Dhaka (Prakash 2008:388).

It is alleged that the ULFA launches most of its operations in the Upper Assam districts from its bases in Myanmar as the militants manage to sneak into India through either Nagaland or Arunachal Pradesh by taking advantage of the terrain (*The Assam Tribune*, 21 February 2007). The camps in that country are maintained along with the NSCN(K). The ULFA also has a council camp in Myanmar, which is headed by senior ULFA leader Jibon Moran, who is responsible for maintaining communication with the leaders of the NSCN(K) (*The Assam Tribune*, 5 October 2007). The recent arrest of a Pakistani Inter-Services Intelligence (ISI) agent in Guwahati city has once again proved beyond doubt that the foreign agency is still active in the north-eastern region. ISI agent SM Alam alias Mojibullah Alam, a Bangladeshi national, who was nabbed by the police recently, frequently visited Bangladesh by taking advantage of the porous international border. During questioning, the arrested ISI agent reportedly admitted before the police that they had links with more than 20 militant outfits of the region, which highlights the gravity of the situation as the Pakistani agency can always engage the militant outfits having links with it to create disturbance in this part of the country without sending its own men to do such dirty work (*The Assam Tribune*, 19 December 2007). According to Assam Public Works, there are thirty-six Jihadi groups operating in the state and said that these groups were in possession of arms that could easily penetrate into the security zone of the Indian Army (*The Assam Tribune*, 25 December 2007). Meanwhile, in the Rajya Sabha, Minister of State for Home Affairs Sri Prakash Jaiswal confirmed that north-eastern insurgent groups were operating from Bangladesh. They had established links with ISI, he said, adding that Government of India had taken up the issue with Pakistan. According to information available with the Indian security agencies, the ULFA has about 250 to 300 militants in the camps located in Myanmar and the headquarters of the 28th Battalion of the outfit is located in the territory of the neighbouring country. 'Available inputs indicate that some Indian insurgent groups active in the North-East region have been using

78 *Shubhrajeet Konwer*

the territory of Bangladesh and have links with Pakistan's ISI.' According to the minister, there were reports of inter-linkages between these outfits for tactical purposes of shelter, hideouts, procurement of arms and training (*The Assam Tribune*, 6 December 2007). The ISI and the Directorate General of Forces Intelligence (DGFI) nexus continues to haunt security forces in Northeast India. A large number of Islamic militants are fleeing Bangladesh and taking refuge in the districts of Assam bordering Bangladesh.

The interference and cross-border assistance to groups like ULFA is perhaps because India's relation with that of its neighbouring countries has seldom been a positive relationship. Once ULFA was born and commenced its operations to destabilise the State and declare war on the so-called 'state machinery', it was but natural that foreign powers inimical to India would extend assistance to them. The ISI, Pakistan's external intelligence agency, is known to have helped ULFA in a big way, particularly in matters of training in camps located in Bangladesh, in the procurement of arms and ammunition and in arranging training and indoctrination to selected cadres in Pakistan and Afghanistan (Hrishikeshan 2002). Neighbouring countries find terror groups in Northeast India and its cross-border affinity as an ideal tool to keep the Indian government under constant pressure. Bangladesh has not been favourably looked upon by the international community for increasingly becoming more fundamentalist in character. In fact, the 'eastward surge of the jihadi elements has gained ground in the wake of Operation Enduring Freedom' (OEF) (Saikia 2003). Officially, Bangladesh continues to deny the presence of terror groups on its territory. Dhaka might continue to push ahead with its stand that no Indian insurgents are located or operating from the country, but may eventually have to move as quietly as possible to neutralise these rebels and choke them off within its territory to escape a possibly foolproof indictment by the international community as a nation that has not done enough to combat terror (Hussain 2005). Bangladesh is a major source of tension in the region. Furthermore, the involvement of ISI in this region may be a policy of the Pakistan state to open up a second front in Northeast India. Pakistan is too keen to see India preoccupied with internal security issues as well as threat from neighbouring countries. It is here that the ISI-DGFI nexus becomes clear. Despite the best efforts of the police and security forces, the routes used by the militants to bring in weapons and explosives from Bangladesh have not been plugged completely (*The Assam Tribune*, 5 November 2007). India needs stable democracies in the neighbourhood to prosper, but unfortunately, India's neighbours are losing their democratic character.

## III

The peace process and ceasefire agreements with different groups that have been signed has had limited effects. The PCG (People's Consultative Group) had three rounds of talks with the central government, but a solution to 'sovereign Assam' was nowhere to be found. The extension of ceasefire with NSCN has still not solved and addressed the issue of 'greater Nagalim'. However, the state governments in this region have achieved some success in their quest for peace. The governments of Assam, Manipur, Arunachal Pradesh and Meghalaya, all neighbours of Nagaland, were from the outset against extending the area covered by the ceasefire beyond Nagaland. This was mainly because they feared that NSCN(I-M) activists would use the opportunity for criminal activities against the civilian population in their respective territories. The Assam government, in particular, is apprehensive about the NSCN(I-M) stepping up its help to militant outfits such as the ULFA and the NLFD (Chaudhury 2001).

The entire top brass of the ULFA who were earlier in Indian custody are now engaged in the peace process. The only top leader of the ULFA still at large is Paresh Baruah, while the outfit's general secretary Anup Chetia is brought to India on November 11, 2015 after extradition from Bangladesh where he was undergoing a jail term since 1997. The arrested ULFA leaders, including Rajkhowa, have been repeatedly saying that they were ready for talks but not in handcuffs – meaning they want to be released. A delegation of the *Sanmilita Jatiya Abhibartan* (SJA) met the Prime Minister and the Union Home Minister in 2011, but the progress of such talks continues to be debated. But the stand of the Government of India on the issue of talks with any militant group is very clear. To start the process of talks, the militant groups must abjure violence and all talks must be held within the framework of the Constitution of India.

On 5 August 2011 seven pro-talk ULFA leaders led by Arabinda Rajkhowa, the chairman of ULFA, submitted a 'Charter of Demands' to the Union Home Minister P. Chidambaram in New Delhi. Rajkhowa, on behalf of the ULFA, reiterates that 'the ongoing issues between Assam and India can be honourably and meaningfully resolved peacefully only by a fresh look at the issues of sovereignty, so as to ensure that the people of Assam can assert their inalienable rights to control their land and their resources therein, which they inherit and occupy from their forefathers, for securing their honourable existence and for developing the economy and the society of their state, according to their needs and aspirations, and also to protect their own identity and develop themselves according to their genius. The people of Assam today feel insecure in their own traditional homeland and have been left far behind. To achieve such objectives, ULFA proposes that

# 80 *Shubhrajeet Konwer*

negotiations be initiated between India and the people of Assam to bring in measures constitutional and otherwise of wide scope and that certain urgent political, economic, social, cultural arrangements be undertaken and completed within a reasonable time frame by the Government of India to ensure a peaceful democratic solution of the historical Indo-Assam conflict' (*The Hindu*, 8 August 2011). While the ULFA wants the government to respond to the 'Charter of Demands', it does face a legitimacy crisis and the people of Assam in 'hush voices' are raising questions about the representative character of the ULFA and the rationality of such demands, but for some, the ULFA's 'Charter of Demands' provides an ideal opportunity for Assam to claim its rightful place under the sun.

The ULFA's offer for dialogue stems from two more problems it now faces, apart from the Bhutan and Bangladesh governments' action which has deprived it of safe bases and heavy loss of cadre in encounters with the security forces. First, the capture of the top brass leadership in neighbouring countries has left little option open for the ULFA other than to seek a dignified outcome. For the other, ULFA is fast losing mass support because of the violence Assam has been experiencing for over a decade. The economy of the state has been shattered as no meaningful development work could be undertaken during the last 15 years. Besides, a good number of ULFA cadres have lost all hope of securing an 'independent Assam' (Chaudhury 2002). Though today the ULFA seems to have moved away from its original plank of Assamese nationalism to a position where it speaks for the 'people of Assam', its main appeal springs from the idea that some form of regional nationalism where all those who have made Assam their home would be bound together by a kind of overall Assamese ethos (Misra 2000:134–36). Although the Assamese do not support or empathise with ULFA at present, tacit sympathy for the local 'boys' has not vanished completely. Though very few support the use of terror tactics by ULFA, there is a general feeling that ULFA's demand for sovereignty is understandable, given the unacceptable attitude of the Union government towards Assam. And if the ULFA has lost popularity amongst the Assamese, this does not mean that the GoI has won wide acceptability either (Nath 2002). There is still a considerable degree of support for the ULFA from leading intellectuals of the state and as well as from numerous civil society organisations, but it may not be as widespread as before.

## IV

The resolution of the crisis is a problem because the state's response to ULFA has been more militarist than political. The Indian Army and paramilitary forces have been employed to deal with the challenge, and in the

*Swadhin Asom* 81

process extreme authoritarian methods have been introduced into the fabric of everyday life, especially in those parts of Assam that are seen as ULFA strongholds (Baruah 1999:144). Since the army has been overused in rural areas in counter-insurgency operations, a certain feeling of scepticism and distrust amongst the villagers has come about towards the Indian state. The villagers see the army as the most visible symbol of presence of the central government and therefore incidence of sexual assault and harassment of villagers is seen as domination and insensitiveness on part of New Delhi. The politics of ULFA is driven more out of a sense of 'neglect' than out of strong nationalist sentiments, which implies that the best way to handle this sense of 'neglect' is to undertake and implement appropriate economic reforms and development projects sensitive to the region's specific requirements (Das 2002). The development strategy followed by the Centre and the state governments of the region has created a totally unbalanced economy in the Northeast. There are differences among the seven states of the region with respect to their resource endowments, levels of industrialisation as well as infrastructural facilities. On the whole, all these economies are underdeveloped agrarian societies with very weak industrial sectors and inflated service sectors (Sachdeva 2000). The high levels of unemployment, corruption and nepotism have contributed to growing frustrations of the youth in the region. 'Rural development' is another lucrative sector, and it is estimated that as much as 70 per cent of all funds available to the state government in Assam under this head is systematically siphoned off under a well-organised network of ULFA and SULFA cadres, contractors, civil servants and members of the political executive (Sahni 2000). A recent report of a committee on Integrated Rural Development Programme (IRDP) in the north-eastern states also mentioned 'an upsurge in insurgency in Assam' as responsible for 'practically no developmental activities in rural areas' and a simultaneous 'flight of capital from the rural areas to urban areas as the former were less secured than the latter' (*Report of the Committee on Credit Related Issues under IRDP* 2000). Perhaps the present fact is that the ULFA's quest for *Swadhin Asom* has obviously been pushed into the remote background by the character of its current activities and associations, and its present agenda is at complete variance – indeed, appears to have nothing to do – with the weighty ideologies, visions, principles and popular aspiration to which it ascribes its origins (Saikia 2001). The split in the ULFA has not helped the people of Assam and has in fact created more challenges for the state. While the pro-talk faction has had several rounds of talks with the government, the anti-talk ULFA faction has stepped up its recruitment and extortion drives. The extortion drive has assumed alarming proportions in Upper Assam, especially in Sivasagar, Tinsukia and Dibrugarh districts.

## 82    Shubhrajeet Konwer

The way forward is never going to be easy especially when Assamese society is witnessing an increase in polarisation of political viewpoints, fragmentation of 'Asomiya' composite culture and proliferation of new insurgent groups. While talks with the ULFA is extremely important for a peaceful solution to the vexed problem of insurgency and underdevelopment, the government and political parties must be able to conduct their activities above party and vote bank consideration. Likewise the civil society too must be neutral in expressing its discontentment and resentment with the state of affairs.

The need of the hour is to seek a political solution rather than a military solution. Military solution is unlikely to result in winning the hearts and minds of the people. Perhaps the army and the government is well aware of that because in spite of 'Operation Rhino and Bajrang' the ULFA is still alive and kicking, capable of hurting state security and infrastructure at will. The support for 'our boys' continues to remain in certain pockets of Assam. It must be recalled that in protest against the custodial killing of a fellow villager by the Indian Army, the villagers of the Kakopathar region in Upper Assam blocked a national highway, stormed army pickets, vandalised vehicles and pro-ULFA slogans and sentiments were openly visible. According to Air Marshal P. K. Barbora, ULFA would die a slow death over the next decade now that the people of Assam have realised how 'a bunch of people sitting in foreign countries and leading lavish lifestyles' were holding the state to ransom (*The Telegraph*, 29 December 2007). While it is easy to make such remarks, it is unlikely to happen so quickly because the government has failed to deliver goods. The current politico-socio-economic scenario of Assam is dismal. Rural development continues to be neglected, unemployment continues to be high, ethnic identity and its assertion is on the rise and corruption is rampant. All these problems are an ideal breeding ground for insurgent groups to grow and strive upon. ULFA is unlikely to be defeated until and unless the cross-border infiltration, issues of development are properly addressed, political parties don't look into the vexed ULFA problem as vote bank politics and linkages between underground and overground rebels are severed. If such conditions are ignored, then the likely result is that the ULFA will not only survive but also result in growth of new and more dangerous ethnic-based insurgent groups.

ULFA on its part must realise that it has taken the battle far too long and that peaceful negotiation is probably the only solution. The issue of 'sovereignty' as it is has lost significance in a globalised world. 'Asomiya' society might render moral support to the group as a symbol of resistance towards New Delhi and its policies, but complete sovereignty is unlikely to be ever accepted. It can be mentioned here that Assam Public Works, an NGO that includes members of ULFA activists' families, conducted an opinion poll,

*Swadhin Asom* 83

and as many as 95.53 per cent of the respondents conducted in nine districts of the state, excluding most of Upper Assam, gave the thumbs down to the militant group's demand for sovereignty (*The Telegraph*, 6 January 2007). Though the ULFA and certain members of civil society have raised doubts regarding the nature and methodology of the opinion poll, it nevertheless is a significant reminder that ULFA cannot take the people of Assam for granted.

A certain degree of soul-searching is required on the part of the ULFA. At a surrender ceremony in Tezpur, ULFA founder-member Bhimkanta Buragohain admitted the futility of the militant group's violent campaign and urged fellow rebels to lay down arms. 'I think the path which we have chosen is the wrong one. This is why I appeal to all ULFA members, even to Paresh Baruah, to introspect. We need to know that peace does not come through the barrel of the gun, but through negotiations' (*The Telegraph*, 27 December 2003). ULFA must stop indiscriminate violence and targeting of innocent civilians. The state in turn must stop atrocities against villagers in the name of counter-insurgency operations. A ceasefire arrangement with the ULFA is unlikely to happen until extortion and hit-and-run missions of the group are not given up. The ULFA's sway and ranks have dwindled, but it often strikes in the heart of Guwahati as symbol of continued resistance. This hurts and in turn further increases the distance between New Delhi and Assam. New Delhi is playing a waiting game, unwilling to negotiate the demand of sovereignty and is expecting the eventual disillusionment and disintegration of the militant outfit, but what it fails to understand is that outfits too are prepared for the long haul. While the Indian Army was pursuing an 'an iron fist in a velvet glove' policy in the troubled areas of the Northeast (*The Hindu*, 18 February 2007), the outfits are unwilling to relent or compromise with their dreams.

Perhaps the need of the hour is 'positive engagement and reciprocity' from all sides which must be facilitated by a fruitful role of the civil society. While civil society groups have repeatedly stressed for the need for peace in Assam, little is known as to what will be the final outcome of the talks with New Delhi. Several issues will delay the arrival to a peaceful solution. First, there is very little consensus amongst Assamese civil society regarding the scope of 'sovereignty' and what it actually stands for. Does sovereignty imply more autonomy while being a part of Indian state or complete severance of ties from the Indian state? The debate is still raging with no clear winners. Second, the ULFA leadership has not clearly addressed the historical demands and counterclaims of smaller communities in Assam and Northeast India. The NDFB has from time to time reiterated its demand for an independent Bodoland, and the demand for a greater 'Nagalim' and

## 84 *Shubhrajeet Konwer*

creation 'supra state body' to enable the Nagas to preserve their culture, identity and customary laws under an umbrella entity has been severely opposed by the government of Assam and Assamese society. The demand for 'independent Bodoland' and 'Nagalim' clearly overlaps the dream of a 'sovereign Assam' and territorial claims contradict each other. And finally, there is little consensus amongst the Assamese society as to what consists of an 'honourable solution'. Does it mean granting of complete amnesty to the ULFA for all its deeds and misdeeds or more privileges, perks and positions for the ULFA's top brass? Again, does honourable solution lie in further devolution of powers from the Centre to the state and more financial autonomy for the state of Assam? Indeed, there is no clear consensus on all these issues in a splintered Assamese society. The onus to arrive an 'honourable solution' lies with the Government of India as well as the ULFA leadership. All parties must clearly spell out their stands on all these three critical issues. Till then, it can be safely predicted that peace negotiations will move painfully slow and arrival at a fruitful conclusion will remain a distant dream.

## References

*The Assam Tribune*, 7 December 2005. 'Centre Faces Flak over Rebel Camps in Bangla'.

*The Assam Tribune*, 21 February 2007. 'Myanmar, India to Launch Joint Action'.

*The Assam Tribune*, 3 October 2007. 'ULFA, NSCN Providing Support to Smaller Outfits'.

*The Assam Tribune*, 5 October 2007. 'ULFA Using Bhutan, Myanmar Soil'.

*The Assam Tribune*, 5 November 2007. 'Cadres Disillusioned with Top Leaders' Activities'.

*The Assam Tribune*, 13 November 2007. 'ULFA Accuses NSCN(I-M) of killing cadres'.

*The Assam Tribune*, 6 December 2007. 'Parliament Concern over Bangla Influx'.

*The Assam Tribune*, 17 December 2007. 'ULFA a Divided Lot, Claims Barbora'.

*The Assam Tribune*, 19 December 2007. 'ISI Activities'.

*The Assam Tribune*, 25 December 2007. 'Govt. Not Taking Steps to Thwart Jihadis: APW'.

*The Assam Tribune*, 14 January 2008. 'External Forces Aiding NE Ultras'.

Baruah, Sanjib. 1999. *India Against Itself: Assam and the Politics of Nationality*. New Delhi: Oxford University Press.

Chadha, Vivek, Lt Col. 2005. *Low Intensity Conflicts in India*. New Delhi: Sage Publications.

Chaudhury, Kalyan. 1999/2000. 'In No Mood for Peace', *Frontline*, 16(27), 25 December 1999–7 January 2000.

Chaudhury, Kalyan. 2001. 'A Cease Fire and Protests', *Frontline*, 18(13), 23 June–6 July 2001.

Swadhin Asom 85

Chaudhury, Kalyan. 2001/2002. 'A Peace Initiative', *Frontline*, 18(26), 22 December 2001–4 January 2002.

Das, Samir K. 2002. 'Assam: Insurgency and the Disintegration of Civil Society', *Faultlines*, 13, http://satp.org/satporgtp/publication/faultlines/volume13/article5.htm.

*Frontline*, 16 January 2004. 'For Sovereign Socialist Assam'.

Hrishikeshan, K. 2002. 'Assam's Agony: The ULFA & Obstacles to Conflict Resolution', *Faultlines*, 12, http://satp.org/satporgtp/publication/faultlines/volume12/Article2.htm.

*The Hindu*, 18 February 2007. 'Insurgency Will Be Dealt with an Iron Fist, Says Army Chief'.

*The Hindu*, 8 August 2011. 'Peace Talks Last Opportunity, Says ULFA Chairman'.

Hussain, Wasbir. 2007. 'Hunting for Rebels, Looking for Peace', *Himal*, February, http://www.himalmag.com/2007/february/analysis4.htm.

Hussain, Wasbir. 2005. 'Insurgency in India's Northeast Cross-Border Links and Strategic Alliances', *Faultlines*, 17, http://satp.org/satporgtp/publication/faultlines/volume17/wasbir.htm.

Kotwal, Dinesh. 2000. 'Dynamics of Unending Violence in Assam', *Strategic Analysis: A Monthly Journal of the IDSA*, 25(3), http://www.ciaonet.org/olj/sa/sa_jun00kod01.html.

Lakshman, Kanchan and Sanjay K. Jha. 2003. 'India-Bangladesh: Restoring Sovereignty on Neglected Borders', *Faultlines*, 4, http://satp.org/satporgtp/publication/faultlines/volume14/Article7.htm.

Misra, Udayon. 2000. *The Periphery Strikes Back*. Shimla: Indian Institute of Advanced Studies.

Nagalim. NL News. 2007. http://www.nagalim.nl/news/00000748.htm.

Nath, Sunil. 2002. 'Assam: The Secessionist Insurgency and the Freedom of Minds', *Faultlines*, 13, http://satp.org/satporgtp/publication/faultlines/volume13/Article2.htm.

Prabhakara, M.S. 2004. 'Rooted in history', *Frontline*, 21(25), 4–17 December, 2004.

Prabhakara, M.S. 2006. 'Fruits of Unrest', *Frontline*, 23(8), 22 April–5 May 2006.

Prakash, V., ed. 2008. *Terrorism in India's North-east: A Gathering Storm*, Vol. 1, Kalpaz Publications.

Ramana, P.V. 2002. 'Networking the Northeast Partners in Terror', *Faultlines*, 11, http://satp.org/satporgtp/publication/faultlines/volume11/article6.htm.

*Report of the Committee on Credit Related Issues under IRDP(GSY) in North-Eastern States*, Ministry of Rural Development, Government of India, 2000.

Sachdeva, Gulshan. 2000. 'India's Northeast: Rejuvenating a Conflict-Driven Economy', *Faultlines*, 6, http://satp.org/satporgtp/publication/faultlines/volume6/Fault6-GSach-F.htm.

Sahni, Ajai. 2000. 'The Terrorist Economy in India's Northeast', *Faultlines*, 8, http://www.satp.org/satporgtp/publication/faultlines/volume8/Article5.htm.

## 86 *Shubhrajeet Konwer*

Saikia, Jaideep. 2001. 'Revolutionaries or Warlords: ULFA's Organisational Profile', *Faultlines*, 9, http://satp.org/satporgtp/publication/faultlines/volume9/Article4.htm.

Saikia, Jaideep. 2003. 'Islamic Resurgence in Bangladesh', *Aakrosh*, 16(21).

Saikia, Jaideep. 2003. 'Terror Sans Frontiers: Islamic Militancy in North-East India', *ACDIS Occasional paper* (July).

*The Telegraph*, 1 November 2002. 'Army Toes Police Line on KLO-ULFA Links'.

*The Telegraph*, 27 December 2003. ' "Dead" ULFA Veteran Surrenders with Peace Cry'.

*The Telegraph*, 3 January 2004. 'Alert Follows ULFA Retaliation Plan – Rebels Flee to Mon Camps from Bhutan'.

*The Telegraph*, 26 July 2004. 'ULFA Feels the Pinch of ANVC Truce'.

*The Telegraph*, 26 January 2006. 'Khaplang Caveat to ULFA'.

*The Telegraph*, 24 October 2006. 'ULFA Back in Bhutan'.

*The Telegraph*, 3 November 2006. 'Police Confirm ULFA Presence in Bhutan'.

*The Telegraph*, 26 December 2006. 'ULFA Breaks Tacit Truce'.

*The Telegraph*, 29 December 2006. 'Assam Wake-up Call for NSCN'.

*The Telegraph*, 6 January 2007. 'Survey Shatters ULFA's Dream'.

*The Telegraph*, 2 February 2007. 'ULFA Cloud on Bhutan, Again'.

*The Telegraph*, 4 May 2007. 'NDFB Whiff in Ramdrama'.

*The Telegraph*, 29 December 2007. 'Barbora Fires Salvo at ULFA: Outfit Labelled "Worst Enemy" of Assamese Society'.

*The Times of India*, 4 March 2012. 'NDFB-P Wants Tribal Areas in Bodoland'.

# Part III

# Migration, contested citizenship and the identity

# 6 Immigration, indigeneity and identity
## The Bangladeshi immigration question in Assam

*Chandan Kumar Sharma*

## Introduction

Assam is located in a unique geo-political space, surrounded by international borders of neighbours. The state constitutes the critical link between South Asia and the South-East Asia. Migrations of different groups of people over a long period of time have laid the foundation of its uniquely diverse demographic landscape. Such migrations made Assam a continental crossroads much before its annexation by the British in 1826. However, while the earlier migrations took place continuously over a protracted period of time, the migrations after the British annexation were much drastic and of different magnitude.

The British established new administrative, economic and social linkages between Assam and the rest of India. The new colonial administrative machinery and other emerging colonial enterprises in Assam required a huge manpower which was locally not available, prompting the colonial regime to bring such manpower from outside. In response to the above situation, since the 1830s various groups of migrants either came or were brought to Assam as traders, as petty officials in the colonial administration, as labourers in the tea plantations and so on. Since the early twentieth century, the state witnessed another surge of migration of the Muslim peasants from the erstwhile East Bengal at the instance of the colonial regime. The new migrations were much more dramatic in that this immigrant population changed the demographic and the socio-cultural landscapes of the region within a matter of few decades, creating serious trepidation among its smaller indigenous communities about their social and political identity. Besides, some of the immigrant groups due to their specific livelihood practices created heavy pressure on land and other resources, triggering serious contestations and conflict between the immigrants and the local communities over access to these resources.

Such conflicts have been most intense centring round massive immigration of the Muslim peasants from the erstwhile East Bengal. After the

90 *Chandan Kumar Sharma*

partition of India in 1947, East Bengal became East Pakistan and the immigrants from there to Assam became illegal immigrants. Immigration continued even after East Pakistan became an independent state as Bangladesh in 1971, leading to acute anxiety among the smaller indigenous communities of Assam about their own place in the political and cultural landscapes of the state.

This chapter recounts the historical backdrop of the East Bengali/East Pakistani/Bangladeshi influx to Assam and the trajectory of the conflict arising out of this issue. It explicates how the long years of deliberate neglect of the problem by succeeding governments has today turned this into an extremely complicated and politically volatile subject undercutting questions of law and rights of citizenship. With new, articulate political formations emerging from the immigrant population in recent times, the resolution of the issue appears all the more difficult.

## Immigration from East Bengal during the colonial period

When the British annexed Assam in 1826 they found a land that was largely unpopulated, full of forests and swamps. Major John Butler who served in the state for 14 years during 1837–51 expressed dismay at the stretches of 'dreary and desolate wilderness' (Butler 1855/1978:23) when he arrived in the state. While towards the end of his stint in the state he saw 'vast improvements' in the Assamese landscape, he was still disappointed that 'immense tracts of forest still remain untilled' (ibid.:249–50). Sanjib Baruah observes that the desolateness of the Assamese landscape appeared all the more striking in comparison to East Bengal, its densely populated neighbour (Baruah 1999:47) and that the 'colonial officials saw land-abundant Assam as a solution to East Bengal's problem of land scarcity . . . (and) expected a spontaneous migration of landless or land-poor peasants from East Bengal to Assam' (ibid.:56). They were disappointed that this did not happen for a long time. However, the situation changed fast since the early twentieth century. The census of 1911 had taken note of the immigration from East Bengal, especially from its Mymensingh district, owing to heavy pressure on land at home.

The British administration encouraged this immigration of peasants, mostly Muslims, hoping to generate higher land revenue by settling them in the fallow and wasteland areas of the Brahmaputra valley. Though the former encouraged this migration since the late nineteenth century, it did not happen as the East Bengal peasants were reluctant to migrate because there was 'no great pressure of population to induce them to migrate' (Misra 2011:105). However, 'the situation changed dramatically in the

*Immigration, indigeneity and identity* 91

first decade of the twentieth century, which saw an exceptional rise in rural densities in several of the Bengal districts bordering Goalpara (district of Assam). . . . This was the result of a pushing forward of the margins of agriculture into the rich alluvial tract of the Ganges and the Brahmaputra' (ibid.:106). This high demographic growth was also accompanied by a situation of impoverishment of the peasantry due to severe exploitation by moneylenders pushing them to migrate into the Assam valley. The rush was such that 'by 1911, more than 118,000 migrants had moved into the district of Goalpara alone . . . leading to a 30 percent growth in the population of the district' (ibid.:107).

It is important to note that already on account of migration from other parts of India, 'non-indigenous elements came to constitute (around) one-quarter of the population of Assam Proper[1] in 1901' (Guha 1988:39). The immigration from the East Bengal thus threatened to transform the demographic landscape of Assam. The Census Report of Assam, 1921, states, 'as to the stream of Bengal cultivators settling in the Brahmaputra valley, it seems that we had only the advance guard in 1911 and that now the main body is just beginning to arrive. The news of the promised land has spread to other districts besides Mymensingh, the colonists are filling up the riverine tracts of the four lower districts of the valley and spreading inland from the Brahmaputra; their number has increased nearly five fold since the last census, and it will not be surprising if they extend further up the valley and if the present number is doubled or even trebled by the next census' (p. 20).

The presence of the immigrants became most conspicuous in the Goalpara district, the Barpeta subdivision of the erstwhile Kamrup district, foothill areas of the Karbi hills in the Nagaon district and the Mangaldai subdivision of the erstwhile Darrang district. The magnitude of the immigration can be gauged from the fact that within 30 years (1911–41) the percentage of Muslim population in the Barpeta subdivision increased from 0.1 per cent to 49 per cent. Similarly, during 1921–31, the Dhing, Lahorighat, Juria, Laokhowa and Bakori *mauzas*[2] in the Nagaon district experienced population growth from 100 per cent to 294 per cent (Barman 1995:30–31). The manner in which this surge of immigration was described by the Superintendent of 1931 Census C.S. Mullan, ICS has now become almost legendary. He writes, '(P)robably the most important event in the province during the last twenty five years . . . has been the invasion of a vast horde of land hungry Bengali immigrants; mostly Muslims, from the districts of Eastern Bengal sometime before 1911 and the census report of that is the first report which makes mention of the advancing host. But . . . the Bengali immigrants censused for the first time on the char islands of Goalpara in 1921 were merely the advance guard . . . of a

## 92　Chandan Kumar Sharma

huge army following closely at their heels. By 1921, the first army corps had passed into Assam and had practically conquered the district of Goalpara' (Mullan 1931:52). He continues, '(W)here there is waste land thither flock the Mymensinghias. . . . Without fuss, without tumult, without undue trouble to the district revenue staffs, a population which must amount to over half a million has transplanted itself from Bengal into the Assam Valley during the last twenty-five years. . . . (I)t is sad but by no means improbable that in another thirty years Sibsagar district will be the only part of Assam in which an Assamese will find himself at home' (Mullan 1931:52).

Mullan's statement has since then served as an ideal fodder to the anti-immigration voices in Assam. Mullan, however, did not mention the fact that the advent of the Mymensinghias was directly patronised by the colonial administration. Yet, although Mullan's statement has been much criticised by a section of the left intelligentsia as an example of the divisionary tactic of the colonial rulers on communal lines (see for example, Barman 1995:31–32; Guha 1988:212–13), it does not seem to be entirely correct to condemn Mullan who might have expressed his own concern which was not unfounded. Moreover, there are many other instances within the colonial regime when its different branches did not only disagree but also bitterly fight over specific colonial policies. It may be noted that the governor of Assam soon rebuffed Mullan's observations in his address to the Assam Legislative Council (Guha 1988:213).

Nevertheless, the Muslim immigration from East Bengal generated disquiet among the Assamese leaders as early as 1915. On 13 March of that year Manik Chandra Barooah, the doyen of the contemporary Assamese middle class and a member of the Assam Legislative Council, complained in his speech in the Council against the large-scale immigration of East Bengal Muslim peasants to Assam and asked the government to take precautions so that they did not come into conflict with the local villagers (Guha 1988:85). Following this, a number of Assamese leaders expressed apprehension about the East Bengal migration.

Assam Samrakshini Sabha (Association for Protection of Assam), floated by the Assamese nationalist leader Ambikagiri Roychoudhury in 1926, was quite vocal on the immigration issue (Guha 1988:211). These concerns later found expression even in the statements of national leaders like Jawaharlal Nehru and Rajendra Prasad (Misra 1988:76). In the years preceding the partition as well as the independence of India in 1947, it was the genuine possibility of Assam being merged with the Muslim-majority East Pakistan that created panic among the Assamese (as well as the tribal) leaders of the time. Though the timely stand taken by the latter led by Gopinath Bordoloi prevented such an eventuality, these developments left a deep impact on the Assamese mindset. This is invoked even today by the

*Immigration, indigeneity and identity* 93

Assamese nationalists whenever there is a debate on the issue of Bangladeshi immigration to Assam.

## The tribal question

The large-scale settlement of the immigrants resulted in the displacement of the indigenous tribal peasantry of Assam from their land in two ways. First and directly, the migrants usurped agricultural land of the tribals who were engaged in *jhum* (shifting) cultivation which included a very large tract. When migrant peasants were settled in these areas, the traditional agricultural practice of the tribal peasants received serious setback because migrants now occupied the land which came under the tract for *jhum* cultivation. Many tribals also abandoned their land and moved to remoter areas and even to forests to avoid living side by side with the strangers (Roychoudhury 1991:23).

Ostensibly, in order to wrest this process of displacement and land alienation among the tribals, provisions for reserved tribal areas were adopted by the then colonial administration. The first such effort could be found in the 'Line System' introduced first in the erstwhile Nagaon district and the Barpeta subdivision of the erstwhile Kamrup district in 1920 (Das 1986:30). It made provisions for settlement of the latter in specified manners in the village areas of Assam. Those villages where the immigrants could settle freely were specified as 'open' villages. Those villages where immigrants could settle only on one side of a line drawn on the village map were specified as 'mixed' villages. And the third category of the villages which were closed to immigrants was known as 'closed' villages.

But this system collapsed under the aggressive land grabbing initiative of the immigrants. The Line System Committee headed by F. W. Hockenhull was instituted to look into the working of the line system, which found that the tribal villagers were the worst victims of the land encroachment ventures of the immigrants. Many tribal villages disappeared in the process and their inhabitants moved into submontane zone (Das 1986:31). The committee, in its report submitted in 1939, favoured creation of 'prohibited areas' for backward and tribal communities. However, the resignation of then Congress-led coalition government under Gopinath Bordoloi and the outbreak of the Second World War put an end to this initiative.

The Muslim League–led coalition ministry under Sir Syed Muhammad Saadulla rejected the suggestions of the Line System Committee by a resolution in June 1940 and instead devised a Land Development Scheme aiming at facilitating the settlement of migrants in all wasteland areas of Assam (Das 1986:33). The enthusiasm of the Muslim League ministry in settling the Muslim migrants had an obvious political objective, which

## 94 *Chandan Kumar Sharma*

was to turn Assam into a Muslim-majority province and then merge it with Pakistan after partition.[3] However, this scheme generated a storm of protest and the Saadulla ministry fell. Saadulla returned to power again on August 1942. Misra writes that by then, the situation was politically quite congenial for him to go ahead with his Land Development Scheme. At the same time, 'pressure was mounting also from the Muslim League government in West Bengal where the state assembly passed a resolution calling upon Assam to open up its reserves to land-hungry immigrants from Bengal. Within a year of his assuming office, in August 1943 the Saadulla ministry adopted a new resolution on land settlement which provided for the opening up of grazing reserve areas and wastelands in the districts of Nowgong, Darrang and Kamrup to immigrants from Bengal as part of the "Grow More Food" programme aimed at helping the war economy' (Misra 2012:36).

While this scheme facilitated the occupation of vast tracts of forest and wasteland by immigrants, the demand for opening up more grazing reserves for the immigrants was still growing. This demand took a militant turn under the leadership of Maulana Abdul Hamid Bhasani.[4] In the Assam Provincial convention of the Muslim League held in Barpeta in April 1944, the demand was raised in the presence of Saadulla that either his ministry gave the immigrants more land or quit power. Bhasani made a scathing attack on the official land policy demanding more land for the immigrants. Saadulla had to rebuff Bhasani by accusing how the greedy headmen (dewanis and matbars) of the immigrant villages had unceremoniously obtained *patta*s for seventy to hundred acres each, with a view to inducting sub-tenants. The Line system was introduced to check such greed and tendencies. He accused these headmen of driving out even the Assamese Muslims from the newly reclaimed lands. Saadulla compared the situation with the unrestricted Jewish migration to the Arab homeland. He argued for the protection of plains tribal population from the onslaught of the aggressive immigrant settlers and appealed for support to this policy. He, however, added that the Line System had already been relaxed to a great deal with a view to ensuring its eventual abolition (Guha 1988:282–83).

However, Saadulla's policy of opening grazing and forest reserves for immigrants faced stiff resistance from the Congress leaders such as Bordoloi. Under sustained protest this policy was modified in January 1945. After going through a process of modification over a period of time, the ideas of today's tribal belts and tribal blocks were implemented eventually by the Gopinath Bordoloi–led Congress ministry in 1946. Villages with 50 per cent or more population of the tribal and backward communities were brought under the jurisdiction of the tribal belts and blocks. For

*Immigration, indigeneity and identity* 95

geographical compactness, even the neighbouring villages with less than 50 per cent tribal population were clubbed with the reserved tribal areas. However, the non-tribal population already inhabiting these reserved areas was allowed to keep their holdings as before. However, transfer of tribal land to non-tribals was prohibited. These provisions were given final shape by the Assam Land and Revenue Regulation Amendment Act, 1947.

## Post-partition scenario

The partition of India in 1947 into India and Pakistan and the merger of East Bengal (as East Pakistan) with Pakistan led to a huge influx of Hindu immigrants from there which had been accorded refugee status by India. However, later on, towards the mid-1950s, the rate of Hindu immigration declined and was overtaken by a surge of poor, landless Muslim immigrants. This triggered a lot of animated discussion among the Assamese leaders both inside and outside state legislative assembly. In fact, the Indian Parliament too expressed concern about the surge of immigrants from the erstwhile East Pakistan. The tribal leaders from Assam were especially vocal on the issue. In order to stem this surge of immigrants, the Government of India brought in the Immigrants (Expulsion from Assam) Act 1950 with effect from 1 March 1950. In the meantime, however, the Nehru-Liaquat Agreement was signed on 8 April 1950, which facilitated the return of many immigrants who left the country after partition.[5]

Nevertheless, the contemporary Indian leadership, not to talk about those from Assam, was quite concerned about the East Pakistani infiltration into Assam.[6] However, an effective law to deport them as 'foreigner' came into force only in 1957 when the word 'foreigner' in the Foreigners Act 1946 (which defined a foreigner as one who was not a natural-born or naturalised British subject) was amended and defined as one who is not an Indian citizen. After this, the GoI issued instructions to all the state governments, including Assam, to deport the illegal Pakistani nationals in India. The 1961 Census report also highlighted the problem of infiltration. In 1962, the GoI introduced a scheme, namely Prevention of infiltration into India of Pakistani Nationals (PIP).

In the meanwhile, the state government also set up a number of tribunals in different parts of Assam to deport the Pakistani infiltrators. While the Congress government of Assam took a tough stand on the illegal immigrants, the then prime minister of India, Jawaharlal Nehru, wanted the Assam government to go slow on deportations evidently in view of the riots in both India and Pakistan at that point of time. However, the then chief minister of Assam, Bimala Prasad Chaliha, refused, saying that 'the problem was so critical that Assam's demography and culture would be

96 *Chandan Kumar Sharma*

permanently changed' (Hazarika 2000:60) if timely action is not taken against it. However, 'a furious revolt by Muslim MLAs against another anti-migrant programme', among other factors, subsequently compelled Chaliha to change his position (ibid.:60–63).

Towards the late 1960s, however, the concern about the seriousness of the immigration problem among the political leadership was on the wane and gradually it evaporated. This seems to have stemmed from the emerging geo-political reality in the subcontinent. The beginning of the popular struggle in East Pakistan for liberation from Pakistan created a new situation leading to the change of position of the Indian leadership on the immigration issue. Apparently, as a strategy to outsmart Pakistan, India not only softened its position on the issue but also legitimised all the illegal East Pakistani immigrants who came to Assam before 25 March 1971 through the instrumentality of the Indira-Mujib Treaty[7] of 1972 after East Pakistan achieved independence from Pakistan as Bangladesh in 1971.

Furthermore, in the post-independence Assam the issue of the state language, closely related to immigration, became most crucial for the Assamese elites and on this they faced stiff challenge from the Bengali language. The latter became the majority language of Assam in the pre-partition days when Sylhet was made a part of the state. Even after partition, the tension persisted. The state witnessed two serious language-centric conflicts in 1960 and 1972. On both the occasions, the Muslim immigrants took the side of the Assamese language and helped the latter retain its majority (and state) language status in Assam. Understandably, the preponderance of the language issue pushed the immigration issue for some time away from the public domain (Deka 2010:34–35).

It is to be noted that unlike the colonial period when the colonial regime encouraged migration of East Bengali peasants to Assam for economic reasons, allegedly the main motive of the post-independence Congress party government (which ruled Assam continuously for 30 years since independence in 1947 and for almost 50 years overall) to settle the immigrants has been political, that is to create 'vote banks' of insecure immigrants for electoral gains. The immigrants settled in the available *chars* (flood sediment islets) of the river Brahmaputra, forests and grazing lands and in tribal reserved areas, often under the patronage of politicians. Inevitably, these immigrants' names also crept into the state's voter list. The freedom movement in East Pakistan during 1970–71 and the Pakistani administration's violent repression of the movement also compelled lakhs of East Pakistani citizens to enter Assam as refugees, many of whom did not return to their homeland even after the formation of Bangladesh. All these contributed to the rising anti-immigrant temperature in the Assamese public discourse.

## The anti-foreigners agitation and the accord

At this juncture, the death of the sitting Member of Parliament of the Mangaldai Parliamentary constituency in early 1979 provided the ideal fodder to the rising anti-immigrant rage. The Election Commission of India (EC) announced a by-election and an updating of the voters' list was undertaken. While the process was on, there were strong allegations about inclusion of many illegal immigrants in the voter list. On reviewing the list, the EC found most of the allegations to be true and the names of almost 45,000 illegal immigrants found included in the voter list. This generated a massive public outcry in Assam. The All Assam Students' Union (AASU) demanded that the voter list of thirteen other parliamentary constituencies of Assam be made public. AASU and several other organisations declared that until and unless the voter lists were cleared of the names of the foreign nationals, no elections would be allowed to be held in Assam. Thus began the anti-foreigners agitation in Assam which in the next six years saw one of the most turbulent phases in the history of the state.

The anti-foreigners agitation, despite all its drawbacks during 1979–85, clearly brought to the fore the Assamese mass concern about the continued large-scale illegal immigration from Bangladesh and how it had posed serious challenge to the political and cultural identity of the indigenous communities. The movement culminated in an accord, popularly known as the Assam Accord, in August 1985 between the Government of India and the leaders of the agitation. AASU originally demanded the deportation of all illegal immigrants who entered Assam after 1 January 1951, the cut-off year for detection of illegal migrants from East Pakistan as per the provisions of the Citizenship Act of India. The National Register of Citizens was prepared on the basis of 1951 as the cut-off year. It was on the basis of this National Register of Citizens (NRC) that detection and investigation of cases under the Foreigners Act was carried to be out. Finally, the accord settled on 1 January 1966 as the base year for detection of foreigners, and accordingly the foreigners who entered Assam after 1 January 1966 and up to 24 March 1971 were to be detected and their names deleted from the electoral list for 10 years. It accepted 25 March 1971 as the cut-off year for identification and deportation of the illegal immigrants. The accord also pledged to provide for the constitutional safeguards for the Assamese people. However, after almost three decades of signing of the accord, the 1966 base year for detection of foreigners is all but forgotten as all the public attention has come to be focused on 1971 as the cut-off year for expelling foreigners. But in all these years only a few hundred foreigners have been deported, and there have been many instances of such deported foreigners coming back to Assam again. According to government data, from 1985

98 *Chandan Kumar Sharma*

to July 2012, only 2,442 illegal migrants have been deported from Assam (GOA 2012:18).

Even the leadership of the anti-foreigner agitation which formed a political party (namely, Asom Gana Parishad) and came to power in the state failed to deliver the goods. Admittedly, there were serious obstacles to the process of detection of foreigners. The provisions of the infamous Illegal Migrants (Determination by Tribunals) Act, 1983, which was legislated by the then Congress government, made it virtually impossible to detect any foreigners. The Act, which was enacted only for Assam, was struck down by the Supreme Court of India as unconstitutional only in 2005.

In the meantime, the immigrants who are illegal as per the Assam Accord have remained in Assam and their numbers have multiplied along with their descendants. The government has also shown no political will to address the issue in right earnest. For example, the functioning of the foreigners' tribunals for expediting the cases against foreigners is in a shambles due to the indifference of successive governments, although even the Guwahati High Court asked the government on a number of occasions to take suitable action to add teeth to the functioning of the tribunals ('HC asks state to speed up trials at foreigners' tribunals' 2013) by providing it adequate manpower and infrastructure.

## The politics of NRC

The updating of the NRC in Assam, which has been generally identified as a crucial instrument of differentiating the legal citizens from the illegal immigrants, has also not been implemented due to lack of political will on the part of the government although it was mandated by the Assam Accord. Finally in 2010, the Registrar General of India notified for a pilot project for updating the NRC in the Barpeta revenue circle in Barpeta district and the Chaygaon revenue circle in Kamrup district. However, after a violent protest by the All Assam Minority Students' Union (AAMSU) in Barpeta against alleged anomalies in the enumeration process on July 21 2010, the government stalled the whole process of updating NRC. Government's approach to the issue came under serious criticism from various organisations and political parties. In the meanwhile, debate also cropped up regarding the base year of the NRC. The AASU and other organisations demand the same to be 1951, the year in which the NRC of the independent India was first prepared, which should be subsequently updated for 1961 and 1971.[8]

Contrarily, AAMSU and other minority organisations and parties demand the 1971 voter list as the basis for updating the NRC. When in March 2013 the Assam government decided, as per the recommendation of a cabinet

*Immigration, indigeneity and identity* 99

sub-committee of the state government, to restart the stalled pilot project to update the NRC of 1951, AAMSU along with 24 other minority organisations declared their strong objections to it ('We will not accept NRC update in Assam: AAMSU President' 2013). On the same issue, the All India United Democratic Front (AIUDF),[9] the main opposition party of the state which has its core support base among the Muslims of immigrant descent, staged a walkout from the state assembly on 1 April 2013 opposing the use of the term 'update' of the NRC as, according to the party, the 1951 NRC is incomplete or non-existent in several districts. Instead, it demanded the NRC be 'prepared' ('AIUDF walks out over NRC "update"' 2013:19) on the basis of the latest (that is 2011) voter list. This is a position that poses to render the very purpose of NRC update to a farce.

The advocates of the process of NRC update point out that in case the names of recognised Indian citizens or their parents were not included in the NRC of 1951 or in the subsequent voter list till 1971, there is a provision under which they can appeal for their inclusion in the NRC on the basis of any one of the sixteen documents such as passport, ration card, account in post office or bank, land ownership document etc. issued to them prior to 25 March 1971. Finally, the government, in the first phase, started the process of NRC update in seven districts in central and upper Assam where 'minimum opposition is expected' ('NRC Update Process Begins' 2013:1).

However, the sluggishness of the process and government's own diffidence about it prompted some civil society organisations in Assam to appeal to the Supreme Court of India (SCI) on the matter. The SCI in its ruling on 18 December 2014 asked the Assam government to publish the updated NRC by the end of January 2016. ('AASU hails court ruling on NRC update' 2014:1). As the process started in March 2015, opposition to 1951 as the base year continued among the civil and political groups representing the immigrant Muslim community.

Incidentally, no political party, including AIUDF, denies that there are illegal immigrants in Assam. However, they are never in agreement on the methodologies for detection and deportation of these immigrants. Furthermore, the question as to where to deport the detected foreigners has always remained a vexed issue as Bangladesh has never admitted the presence of its citizens in India. Moreover, there is no treaty between India and Bangladesh for deportation of foreigners. Therefore, identified Bangladeshi nationals are deported mainly through the 'push back' method by which the Indian Border Security Force pushes the former back to Bangladesh (GOA 2012:21).

It has already been mentioned earlier that a large section of the Muslim immigrants in the Brahmaputra valley have identified themselves as

100 *Chandan Kumar Sharma*

Assamese speakers in the successive censuses since 1951, which has helped Assamese to retain its status as the majority language in Assam till date. Otherwise, in the event of the immigration of a number of large linguistic groups from other parts of India and the tendency among several erstwhile ethnic groups in the state to identify themselves as the speakers of their own ethnic languages instead of Assamese in recent censuses, it would be almost impossible for Assamese to retain its majority status in the state. This point is underscored by a significant section of the Assamese intelligentsia too which believes in facilitating the process of assimilation of the Muslim immigrants into the Assamese society rather than alienating them by divisive rhetoric (Gohain 1985:27; Roychoudhury 2009; Sharma 2009).

But the charges that underwrite the campaign against the Muslim immigrants is that once they become a majority community they will abandon such an assimilative approach and stake their own claim on power. Such tendencies among the immigrants have already been observed. In June 2007, an AIUDF legislator Rasul Haque Bahadur made a public statement that on the basis of their present population the Muslims of Goalpara, Dhuburi, Bongaigaon and Darrang districts of Assam should get an autonomous council under Indian Constitution. It is a different matter that the latter does not have such a provision. AIUDF also distanced itself from this statement (Nath 2011:238). The same leader, though no more with AIUDF, again stirred a controversy in April 2013 when he asserted that there were about 12 million Muslims in Assam and no one could stop a Muslim leader from becoming chief minister of Assam after the Assembly election in 2016 ('Muslim panel calls 12-hr strike – Autonomous Council Plea' 2013:19). His statement came close on the heels of the claim of the AIUDF leader Sirajuddin Ajmal on 2 April that Badruddin Ajmal, the AIUDF supremo, would become the chief minister of Assam in 2016 ('Ajmal's Dream' 2013:1). These statements have also contributed to the prevailing apprehension among the indigenous communities that they would soon lose control of political power in the state.

Similarly, although a large section of the immigrant Muslims identified themselves as Assamese speakers in successive censuses, prior to the census of 1991, a section of the immigrant Muslim politicians campaigned in the immigrant-dominated areas for adopting Bengali in place of Assamese. This situation recurred prior to the 2011 census when some immigrant Muslim politicians advocated the cause of what was called a 'Miyan'[10] language for the immigrant population. Under influence of such campaigns, on both the occasions, sections of immigrant Muslims identified themselves as speakers of either 'Bengali' or 'Miyan' language (Nath 2011:242–43).

# Number of illegal immigrants

All these account for the persistent cause of concern and indignation among the indigenous communities of Assam at the rapid growth of Muslim population in the state (Table 6.1). The provisional census figures of 2011 showed the continuation of the same trend as the percentage of the Muslim population in Assam reached 34.2 from 30.9 in the 2001 Census, registering the highest increase in share of Muslims among all the states in India ('Census 2011: Assam records highest rise in Muslim population' 2013). Census figures also show that in terms of total population growth during 1971–91 the Hindu population in Assam grew by 41.9 per cent while during the same period the Muslim population grew by 77.4 per cent. Again, during 1991–2001, while the Hindu population grew by 15 per cent the Muslim population witnessed a growth of 31 per cent (Deka 2010:86). During these periods, several Hindu-majority districts of Assam have also turned into Muslim-majority districts. While in 1971 there were only two districts in Assam where Muslims constituted more 50 per cent of the total population, in 2001 this figure reached six, while in four other districts they have a strong presence. The indigenous Muslim community of the state being a small minority, it can be easily surmised that the majority of the Muslim population of the state are of immigrant descent.

Again as the Indo-Bangla border is extremely porous, it is quite possible that a significant section of the immigrant Muslim population of the state

*Table 6.1* Variation of religion-wise demographic pattern in Assam 1901–2001

| Year | Hindus (%) | Muslims (%) | Others (%) |
|------|-----------|-------------|------------|
| 1901 | 71.03 | 12.40 | 16.57 |
| 1911 | 67.95 | 16.69 | 15.36 |
| 1921 | 67.33 | 19.41 | 13.26 |
| 1931 | 70.09 | 23.41 | 6.50 |
| 1941 | 46.84 | 25.72 | 27.44 |
| 1951 | 72.01 | 24.68 | 3.31 |
| 1961 | 71.33 | 25.26 | 3.41 |
| 1971 | 72.51 | 24.56 | 2.93 |
| 1991 | 67.13 | 28.43 | 4.44 |
| 2001 | 64.89 | 30.92 | 4.19 |

Source: Government of Assam (GOA) 2012: 42–43.

102  *Chandan Kumar Sharma*

could be illegal immigrants. The rapid growth of their population as per census data in the districts bordering Bangladesh also suggests this. The figure of illegal immigrants in Assam, however, is a much contested issue with different organisations, newspaper reports and studies fixing their numbers at several millions. Way back in April 1992, Hiteswar Saikia, the then chief minister of Assam, stated in the state assembly that there were two to three million illegal Bangladeshi immigrants in Assam only to retract this statement two weeks later under threat from the immigrant Muslim political leaders (Prabhakara 2003). Subsequently, Indrajit Gupta, the then home minister of India, stated in the Parliament on 6 May 1997 that there were ten million illegal migrants residing in India. Quoting Home Ministry/Intelligence Bureau source, the 10 August 1998 issue of *India Today* estimated the illegal migrants in Assam at four million (Sinha 1998). The statements of many other senior ministers, group of ministers, top police officials and others at different junctures in the following years have also fixed the number of illegal Bangladeshi immigrants in India (and Assam) at several millions. The Report of Lt Gen. (retd) S.K. Sinha, former governor of Assam, on illegal migration into Assam which was submitted to the President of India in November 1998 gave a detailed account of the magnitude of the problem, which brought the issue again to the centre stage.

## The indigenous discontent

It goes without saying that this rise in their population also has considerable impact on the electoral politics of the state, causing much consternation among the indigenous communities including the indigenous Muslim population which are fast losing out their political space to the immigrants communities. The indigenous groups are upset with the government not only for its inaction in tackling the illegal immigration, they are also indignant about the way the government is actually facilitating the latter's recognition as genuine citizens by making adequate legal provisions or by its dilly-dallying attitude with regard to the illegal immigration issue. While the Assam Accord accepted 1971 as the cut-off year as a pragmatic step to resolve the issue, the IM(DT) Act made even the expulsion of the post-1971 illegal migrants an uphill task. Although the IM(DT) Act was annulled in 2005, the illegal migrants certainly got the benefit of the Act. After four decades of their residence in Assam (along with their descendants), deporting them to Bangladesh appears to be a highly unrealistic idea and their Indian citizenship appears to be a *fait accompli*.

The challenges that the Muslim immigrants have posed to the indigenous communities are multidimensional. Yet, unlike the Hindu Bengali immigrants, they hardly posed, at least till recently, any threat to the Assamese

## Immigration, indigeneity and identity 103

*Table 6.2* Trend of population growth in Assam and India: 1901–2011

| Year | Percentage of decadal variation | |
|---|---|---|
| | Assam | India |
| 1901 | 0 | 0 |
| 1911 | 17 | 5.8 |
| 1921 | 20.5 | 0.3 |
| 1931 | 19.9 | 11 |
| 1941 | 20.4 | 14.2 |
| 1951 | 19.9 | 13.3 |
| 1961 | 35 | 21.5 |
| 1971 | 35 | 24.8 |
| 1981* | 0 | 24.7 |
| 1991 | 24.2 | 23.9 |
| 2001 | 18.9 | 21.5 |
| 2011 | 16.9 | 17.6 |

Source: GOA 2012: 38.

* No census was conducted in Assam in 1981.

middle class in the sphere of the job market. They came to Assam as poor, landless peasants. A considerable section of them are still very poor and illiterate. However, they have usurped lands, often under political patronage, everywhere in Assam – right from the fallow government land to reserve forests to even agricultural land belonging to indigenous people in more remote areas. The traditional common property resources of the indigenous communities also have been encroached upon. It is to be noted that the tribal communities of the state are engaged mostly in consumption-oriented agrarian economy which finds it extremely difficult to compete with the immigrant Muslim peasants with a long tradition of commercial production. In the immigrant Muslim–dominated areas it is now a normal practice for the indigenous landowner, tribal or non-tribal, to lease out land to the former either out of compulsion or expediency and eventually lose possession of their land due to various factors even though that land belongs to a tribal reserve area. This adds a new dimension to the process of tribal land alienation in Assam (Sharma 2012a). In fact, the two major conflicts (Udalguri in 2008 and Kokrajhar in 2012) that the state saw in

104   *Chandan Kumar Sharma*

recent times between the immigrant Muslims and indigenous tribals mainly centred around the question of land.

The immigrant Muslims, most of them being landless peasants, always look for new land, if necessary even in distant areas. In the process, their presence is seen everywhere from forest reserves to village commons where their villages spring up in no time. This horizontal growth, however, may not necessarily be matched by a corresponding vertical growth in their population in all places. But it adds to the popular perception that their population is also fast increasing. Such usurpation of land is not experienced in case of other immigrant communities. This would not have been possible without political patronage.

In this connection, it is worthwhile to note that the process of parting with a village for land or livelihood somewhere else does not seem to be socially, culturally and emotionally a very violent process for the immigrant villagers who came to Assam under extreme destitution in their place of origin. Unlike the indigenous villages, many of the immigrant villages are relatively new and lack any strong historical or cultural roots to cause serious emotional distress among the outgoing villagers. Second, a large section of the later immigrants settled in riverine as well as the *char* areas which are extremely vulnerable to flood and erosion, compelling many of their inhabitants to move out at regular intervals in search of land and livelihood. Third, rampant poverty, rapid population growth and scarcity of land always tend to push the immigrants out of their villages in search of new opportunities. Their dwelling units are also often of makeshift kind, thus enabling them to migrate at relative ease.

On the other hand, the impact of parting with their villages is just the opposite for the indigenous peasants. Their villages are relatively older with which the villagers share deep social, economic and cultural relationships. Thus their tendency to migrate out of their villages is much less in comparison to the immigrant villagers. This is not to deny that historically the Assamese peasants also migrated to various places to reclaim new land under various circumstances. The tribal peasantry in Brahmaputra valley too was engaged in shifting cultivation. However, the nature of such migrations was quite different.

Besides, with their sheer demographic strength, the immigrant Muslims of Assam are today emerging as a powerful force in the social and the political landscape of the state. In this context, it is interesting that the indigenous Assamese Muslims have become vociferous in recent times about their rights as minorities who allege that the immigrants have usurped all the rights and privileges due to the indigenous Assamese Muslims. Their marginalisation, they argue, has been most acute in the domain of politics which has been overwhelmed by the immigrants who with their numerical

*Immigration, indigeneity and identity* 105

strength have emerged as the only 'voice and face' of the religious minorities of Assam.[11]

## Resolving the tangle

It is clear that the conflict around the issue of Bangladeshi immigration in Assam stems from the apprehension of the indigenous people of the state of getting politically, economically and culturally marginalised in their own homeland. That the issue is of international nature only adds to its complexity. Evidently, any solution to the issue involves a two-pronged strategy: one, deporting the already existing illegal immigrants and two, bringing such cross-border immigration to an end. Both are daunting exercises.

Insofar as the deportation of the illegal immigrants is concerned, it entails a massive political, social and economic exercise. The identification of illegal immigrants itself has been a major political issue, and successive governments have refrained from taking any decisive step in this matter fearing adverse electoral fallout. The fact that even after three decades of the signing of the Assam Accord only a couple of thousand immigrants have been deported to their home country speaks volume of the politics of deportation. Another major complication in the issue is that Bangladesh is yet to officially acknowledge that illegal immigration of its people to India has occurred at all. There also has not been any effort on the part of the GoI to bring into effect any bilateral agreement on this issue with Bangladesh. However, after the bloody violence between the indigenous Bodo ethnic group with the immigrant Muslims in western Assam in July 2012 (see e.g. Misra 2012), the urgency for such an agreement has been forcefully raised by various organisations and political parties in Assam.

The western Assam carnage also led various organisations to demand from the government of Assam a white paper on the issue of illegal immigrants in Assam. Subsequently, under popular pressure, the government published a white paper in October 2012. Although this document included important information about the illegal immigration to Assam and actions that the government has taken over the years to check it, it came under criticism from various Assamese organisations. AASU criticised the document for making no mention of a road map to ensure implementation of the Assam Accord. It also criticised the white paper as a cleverly crafted document to protect the interests of the illegal migrants ('White paper on influx a white lie': AASU 2012).

Insofar as stemming the flow of influx is concerned, the most commonly proposed solution is the construction of barbed wire fencing along the Indo-Bangladesh border. Under the provision of the Assam Accord, the task of a 272-kilometre-long border fencing is already under way. But

106 *Chandan Kumar Sharma*

even after a prolonged period the task is not yet complete. This for long has been one of the most passionate issues in the Assamese public domain. However, it is to be noted that the topography of the Indo-Bangladesh border also has stood in the way of construction of the border fencing. Rivers generally serve as natural boundaries. But rivers in the Indo-Bangladesh border frequently change their courses, rendering it extremely difficult to fix boundaries (Hazarika 2000:125–27). However, it is pointed out that this problem can be addressed by increased river patrolling.

It is worthwhile to mention that the illegal immigration across border has been possible because of the nexus of the corrupt border guards, local officials and politicians. The stranglehold of the local politicians on the illegal immigrants continues till much later. They secure various citizenship documents for the immigrants, who become handy instruments in fulfilling the vested interests of the politicians. Cases of arrest of illegal Bangladeshi immigrants with such documents are often reported in the media.

For example, quoting police sources, a news item published in a respectable daily in Assam reported that between July 1999 and June 2000, the city police had pushed back 187 infiltrators arrested in the Guwahati city, out of which 182 infiltrated freshly and five re-infiltrated after being pushed back before. The news item also highlighted a case in Nagaon district which offered a telling commentary of the nature of infiltration in Assam. A Bangladeshi citizen named Md. Kamaluddin was arrested in Nagaon town in February 1998. It was found that he obtained a passport through illegal means to enter India in 1994 and arrived at Murajhar in Nagaon district. After his arrest, he was deported to Bangladesh. But he soon returned and filed a case in the Gauhati High Court challenging his deportation and stating that he was a citizen of India and a resident of Kapahbari under P.O. Murajhar with landed property in the village. He also claimed that his name was there in the voter list and that he even contested election from the Jamunamukh Legislative Assembly constituency in 1996. The state government contested Kamaluddin's claims and produced before the court documents seized from him which included a passport issued to him by the Government of Pakistan in November 1994 and a boarding pass of the Pakistan International Airlines which he used to travel from Karachi to Dhaka. After hearing the case, the court vacated the stay order, passed earlier, on the deportation of Kamaluddin and ordered his immediate deportation. The court expressed displeasure and annoyance with regard to the casual and cavalier manner in which voters' list is prepared in Assam which allowed even a foreigner to contest elections ('Bangla infiltrators swamping city' 2000).

In an interesting study, Kamal Sadiq demonstrates that the scenario in Assam is an outcome of the document-centric notion of citizenship of

*Immigration, indigeneity and identity* 107

modern states (Sadiq 2009:139). Referring to the millions of illegal immigrants from Bangladesh in India and elsewhere that he writes, '. . . documentary citizenship opens the door not only to the exercise of suffrage by illegal immigrants, but also to public office, thus directly challenging the boundaries . . . between immigrant and citizen. The recruitment of illegal immigrants as voters also advantages certain political parties. . . .' (Sadiq 2009:140). Documentary citizenship thus does not only 'enfranchise illegal immigrants, but the political participation of these individuals can alter political outcomes in favour of governments that enable illegal immigrants to acquire proof of citizenship and the ability to vote. In effect, illegal immigrants may vote in order to secure their identity and citizenship status' (Sadiq 2009:140–41).

Referring to Assam, Sadiq explains how the massive illegal Bangladeshi immigration to the state and their participation in the elections have created considerable amount of insecurity among the indigenous groups of the state about their political future in their own homeland (Sadiq 2009:148). However, he suggests that the frenzied discourse around the question of citizenship of the illegal immigrants has not only facilitated a more active role for the pro-illegal immigrant parties and organisations in the state as saviours of the immigrants, but it also possibly has 'raised awareness among illegal immigrants from Bangladesh that more trustworthy types of paperwork would have to be collected, either illegally or legally through networks of complicity' (ibid.:152). Naturally, for the pro-immigrant political parties such 'document-wielding illegal immigrants make for an active and loyal electorate' (ibid.:155). Thus, Sadiq maintains, some political 'parties and immigrants both have an interest in preserving the irregularities of documentation and collaborate to that end' (ibid.:167).

Some scholars and organisations in Assam advocate the case for 'work permit' for the illegal immigrants (Hazarika 2000:261–62). They argue that the prime reason behind illegal Bangladeshi influx being economic, facilitating conditions of employment as well as license for trade would largely eliminate the ground for illegal border crossing and encourage the intruders to immigrate with proper documents. This will also allow the government to keep track of the immigrants.

It is well acknowledged that north-eastern India, especially Assam, presents itself as a natural living space (lebensraum) for the densely populated Bangladesh. It is also worthwhile to note that the available living space in Bangladesh is shrinking due to flood and erosion. The country has also lost a significant area of its coastline to the rising sea level. These have left a huge number of poor Bangladeshis without any livelihood or living space (IPCC 2007; Sarwar and Khan 2007; World Bank 2009). Assam has already been the destination for the impoverished masses from Bangladesh,

## 108 Chandan Kumar Sharma

leading to indigenous–immigrant conflict therein. The climate refugees would only add to this conflict (Swain 1996). Taking cognizance of the impact of environmental onslaught on Bangladesh, historian H. K. Barpujari observed that under such circumstances, immigration is inevitable. He, therefore, suggested that the Indian government, in collaboration with Bangladesh and other international neighbours and agencies, should contribute to the growth and development of Bangladesh's economy along with emphasis on soil conservation, irrigation and river valley projects (Barpujari 1999:122).

The cultivable land in the narrow strip of the Assam valley is also fast shrinking owing to huge population pressure and devastating flood and erosion every year. This has resulted in massive illegal encroachment of various reserved areas, including forests, all over Assam by the landless people posing a serious environmental threat to the entire region. Simultaneously, this has also given rise to a serious conflict situation among various groups over the limited available land resources. Original inhabitants, wherever the case applies, often find such encroachment by new settlers as an invasion on their traditional community resources. This conflict over access to land and other resources to a great extent explains the ethnic clashes in Assam in the recent times.

There is a strong ground to argue, as mentioned earlier, that the immigration from Bangladesh is rooted in the prevailing asymmetric economic development in the region. However, such asymmetries can be taken care of by adequate policies towards a uniform economic development of the region as one common economic zone. Unfortunately, enough attention has not been paid to this by the Indian policymakers. Adequate policies in this regard would take care not only of immigration but also of the heavy revenue loss that India suffers due to illegal border trade. Such economic measures can also address the pitfalls of 'documentary citizenship' as illustrated by Sadiq (Sharma 2012:306–7).

Sanjib Baruah draws a parallel between the indigenous–immigrant conflict in Assam and countries such as Malaysia and Fiji and comments, 'Assam's political turmoil since 1979 has some structural similarity to the political crises in Malaysia and Fiji' (Baruah 1999:67). In all these three places with considerable immigrant population, there has been a 'long history of demands on the part of those claiming to be 'indigenous' for primacy of official cultural symbols, economic opportunities, and even political power' (ibid.). Baruah points out that while Malaysia and Fiji have tried to respond to 'indigenous' demands in their countries in their own unique ways, in Assam, there has been a very little direct acknowledgement of this central problem by the authorities, which accounts for the continuous high levels of immigration to Assam unlike Malaysia and Fiji (ibid.). Successive

*Immigration, indigeneity and identity*  109

governments in the Centre and Assam have only soft-pedalled the anxieties of indigenous groups to their utter frustration. As citizenship in India is a federal issue, it is the bounden responsibility of the central government to respond to the situation in Assam with a robust policy.

Various other suggestions to address the nagging immigration tangle in Assam have also come from different corners. A senior journalist of an influential Assamese daily advocates for preserving those legislative constituencies for indigenous communities which had less than 50 per cent of religious minority (Muslim) population prior to a specific cut-off year which is to be determined. He also suggests curtailment of rights of the immigrant population to vote or to purchase land in the areas to which they migrate in search of livelihood. The latter provision is there in the tribal hill districts of Assam under the Sixth Schedule of the Indian Constitution ('Bideshi Prasangat' 2013). An influential peasant leader of Assam also suggests a number of measures to address the problem. The significant among them include a comprehensive land survey in Assam for identifying and classifying all kinds of land in the state, strict protection of forest land to keep it free from encroachment, issue of work permit, protection of land for the indigenous people with special provisions etc. (Gogoi 2013:209–10).

## Conclusion

There is no doubt that Assam needs a multi-pronged strategy to address the long-standing issue of illegal immigration. One has to recognise the genuine fear of the state's smaller indigenous communities, including indigenous Assamese Muslims, which have already become irrelevant in the majoritarian political discourse of the state.

It is, however, also important to take cognisance of the changing demographic landscape of Assam today. Any policy that undermines the interest of the state's large immigrant population would be practically unsustainable. The Muslims of immigrant descent, for example, today constitute close to 30 per cent of the total population of Assam (the percentage of total Muslim population in Assam being 34.2 according to the 2011 Census), a very significant number in a multi-ethnic state. Divisive rhetoric and politics in such a situation will only contribute to further polarisation of indigenous–immigrant relationship in the state. After all, millions of people of immigrant descent, many of whom came to the state nearly a century ago, have now become an inseparable part of the demographic landscape of the state.

Despite their growing demographic and political presence, however, the immigrant Muslims remain more or less ghettoised due to lack of education and development, which makes them vulnerable to the machinations of divisive political forces. It was incumbent on the government to

110  *Chandan Kumar Sharma*

expedite the process of social development of these people. But successive governments, either in Centre or in the state, have neither undertaken any measures to assuage the apprehension of the indigenous people nor have cared to bring the masses of immigrant Muslims to the mainstream sociopolitical discourse resulting in growing polarisation between them. Thus, while the government must take effective measures to stop illegal boundary crossings and deport all illegal immigrants, taking the legal immigrants into confidence in doing so is also equally important. This underscores the need of an inclusive policy on the illegal immigration issue in Assam informed by the state's contemporary geo-political reality which not only effectively protects the indigenous interest but also offers enough space for a progressive inclusion (or assimilation) of the immigrants into the mainstream socio-political dispensation of the state so that the existing indigenous–immigrant dichotomy is not further perpetuated.

## Notes

1 The districts of the Brahmaputra valley.
2 A *mauza* is a revenue unit constituted of several revenue villages.
3 The Muslim League began its demand for a separate Pakistan with the Muslim-majority areas of India since the late 1930s. By the end of the Second World War, the six provinces with a large Hindu majority that the Muslim League leader M.A. Jinnah demanded for Pakistan also included Assam (Anderson 2012: 79).
4 Hailed from the Pabna district of East Bengal, Bhasani migrated to Assam in 1928 and became an undisputed leader of the Muslim immigrants. In 1937, he became a member of the State Legislative Council and then a state president of the Muslim League in Assam. Bhasani played a critical role in the state politics till the eve of India's independence in 1947 (Roychoudhury 2009: 31).
5 The number of migrants to Assam was estimated at 1,61,360 (GOA 2012: 7).
6 The report of the Registrar General of Census on the 1961 Census estimated that 2,20,691 infiltrators had entered Assam (GOA 2012: 8).
7 This treaty was signed between Indira Gandhi and Mujibur Rahman, the prime ministers of India and Bangladesh, respectively.
8 It is to be noted that since 1951 no updating of NRC has taken place in Assam.
9 AIUDF has its main support base among the immigrant Muslims. Led by the millionaire businessman Maulana Badruddin Ajmal, AIUDF has made rapid strides in the electoral politics and poses a serious threat to the Congress party in retaining its minority vote bank.
10 Though there is nothing called the *Miyan* language as such, one can see that the aim was to present it as the language of the East Bengali/East Pakistani immigrants who are commonly referred to as the *Miyan*s.
11 There are regular reports in the Assamese media on this (see e.g. Pratidin Correspondent, 'Asamot Bangiya Musalmanor Adhipatyat Astitvar Sankatot Bhugise Khilonjiya Musalmane').

# References

Anderson P. 2012. *The Indian Ideology*. New Delhi: Three Essays Collective.

*Asomiya Pratidin*, 2010. Asamot bangiya musalmanor adhipatyat astitvar sankatot bhugise khilonjiya musalmane (Dominance of Bengali Muslims Causes Identity Crisis among the Indigenous Muslims in Assam). Guwahati.

*Amar Asom*, 2013. 'Bideshi Prasangat' (On the Foreigners Question). pp. 1, 6 (Prasanta Rajguru).

*The Assam Tribune*, 2000. 'Bangla Infiltrators Swamping City'. pp. 1, 3.

*The Assam Tribune*, 30 October 2012. 'White Paper on Influx a White Lie: AASU', *The Assam Tribune*, 30 October 2012, http://www.assamtribune.com/scripts/detailsnew.asp?id=oct3012/at07 (accessed 4 April 2012).

Barman, S. 1995. *Asamor Janajati Samasya (The Tribal Problem of Assam)*. Guwahati: Progressive Book House.

Baruah, S. 1999. *India against Itself: Assam and the Politics of Nationality*. New Delhi: Oxford University Press.

Butler, J. 1855. *Travels and Adventures in the Province of Assam*. London: Smith, Elder, and Co.

Das, J. N. 1986. 'Genesis of Tribal Belts and Blocks of Assam'. In B. N. Bordoloi (ed.), *Alienation of Tribal Land and Indebtedness*, pp. 28–38. Guwahati: Tribal Research Institute, Government of Assam.

Deka, H. 2010. *Prabrajan Aru Anupravesh (Immigration and Infiltration)*. Guwahati: Aank-Baak.

Gogoi, A. 2013. *Bideshi Samasya Aaru Jatiya Anandolanar Path (A Study on Immigration and Nationality Question in Assam)*. Guwahati: Aank-Baak.

Gohain, H. 1985. *Assam: A Burning Question*. Guwahati: Spectrum.

Government of Assam. 2012. *White Paper on Foreigner's Issue*. Guwahati: Government of Assam Press.

Guha, A. 1988. *Planters – Raj to Swaraj: Freedom Struggle and Electoral Politics in Assam 1826–1947*. New Delhi: People's Publishing House.

Hazarika, S. 2000. *Rites of Passage: Border Crossings, Imagined Homelands, India's East and Bangladesh*. New Delhi: Penguin.

IPCC 'Summary for Policymakers: A Report of Working Group I of the Intergovernmental Panel on Climate Change', 2007. http://www.ipcc.ch/pdf/assessment-report/ar4/wg1/ar4-wg1-spm.pdf (accessed 21 July 2011).

Lloyd, G. T., ed. 1921. *Census of India, Vol. 3: Assam*. Shillong: Government Press.

Misra, S. 2011. *Becoming a Borderland: The Politics of Space and Identity in Colonial Northeastern India*. New Delhi: Routledge.

Misra, Udayon. 1988. *North-east India: Quest for Identity*. Guwahati: Omsons Publications.

Misra, Udayon. 2012. 'Bodoland: The Burden of History', *Economic and Political Weekly*, 47(37): 37–42.

Moffat Mills, A. J. 1984. *Report on the Province of Assam*. Guwahati: Publication Board Assam.

## 112   Chandan Kumar Sharma

Mullan, C. S., ed. 1931. *Census of India. Vol. 3: Assam*. Shillong: Government Press.

Nath, M. K. 2011. *Asamor Rajnitit Musalmam (Muslims in Assam's Politics)*. Nagaon: Krantikal Prakashan.

Prabhakara, M. S. 2003. 'Chasing a Mirage'. *Frontline*, 20(13), http://www.frontline.in/navigation/?type=static&page=flonnet&rdurl=fl2013/stories/20030704001904100.htm.

Roychoudhury, A. 2009. *Asamot Bangladeshi (The Bangladesh Is in Assam)*. Nagaon: Jagaran Sahitya Prakashan.

Sadiq, K. 2009. *Paper Citizens: How Illegal Immigrants Acquire Citizenship in Developing Countries*. New York: Oxford University Press.

Sarwar, G. M. and M. H. Khan. 2007. 'Sea Level rise: A Threat to the Coast of Bangladesh', *Internationales Asien Forum*, 38: 375–97, http://www.undp.org.bd/library/policypapers/Asienforum_Sarwar_Khan.pdf (accessed 18 July 2011).

*The Sentinel*, 3. April 2013. 'Ajmal's Dream'. Guwahati, p. 1.

Sharma, C. K. 2000. 'Assam: Tribal Land Alienation: Government's Role', *Economic and Political Weekly*, 36(52): 4791–95.

Sharma, C. K. 2012. 'The Immigration Issue in Assam and Conflicts Around It', *Asian Ethnicity*, 13(3): 306–7.

Sharma, C. K. 2012a. 'Assam's Illegal Migrants: Neither Myth Nor Complete Reality', 23 August, http://www.firstpost.com/india/assams-illegal-migrants-neither-myth-nor-complete-reality-427393.html (accessed 23 August 2012).

Sharma, D. 2009. *Migration and Assimilation: Society, Economy, Politics of Assam*. New Delhi: Jorhat College and Daanish Books.

Sinha, S. K. 1998. 'Report on Illegal Migration into Assam: Submitted to the President of India', http://www.satp.org/satporgtp/countries/india/states/assam/documents/papers/illegal_migration_in_assam.htm (accessed 27 April 2010).

Swain, A. 1996. 'Displacing the Conflict: Environmental Destruction in Bangladesh and Ethnic Conflict in India', *Journal of Peace Research*, 33: 189–204.

*The Telegraph*, 2 April 2013. 'AIUDF Walks Out over NRC "update"'. Guwahati, p. 19.

*The Telegraph*, 18 December 2014. 'AASU Hails Court Ruling on NRC Update'. Guwahati, p. 1.

*The Times of India*, 5 January 2013. 'HC Asks State to Speed Up Trials at Foreigners' Tribunals'. 2013. http://articles.timesofindia.indiatimes.com/2013-01-05/guwahati/36160953_1_tribunals-high-court-proceedings (accessed 1 April 2013).

*The Times of India*. 2013 .'Census 2011: Assam Records Highest Rise in Muslim Population'. http://timesofindia.indiatimes.com/india/Census-2011-Assam-records-highest-rise-in-Muslim-population/articleshow/45972566.cms.

*The Times of India*, 26 March 2013. 'We Will Not Accept NRC Update in Assam: AAMSU President', http://articles.timesofindia.indiatimes.com/2012-03-26/guwahati/31239803_1_aamsu-nrc-abdur-rahim-ahmed (accessed 31 March 2013).

*Immigration, indigeneity and identity* 113

Weiner, M. 1978. *Sons of the Soil, Migration and Ethnic Conflict in India*. Princeton, NJ: Princeton University Press.

World Bank 2009. 'South Asia: Shared Views on Development and Climate Change', http://web.worldbank.org/WBSITE/EXTERNAL/COUNTRIES/SOUTHASIAEXT/0,contentMDK:22038355~pagePK:146736~piPK:146830~theSitePK:223547,00.html (accessed 10 July 2011).

# 7 The state and the migrants

## Contextualising the citizenship debate in Assam

*Rumi Roy*

Citizenship is one of the most contextualised concepts in political theory and practice. In today's modern states, citizenship represents a symbolic reality of equality of the members of a community (Heater 1999:1). It signifies a bundle of rights, a sense of belonging to live in an environment of social cohesion (Kymlicka and Norman 2000:1–41). The principle of citizenship answers to the political imperative of what draws a body of citizens together into a coherent and stable organised political community and keeps that allegiance. Yet at the same time it lays down certain criteria for inclusion and exclusion, for attaining membership in a political community. Citizenship is inextricably tied with the processes of state formation. Both governmentality and state are intertwined and this is affirmed through the exercise of state sovereignty. Thus, alongside the citizens, the state produces the 'constitutive outsiders', the indifferent outsiders, namely aliens and foreigners, and disruptive categories of 'illegal migrants'. It is the effective presence of these contending categories which generate the crisis within citizenship. Drawing on the theoretical framework of the debate around citizenship and migration in contemporary perspective in general, and Assam in particular, this chapter examines how boundaries are constructed around the notion of citizenship in the state to create the figure of the 'migrant'. The subjectivity of the migrant highlights the deep and lasting impact of manifestation of state sovereignty in the constructions of citizenship in Assam in context of the Illegal Migration (Determination by Tribunal) Act, 1983. The distinction between the citizen and foreigner often becomes a ground of contestation between the Centre and the state government in implementing the citizenship practices in state. This has further aggravated the already complicated issue of migration and emerging political formations accompanying them. Political instability prevailing in the state at present times can be relegated to the incompatibility and antagonistic nature of the Centre and the state in implementing laws relating to the detection of an illegal migrant.

*The state and the migrants* 115

The chapter further illustrates how the state legitimises itself as the sole arbiter in the delineation of citizenship claims, by determining the status of the migrant category on its own terms. The Indian Supreme Court decision further highlights the continued salience of state sovereignty in context of the challenges posed by Bangladeshi migrants crossing the border into Assam. An inquiry into the relationship between citizenship practices and the state sovereignty in context of migration in the state draws out attention on how the migrant is perceived as illegal and is trapped in legal ambiguity. Such an ambiguity in delineation of citizenship is a revelation of the fissures between the federal authority and the state.

## Theoretical perspective on citizenship, migrant and the state

Citizenship as a basic institution in the modern state found expression in the Marshallian definition of citizenship. The dimension of citizenship that emerge from Marshall's account is that of rights and responsibilities which the state owes to the citizens and citizens owe to the state and citizens owe to each other (Marshall 1998:75–101).Thus, citizenship viewed in Marshallian terms evokes state control over the terms of membership of a political community. Marshall provided a traditional account of the citizenship discourse. The aim here is not to provide a comprehensive definition of citizenship given the complexity and exhaustive nature of the concept. Instead the aim is to highlight the construction of citizenship in the contemporary period. An insight into the understandings of citizenship practices from the perspective of the migrant will be explored.

In the contemporary times, migration flows have raised fundamental issues about who is in and who is out, thus unfolding the boundaries of citizenship. It lays claim to the fact that the states are engaged in surveying the borders of citizenship. A contemporary scholar, Yuval-Davis conceives citizenship in statist terms. She argues that the state follows the patterns of inclusion and exclusion in the discourse of citizenship by integrating some on one hand and keeping out others on the other hand. Construction of boundaries around the notion of citizenship in accordance with various inclusionary and exclusionary criteria, relating to ethnic and racial divisions including class and gender, is one of the important areas of struggle concerning citizenship (Yuval-Davis 1997:4–27). Such notion affirms our belief that citizenship is a status awarded by the state through specified criteria. This has an important bearing on the migrant figure in the delineation of citizenship practices.

The modern regime of citizenship as it appears does not aim to keep migrants out; rather, it seems to foster the inclusion of a selective few as

## 116   *Rumi Roy*

determined by using its own criteria. This process, Balibar argues, produces multiplicity of legal positions and hierarchies in the citizenship practices of the state, opening conditions of apartheid. The word 'apartheid', according to him, must be taken literally, because what needs to be put at the centre of the theoretical and political debate is 'the process of constitution of a population made inferior (in rights and thus in dignity) that is the object of violent forms of "security" control and coerced into permanently living "at the border", neither wholly inside nor outside'. In a manifestation of 'lesson of otherness', as Balibar calls it, citizenship produces the 'constitutive outsiders', 'as an indispensable element of its own identify, its virtuality, its power'. Denoting differential or layered membership in the political community, 'otherness' is not a relationship of 'simple opposition' which manifest itself in exclusion. Rather, the relationship is one of forclusion, where the outsider is present discursively and constitutively in delineations of citizenship (Balibar 2003:39). Mezzadra, describing the migrant as a weak figure, relegates him to an inferior position, thus denying him any possibility of becoming a subject. As they become objects themselves, divorced from any personal dimension of being, they are subjected to a crude generalisation, numbering and classification implicit in the mainstream treatment of migratory processes (Roy 2008:48). What follows from the above discussion is that the migrant outsider becomes an indispensable element in the identification of a citizen. The migrant occupies significant importance in the deliberation and delineation of citizenship. The migrant is also manipulated by conferring multiple positions at the discretion of the state.

### The citizen and the migrant in Assam

While in the context of India the state not only grants citizenship embedded in the Constitution but also creates a legal judicial system to protect them. In the changing political scenario, marked by the flow of migrants, many undercurrents have occurred in the state–citizen relationship. Citizenship in the post-colonial India has not been conceived exclusively within the confines of the modern nation-state (Shafir (ed.): 1998). The legal framework of citizenship in India as it came into being with the enactment of the Citizenship Act of 1955 by Parliament laid down that any person born in India was a citizen of India, irrespective of the nationality of his or her parents. In 1986 following the famous Assam Accord an amendment to the Act was enacted by the Parliament, wherein Article 6A was inserted to address the people coming from Bangladesh. The category of the migrant made its first appearance in the legal regime of citizenship in India through the amendments in 1986 and again in 2003 and 2005 (Roy 2003:231). These changes allowed for the introduction

*The state and the migrants* 117

of the Citizenship (Registration of Citizens and Issue of National Identity Cards) Rules, 2003. These changes projected increased control of the state over the citizenship practices. Religious identity, cultural identity and principles of descent and blood ties are considered central to the Indian Constitution. The granting of group-differentiated rights to citizens giving cultural minorities the right to reserve their own culture has become an overriding consideration of exercise of state sovereignty. The migrant subject is an outcome of such specified legal proceeding of the state. It is to be noted that the amendment of 1986 referred to the identification of the illegal migrant from Bangladesh in specific context to the state of Assam (Roy 2003:231). The peculiarity imbricated in the Act escalated the government's punitive response to citizenship practices in Assam and the differential treatment meted out in this regard. Provided the given backdrop it is observed that the migrant is deeply imbricated in the constitution of citizenship in Assam. The migrant's identity and citizenship were by and large constructed in relation to the Assamese national identity formation during the movement days. Within this backdrop, this paper explores the ways of Indian practice of citizenship in Assam. It delves into the complex process in which attribution of illegality is associated with the figure of the migrant in the delineation of citizenship rights and the crucial role of the state. It interrogates how the migrant addressed through a spectrum of legal rules is reminiscent of the sovereign encounter practised by the state.

Under the strict statist regime the migrants are often subjected to judicial and bureaucratic scrutiny to determine their 'evidentiary value' (Kapur 2007). The category 'migrant' also designates crisis and associated conditions of poverty and marginalisation. Often, they are accused of invading the political space of the citizens and becoming sites of conflicts. In Assam, the state enjoyed unfettered authority, over the questions of deliberating and delineating citizenship. By demarcating the boundaries around the notion of citizenship in lines of the Assam Movement, a strict legal regime made its appearance for sifting out non-citizens in the state. Instead of resolving the problem, the new enforcement priorities escalated the government's punitive response to the migration issue in Assam and rest of India. The polarisation and political salience of the problem of migration deepened. It persisted and grew larger with time through the machinations of the politicians who were hell bent on securing electoral votes. Viewed in the larger context of a restrictive, and in many ways regressive, citizenship politics in post-partition India, the poor migrant became the symbol of continuing assertion of sovereignty by the state and growing political polarisation. The deepening polarisation of its society and polity has led to the relations between its multiple sub-nationalities being driven along

118  *Rumi Roy*

ethnic and communal lines. Democratic politics is seen to be overshadowed by ethnic politics in contemporary Assam.

## The crisis of citizenship in Assam: implications of the IMDT Act 1983

The figure of the migrant produced much anxiety leading to crisis of the citizenship regime in Assam. The Assam Movement, popularly known as the anti-foreigners' movement, laid claims for a distinctive citizenship regime for the people of the state. The term 'ethnic Assamese' was popularised by the movement which was non-existent before the movement (Baruah 1999:25). It led to the creation of a distinct Assamese identity, giving it a distinct local accent. The predicaments of the movement and harbouring notions of 'Swadhin Asom'(Misra 2000:183) posed a challenge to the universal notion of citizenship, showing the assertion of different concern from the national discourse. The propagation of regional assertion as projected by the Assam Movement created a regime of differentiated citizenship. In this complex configuration of the citizenship regime, the controversy engulfing the status of the migrant arose. Within the pan-Indian discourse, the Accord sought to solve the problems confronting the state within the national boundaries, but the radical group of the movement, the United Liberation Front of Assam (ULFA), a banned outfit now, wanted a solution to the problem outside the national political space. This brought to fore the complex configurations and twists in the convoluted situation of the state. The identification of the migrant as 'illegal' remained a central concern to define the Assamese universal and in delineating citizenship for the Assamese. The Assam Accord 1985 signed between the Centre, the state government and the leaders of the Assam agitation resulted in the 1986 amendment whereby a new form of identification and deportation of the illegal migrant was created and was made applicable only in Assam. The ambivalence in the articulation of citizenship along the eastern border has resonated in the amendments to the Citizenship Act in 1986, manifested the ways in which migration across the eastern borders, particularly in Assam, was sought to be addressed (Roy 2008:219–48).

The citizenship question became more complicated with the adoption of the historic Illegal Migration (Determination by Tribunal) Act, 1983, hereafter referred to as the IMDT Act, an extraordinary piece of legislation empowered by the central government to deal with the illegal migrants coming from Bangladesh to Assam after the formation of Bangladesh. The IMDT Act 1983 formalised Assam as an exception to India's citizenship laws by applying the Act particularly in Assam and by giving legitimacy to the questionable citizenship practices prevalent in Assam. The application

*The state and the migrants* 119

of the law particularly in Assam reiterated the claims of the state to dictate the terms of citizenship. The IMDT Act was passed on 15 October 1983 to detect and deport the illegal migrants in the state coming from Bangladesh in response to the Assam Movement of 1979–85 that began when the electoral rolls were being revised. Amid allegations that a large number of Bangladeshi Muslim immigrants were being included in the rolls, the Election Commission asked the Assam government to identify constituencies with a big rise in the number of voters. The revelation of the presence of number of doubtful citizens in the voters caused widespread disturbances in the state. The Nellie incident leading to the death of innocent lives was an outcome of such outburst. There was widespread demand by AASU activists to boycott the polls. People supported the cause; elections could not be held in seven out of twelve constituencies. The passing of the Act took place when there was no representation in the Parliament and the state was ruled by the Congress party under the leadership of Hiteswar Saikia reflected the political opportunism of the parties both at the Centre and state level. It underlined the political dynamics of the parties in the politics of citizenship in Assam (Prabhakara 2005:1).

Born under such controversial circumstances the Act was considered a contentious piece of legislation in the polemics of Assam politics. The Act became a major irritant for the agitation leaders. They were apprehensive of the Act which had an overriding effect over the Foreigners Act, 1946, or the Act legislated immediately after independence, The Immigrants (Expulsion from Assam) Act, 1950, which was applicable universally in the rest of the country and indeed in Assam as well until then. They suspected that the new legislation was adopted only as a protective measure that the state could not do without, initiated by a leader and a government which they continued to insist was illegal (Prabhakara 2005:1). The agony over the Act was further compounded by the constraints imposed by the lack of clarity as to who constitutes a foreigner and a citizen. The rest of India, which had the Foreigners Act, 1946, puts on the accused the onus of proving his/her Indian nationality. IMDT defined foreigners as those who settled down in Assam after 25 March 1971 and puts on the one who denounces a person the onus of proving that he/she is a foreigner. Complicating the process further is the Assam Accord (Assam Accord 1985:1369–70) which distinguishes three streams of such migrants: those who came to Assam before 1 January 1966, whose presence is to be regularised; those who came after 1 January 1966 but before 25 March 1971, in respect of whom the Foreigners Act, 1946, will apply; but only to the extent that they would be detected and their names would be deleted from the electoral rolls for a period of 10 years and those who came after 25 March 1971, in respect of whom the provisions of the IMDT Act, 1983, will apply (Prabhakara 2005:2).

120   *Rumi Roy*

The key component of the Act, the tribunals were ineffective in its functioning. The application of the IMDT Act only in Assam when in the rest of India the Foreigners Act prevailed was condemned at various levels as it pointed out the discriminatory treatment meted out to the people of Assam by the central government.

The infirmities of the Act became a ground of contestation at the sociopolitical level in Assam. One of the central issues that the Act contemplates is the relationship between citizenship and the enabling institutions which endow persons to act as citizens. In practice, the IMDT Act was found to be impractical. There was great impasse between the state and central governments over the functioning of the tribunals. The state government was blamed for the inefficient functioning of the tribunals as out of sixteen tribunals only four were functional. There were also disagreements between the state and the Centre with regard to the amendments in the IMDT Act. The contradiction was generated by the Centre by application of two Acts, the Foreigners Act as provided by the Accord and the IMDT Act which stood diametrically opposed to each other at the same time. The specificities in the legal framework of citizenship laid down by the Centre for the people of Assam was viewed as discriminatory for it meted out a differential treatment to the people of Assam. Speaking in this context, Udayon Misra pointed out that:

> By enacting two laws, one for the rest of India and one for the Assamese, the Centre facilitated the growth of differential feeling because laws enacted for foreigners' were different. The dichotomy in enactment of the laws dealing with the foreigners' needs to be changed.
>
> Misra (2000:37)

The impediments in the provisions of the IMDT Act, 1983, constrained the detection and deportation of the foreigners in Assam. The migrant's status under two different regimes gave birth to contradictions. This caused resentment among the people and the leaders of the Assam Movement. The simultaneous application of the IMDT Act and the Foreigners Act, 1946, to deal with migrants who came before 1971 amounted to difficulties in expeditious and effective detection and deportation of illegal migrants as both the Acts provided two different criteria which were contradictory to each other. Demands were made by the AASU and AAGSP to scrap the Act. However the decision to scrap became contested with different political parties at the Centre and state adopting different positions regarding the striking of the Act. The contests continued till the Supreme Court scrapped the Act on 12 July 2005 considering an appeal made by Sarbananda Sonowal, the then Member of Parliament belonging to the Asom Gana

The state and the migrants  121

Parishad, in the form of a public interest litigation. A three-judge bench comprising Justice G. P. Mathur, Justice P. K. Balasubramanyan and Chief Justice R. C. Lahoti delivered the judgement, leading to scrapping of the IMDT Act, 1983.

## The judicial interpretation of the IMDT Act

The Supreme Court struck down the Act acting on the writ petition filed by Sarbananda Sonowal, MP of Asom Gana Parishad (AGP), under Article 32 of the Constitution of India by way of a public interest litigation. While striking down the Act, the Supreme Court said that the Act was a failure in detecting and deporting illegal migrants from the state of Assam. Ironically, the Court agreed with much of what the leaders of the Assam Movement had argued regarding the built-in impediments in the provisions of the Act. It is to be noted that the IMDT Act, 1983, outlived the Accord, which was signed in 1985, and persisted in the political space of Assam until it was struck down in 2005.

The judgement questioned the constitutional validity of the Act and declared it unconstitutional. While delivering the judgement the bench directed that all the tribunals constituted under the IMDT Act for identification of illegal migrants from Bangladesh to cease functioning with immediate effect and directed that the cases pending before the tribunals under the IMDT Act would be transferred to the tribunals under the Foreigners Act. The state government was directed to constitute tribunals under the Foreigners Act to deal with the pending cases under the IMDT Act (Venkatesan 2005:1). By doing so the judgement reiterated to the state to decide the terms of legal membership of the foreigners in Assam. According to the Court the burden of proving his or her Indian citizenship on the person accused seemed completely unreasonable, since the person accused has the best means of knowing and proving whether he is an Indian or a foreigner.

Another discriminatory aspect justified by the Court for scrapping the Act was the constitutional validity of the Act under Article 355 of the Constitution of India. The Court provided that as per the provisions under Article 355, it is the foremost duty of the Union to protect the state against external aggression. While the word 'aggression' was widely interpreted by the judges (Sonowal 2005:Para 32–33), in case of Assam the judges remarked that aggression was caused due to the presence of the migrants who pose a threat not only to the demography of the state but also to the security of the country as a whole. It is to be noted that the judges were aware of the limitation that an Act of Parliament cannot be declared void merely because it had not succeeded in its objective. It could only be

## 122 *Rumi Roy*

struck down if the Parliament lacked legislative competence to enact it, or if it violated a specific provision of the Constitution. A wide reference was made to the report submitted by the then governor Gen. S. K. Sinha while deliberating on the issue of constitutional validity of the Act by the judges. The demographic account and security perspective which the report underscored exerted considerable influence on the judgement. The report's reference to the illegal migrants mostly comprising the Muslim population assumed significant importance in the judicial interpretation of the provisions of the Act which were in the Court. Such a disjunction exhibited them not only as outsiders while defining the borders of citizenship by the state but also as a suspicious category supporting unlawful activities like Islamic fundamentalism and insurgency. The attribution of illegality to the Muslim migrants displayed a communal overtone based on religious consideration while delivering the judgement. In doing so, the Court constructed institutional borders around the notion of citizenship marking out the outsider as a constructed category of the state often subjected to suspicion and marginalisation (Roy 2009:54). The Court's heavy reliance on the report manifested in the cultural identity and specified special connotation to a particular category in its approach to the issue of citizenship. Thus the 'Bangladeshi Muslim migrant' was cast as an aggressor causing a security threat to the nation as a whole and further problematising the normative definitions of who belongs and who does not. The decision recognised this reality that the threat was specifically identified as 'Muslim threat'. The boundary of citizenship which the judgement created is deeply anchored towards ghettoisation and the feeling of marginalisation of a particular category living under a constant shadow of suspicion.

The Court also justified the scrapping of the Act on grounds of the power to deal with the entry, presence and departure endowed on the tribunals constituted under the provisions of the Act, which deprived the Union to legislate over the question on the status of the foreigners in Assam. The Court substantiated the position of the state by pointing out that the state has the absolute right to throw an illegal migrant out of the country and that the IMDT Act was a barrier in detecting and deporting the illegal migrant from the state and hence it needed to be declared unconstitutional. The judgement was seen as reflecting an authoritarian mindset in giving the state machineries the power to decide the terms of citizenship for the migrant. On another account where sovereignty was redefined for the state, justification was provided under Article 355 of the Indian Constitution 'where it is the duty of the Union to protect a State against external aggression'. The Court justified the position of the state to expel foreigners on the ground that it does not amount to violation of Article 21, as expulsion of a foreigner by the state does not deprive one of his life or

*The state and the migrants* 123

liberty (Sonowal 2005: Para 47). The Court interpreted the word 'aggression' in a bloated manner by adding it into the ambit of Article 355 (Kapur 2007:557). The Court justified the scrapping of the Act on grounds of violation of the provisions of the Constitution, by underscoring the presence of migrants as causing aggression threatening the security of the country.

## Shifting trends and party positions

The decision to scrap the Act was both supported and opposed. Congress and Bharatiya Janata Party (BJP) held diametrically opposite views on the Act. While the former always stood by the law arguing that it proved to be a deterrent against arbitrary detection and deportation of Bengali-speaking Indian nationals from Assam, the latter demanded for scrapping the Act, alleging that it had been ineffective in detecting the Bangladeshi immigrants. The onus of laying the burden of proof on the complainant as provided by the Act came under severe criticism and condemnation at various grounds under various levels. It was opposed on the grounds that it would lead to further polarisation of society. It was welcomed on the ground that the vexed problem of citizenship status of the foreigners will be solved once the Act is gone. Lt Gen. S. K. Sinha's, the then governor of Assam, report focused on changing demography of the state owing to large-scale migration from Bangladesh (Sinha 1998). Sonowal's affidavit relied much on the report by Lt Gen. (retd) S. K. Sinha to the President which expressed grave concern at the unabated influx of illegal migrants from Bangladesh to Assam which, in his opinion, threatened to reduce the Assamese people to a minority in their own state. Illegal migration was considered to be the major contributory factor behind the insurgency in the state. However, Sinha's report only referred to the migrants as the ones coming from Bangladesh and particularly the Bangladeshi Muslims or *Miyas* as they are addressed in Assam today (Talukdar 2012:1). The report in a prejudiced manner blamed the illegal migrants as the cause of insurgency threatening the security scenario of the state and causing conflicts in the region (Sinha 1998:2–3). The politics of migration and citizenship grew even more complicated after term Muslims and *Miyas* came to be used interchangeably. This has posed a threat to the indigenous Muslims of the state. The strengthening and spreading this flawed perception of Muslims as *Miyas* is growing. It would be worthwhile to discard such communal and ethnic prejudices for harmonious co-existence.

The affidavits produced for scrapping the Act exhibited the antagonistic nature of the Centre and the state. The migrant occupied varying positions with each party adopting a different and antagonistic stance than the other. While the NDA government's affidavit focused on the demographic

## 124   *Rumi Roy*

change in the state, religious and economic reasons and implications and issues of national security due to illegal migration, the AGP government focused on the change in the demographic profile of Assam, in particular the rise of Muslim population and the role played by it in the Assam Movement. They laid more stress on what they did in the yesteryears for the people of Assam. The Congress party in filing the third affidavit reversed the position taken by the previous AGP government that the IMDT Act was unconstitutional and hence saw no reason to scrap it. The fourth one filed by the NDA Government in response to the Congress government in Assam reiterated its stand on the IMDT Act, demographic change and national security, and exposed the duplicity of the Congress government on the recommendations of the Law Commission report. The fifth one, passed by the UPA government led by the Congress, focused that the IMDT Act was protective of the genuine Indian citizens by enabling judicial scrutiny. The minority appeasement policy adopted by the Congress by objecting to the scrapping of the Act exhibited the extent to which the party laid stress on retaining the Act. The AGP government kept emphasising their agitation days during the Assam Movement to drive out the illegal Bangladeshi immigrants from the state. The BJP-led NDA government focused on the demographic and security perspective (Roy and Singh 2009:37–60). The oscillating positions adopted by each party seemed to be guided by political compulsions of vote bank politics. After much deliberation the Act was struck down by the Supreme Court of India. However, by striking down an Assam-specific law that had been in force for over 20 years, the Supreme Court put a question mark over the faith of lakhs of Muslims who were suspected to have illegally migrated from Bangladesh since 1971.

## Implication of the judgement in the polity of Assam

The judgement evoked mixed response in the state. It was hailed by the influential AASU and the major Opposition parties, the AGP and the BJP. The AAMSU called for Assam bandhs following the judgement to protest the failure of the Congress-led government in the state to prevent the scrapping of the Act. Immediately following the judgement, the Union Government headed by the Congress set up a Group of Ministers (GOM) to study the ruling and take further action in this regard. Fresh notifications were issued by the government to amend the Foreigners (Tribunals) Order, 1964. The opposition consisting of the AASU, BJP and AGP took the battle to the Supreme Court, filing two separate petitions seeking the quashing of the notifications (Talukdar 2006:8). Following the scrapping of the Act there has been attempted resurrection of the Act by amendment and modification of the foreigners tribunals. The problem of 'D voters or

*The state and the migrants* 125

doubtful voters' came to the forefront. D voter is a category of voters who have been declared 'doubtful' by the Election Commission, because they have failed to produce legal documents of citizenship. The foreigners tribunals were formed to resolve the problem of doubtful 'D' voters. By 2006, there were altogether thirty-six tribunals, including the then existing fifteen, working in Assam to detect and deport foreigners; 57,465 'D' voters were identified and the foreigners tribunals managed to dispose of 83,471 cases. But only in 6.7 per cent of the cases, the accused have been declared as illegal immigrants (White Paper on Foreigners' Issue 2012:1–46).

The judgement which led to the scrapping of the Act brought an end to the Act which was a major cord of discontent among the people of Assam. It upheld the right of the executive government to expel the Bangladeshi migrants who have trespassed into Assam or other parts of the country illegally. Thus, the Bangladeshi Muslims, as depicted in statist terms who have crossed the border, cease to have any legal right of any kind to remain in India and hence are liable to be deported by the state. The judicial treatment of attribution of illegality with the Bangladeshi Muslims shows how boundaries of citizenship were solidified against a particular category of people. The trajectory that follows from this is that the subjects of Indian citizenship is defined by the state at its own discretion, a significant way by which sovereign power is exercised by the state. The Supreme Court in scrapping the Act restored sovereign powers back to the state in matters of citizenship, giving a new definition of citizenship which emerged along the ethnic lines of a community within the legal framework of citizenship in India. It provided an exclusivist framework by unduly targeting the Muslim population. Though the judgement scrapping the Act was justified on grounds of legal procedures, by laying its focus from the issue of influx onto the status of minorities, the judiciary entered the debate on the politically divisive migration issue in the state, thus giving a new interpretation of the legal definition regarding the foreigner and citizen in Assam. The judicial pronouncement reiterated that defining boundaries of citizenship is a manifestation of state's sovereign powers, giving legitimacy to the state to determine the entry, presence and departure of the migrant at its own discretion. The Apex judiciary by marking out the outsider migrant as Muslims shaded its secular character and delineated citizenship of the foreigner migrant based on religious consideration (Roy and Singh 2009:55). The Muslim community came to perceive any move to do so with suspicion and as attempts to strip them of citizenship and rights.

A significant reaction in the aftermath of the judgement was the formation of a new party, popularly known as the Assam United Democratic

126  *Rumi Roy*

Front (AUDF), presently known as All India Assam United Democratic Front, by perfume baron Badruddin Ajmal. Dissatisfied with the failure of the Congress government to defend the IMDT Act, the AIUDF presented itself as a replacement for the Congress, for the protection of minority interests. Gradually the party succeeded in garnering support among the minorities of Assam and eventually the party became the main player as the third front with the party winning 10 of the 126 assembly seats in the 2006 state elections. D voters became significant in the politics of identity in Assam. There are Muslim D voters, and there are Hindu D voters. For the AGP, both are equally despicable. While the BJP demanded a clemency regarding the D voters, the Congress party expressed fear about the steady loss of its support base among Bengali-speaking Muslims, who are believed to be leaning heavily towards the newly formed Muslim-centric party the AIUDF. The rise of AIUDF can be seen as the emergence of new narratives surfacing in the political environment of the state.

## Changing electoral trends of post IMDT Act

Migration in Assam has been a rallying point for political mobilisation since Independence. The Assam agitation of the 1980s, followed by passing of the IMDT Act and signing of the Assam Accord in 1985, had wide ramifications on the electoral profile of the state of Assam. The IMDT Act, which was enacted at the height of the Assam Movement, brought about new dynamics in the political equations of the state. The provision of the Act ghettoised Assamese society in a different way and created exclusionary citizenship regime in Assam by marking the migrant as an outsider. Even though the Act was scrapped, the migration issue lacks a viable solution. The emergence of 'D voters' further complicated the scenario. The central government made it compulsory for every citizen of the country to register in a National Register of Indian Citizens (NRIC) as per Section 14A of the Citizenship Act 1955 as amended in 2004. The NPR is the first step towards preparation of the NRIC. However the decision to update the National Register of Citizens on the basis of the cut-off date of 24 March 1971 to detect illegal migrants in the state was met with much opposition by several groups in Assam on the ground that it would include many illegal migrants staying in the state. The infiltration of migrants from Bangladesh has not come to an end despite the annulment of the IMDT Act, 1983, and decision to update the National Register of Citizens by the state in recent time. This is because of the ambiguity in the procedures laid down for identification of the illegal migrants and the mechanism by which their cases for deportation are processed. Also there has been an irrevocable

The state and the migrants    127

shift in the balance of forces in Assam; the entrenched presence of the migrants in the state, legal or illegal, and the increasingly decisive assertiveness of their influence in the politics of the state.

Assam politics have grown far more complex in the post-IMDT scenario. Politics of citizenship is a dominant discourse in the political landscape of Assam. A wide range of political developments following the scrapping of the Act changed the power equations within the political system and have also influenced the nature, course and direction of electoral politics in the state. The electorate underwent significant changes. A fragmented electorate descended in the political scene in Assam post scrapping of the Act. Such changed trends were visible in the 2006 assembly elections that took place immediately after scrapping of the Act. The results clearly reflected the deep-rooted fractured politics with every community asserting its identity. The major national parties, namely the ruling Congress and the BJP, fought the elections alone. The opposition party, AGP, could only work out seat adjustments with CPI, CPM, ASDC, Samajwadi Party, Trinamool Gana Parishad and the Rabiram faction of the BPPF. There was no alliance based on a common programme (Baruah and Goswami 1999:2492–501). The Congress party emerged as the single largest party in Assam by winning fifty-three seats. Many changes were apparent in the political equation with the Congress party forming a government with support from a Bodo party. There was erosion of the traditional base of the Congress which is largely attributed to the growing influence of the AIUDF among the minorities who constituted the electoral vote bank of the Congress in the previous elections. Another aspect of this change was visible in the announcement made by the AGP to enter into alliance with the AUDF, the Muslim party in the state. However, the AIUDF distanced itself from the AGP following its decision to enter into poll alliance with the BJP for the 2009 elections, although it was made clear by the AGP that it would be limited to only seat sharing between the two (Talukdar 2006:1–5). In the 2009 parliamentary elections, AGP–BJP camaraderie won five seats, with the BJP winning four and AGP wining one. The BJP's 2009 election manifesto's emphasis on launching a massive program to detect and deport illegal immigrants helped the party to garner support among the upper caste Hindus in Assam (BJP election manifesto 2009:10–11). The Congress party came back to power again in the 2011 assembly elections by securing an absolute majority winning seventy-eight seats. The changing contours of Assam politics is a manifestation of ambiguity in the procedures of citizenship practices in the state undertaken at the discretion of the state machinery. While on one hand anti-foreigner campaign has found an influential supporter in the BJP and started gaining popularity in the polemics of Assam politics, on the other hand the people of Assam saw the waning

128   *Rumi Roy*

of the AGP, the only regional party who sloganeered for driving out the illegal migrants from the state during the Assam Movement, and saw the rising of AIUDF as the main opposition. Fragmentation of politics along ethnic lines was visible in this election with emergence of new political parties like the AIUDF and BPPF. The emergence of AIUDF, a Muslim-based party, did manage to garner a portion of the immigrant Muslim votes which earlier was considered to be the vote bank of Congress party. However the Congress did manage to regain its lost power by strengthening its support base among the Bengali Hindus and the Assamese Muslims who earlier aligned with the AGP and the BJP (Goswami 2001:1584–86). The 2011 assembly elections saw the rise of new form of politics emerging in the state. Changing trends were noticeable in the electoral politics in the Assam with the formation of smaller ethnic parties, causing even greater political and ethnic fragmentation. Politics of ethnicity emerged as visible forces with the success of ethnic parties like AIUDF. The BJP's stance on illegal migration paved them to win seven of the fourteen parliamentary seats in Assam, where locals have long resented growing numbers of Muslims of Bengali origin, whom they believed were illegal migrants from Bangladesh. However, the recent violence and bloodshed in the western parts of Assam has raised doubts about what could potentially happen. How the Assam violence is dealt with could be a deciding factor in votes in certain states in the coming elections. Moreover, the ongoing ethnic conflicts in the region may fan communal politics in a country where simmering tensions between Hindus and Muslims have often been exploited for electoral gain. Assam has the most complex problem of illegal migration that will test the acumen of politics in the coming days.

## Conclusion

The suturing of state sovereignty continues to set the discursive stage on which the merging debates on the citizen, the migrant and the foreigner are being played out. While the formal legal status is significant, this can be easily compromised or nullified at the discretion of the state. The Centre–state relation based on consensual and antagonistic approach marks a relation of contradictory cohabitation in delineating citizenship depending on the nature of politics. The state maintained ambiguity in this regard through a set of legal and political manoeuvres. The boundaries formed by adopting such approach exhibits how our diverse polity imagines and exercises state sovereignty. The judgement which led to the scrapping of the Act was also seen a fickle form of strategy that relied solely on electoral politics. The terms of exclusion and inclusion as highlighted in the judicial treatment of the Bangladeshi Muslim unmask the complex and contradictory narratives

*The state and the migrants* 129

of boundaries around citizenship practices in Assam. The volatile and often ambivalent configuration of citizenship and sovereignty constructed the migrant as a constructed category often subjected to suspicion and marginalisation. The persistent problem of migration is seemingly an intractable problem pertaining to the state of Assam. A resolution to the problem would warrant an early and concerted action on the part of political leadership across the spectrum which is devoid of narrow selfish interests.

## References

Assam Accord. 1985. *Economic and Political Weekly*, 20(33): 1369–70.

Balibar. 2003. 'Europe, an Unimagined Frontier of Democracy', *Diacritic*, 33(39): 26–44.

Baruah, Apurba K. and Sandhya Goswami. 1999. 'Fractured Identities: Politics in a Multi-Ethnic State', *Economic and Political Weekly*, 34(35): 2492–501.

Barpujari, Indrani. 2005. *Illegal Migrants (Determination by Tribunal) Act 1983 Promulgation and Repeal: A Contextual Analysis.* Guwahati: Omeo Kumar Das Institute of Social Change and Development.

Baruah, Sanjib. 1999. *India against Itself: Assam and the Politics of Nationality.* New Delhi: Oxford University Press.

Baruah, Sanjib. 2005. *Durable Disorder. Understanding the Politics of Northeast India.* New Delhi: Oxford University Press.

'Bharatiya Janata Party: BJP Manifesto for General Elections', 2009, http://www.bjp.org/images/pdf (accessed June 2009).

Gokhlae, Nitin and K. Samudra Gupta. 2004. *Legal Protection to Illegal Migrants: A Case for the Effective Repeal of the IMDT Act in Assam.* Mumbai: Rambhau Mhalgi Prabodhini.

Goswami, Sandhya. 2001. 'Assam: Changing Electoral Trends', *Economic and Political Weekly*, 36(19): 1584–6.

Hazarika, Sanjoy. 2000. *Rites Passage: Border Crossings, Imagined Homelands, India's East and Bangladesh.* New Delhi: Penguin Books.

Heater, D. 1999. *What Is Citizenship?* Cambridge: Polity Press.

*Indian Kanoon*, 2005, 'Sarbananda Sonowal vs. Union of India and Anr', http://indiankanoon.org/doc/907725/pdf (accessed January 2009).

Kapur, Ratna. 2007. 'The Citizen and the Migrant: Postcolonial Anxieties, Law, and the Politics of Exclusion/Inclusion', *Theoretical Inquiries in Law*, 8(2): 538–69.

Kaushik, Narendra. 2010. 'BJP to Rid the Bangladeshi Infiltrators Out of India', http://www.asiantribune.com/2004/11/05/bjp-rid-infiltrators-out-India.html (accessed July 2010).

Kumar, B. B., ed. 2006. *Illegal Migration from Bangladesh.* New Delhi: Astha Bharati Publications.

Kymlicka, W. and Norman. 2000. 'Citizenship in Culturally Diverse Societies: Issues, Contexts, Concepts'. In W. Kymlicka and W. Norman (eds), *Citizenship in Diverse Societies*, pp. 1–41. Oxford: Oxford University Press.

130 *Rumi Roy*

Marshall, T. H. 1998. 'Citizenship and Social Class in the Citizenship Debates'. In Gershon Shafir (ed.), *The Citizenship Debates: A Reader*, pp. 75–101. Minneapolis: University of Minneapolis.

Mezzadra, Sandro. 2006. 'Citizen and Subject: A Post-Colonial Constitution for European Union', *Situations*, 1(2): 31–42.

Misra, Udayon. 2000. *The Periphery Strikes Back: Challenges to the Nation-State in Assam and Nagaland*. Shimla: Indian Institute of Advanced Study.

'175th Report on the Foreigners' (Amendment) Bill', Law Commission of India, Delhi, 2000.

Prabhakara, M. S. 2005. 'An Act Undone', *Frontline*, 15(16).

Roy, Anupama. 2006. 'Between Encompassment and Closure: The "Migrant" and the Citizen in India', *Contributions to Indian Sociology*, 42(2): 219–48.

Roy, Anupama and S. Ujjwal Kumar. 2009. 'The Ambivalence of Citizenship, The IMDT Act (1983) and the Politics of Forclusion in Assam', *Critical Asian Studies*, 41(1): 49–51.

Roy, Anupama and S. Ujjwal Kumar. 2010. *Mapping Citizenship in India*. New Delhi: Oxford University Press.

Sinha, S. K. Lt Gen. (retd). 1998. 'Report on Illegal Migrations into Assam, to the President of India', http://www.satp.org.pdf (accessed December 2010).

Talukdar, Sushanta. 2006a. 'Politics of Migration', *Frontline*, 23(25).

Talukdar, Sushanta. 2006b. 'Foreigners Issue to the Fore in Assam', *The Hindu*, 8 December, http://www.thehindu.com/foreigners-issue-to-the-fore-in-assam/article3031027.ece (accessed June 2010).

Talukdar, Sushanta. 2010. 'Assam's Sorrow', *Frontline*, 29(16).

Venkatesan, J. 2005. 'Illegal Migrants Act Struck Down', *The Hindu*, 13 July, http://www.thehindu.com/2005/07/13/stories/2005071313320100. htm (accessed September 2009).

'White Paper on Foreigners Issue', 2012, http://online.assam.gov.in/web/homepol/whitepaper (accessed March 2012).

Yuval-Davis, Nira. 1997. 'Women Citizenship and Difference', *Feminist Review*, 57: 4–27.

# Part IV

# National consciousness

## The role of students and literary bodies

# 8 Identity consciousness and students' movement
## The role of AASU

*Protim Sharma*

The idea of nation and nationalism is largely inherited by the post-colonial societies from the West. In the post-colonial world, the emerging middle class spearheaded the movement for ethnic solidarity and nation-building projects in the line of Eurocentric notion of nationalism through espousing nationalistic sentiments. Throughout the colonial and post-colonial period, Assam has been witnessing such nationalistic movements arising out of middle-class consciousness. In this context, student bodies, particularly the All Assam Students' Union (AASU), have been playing a very significant role in shaping Assamese nationalism. The chapter intends to analyse the factors responsible for the formation of Assamese national identity in the post-colonial period and the role of the educated middle class in consolidating that identity in the consciousness of the Assamese people. In that line, the chapter particularly analyses the role of the AASU in carrying forward the sense of Assamese national identity and strengthening it through identity-based nationalistic movements in the post-independence period.

Historically, the nationalistic movements have largely been taking place in Assam with the emergence of the educated middle class. Sharma opines that 'with the emergence of this middle class we see the ideas of western liberalism taking roots in Assam and beginning to influence almost all sections of the Assamese society, as these ideas became the ideas of the hegemonic class' (Sharma 2002:62). Organisations such as *Asom Chatra Sanmilan* (All Assam Students' Conference) of 1916 or *Asom Sahitya Sabha* (the most revered literary body of Assam) of 1917 down to the All Assam Students' Union of 1967 have by and large carried out their activities taking into account the Assamese middle-class aspirations. For these organisations 'the emphasis on the development of Assamese literature and language, on Assamese nationalism, on dignity of man leading to the ideas of self-reliance and the betterment of the individual, were the ideas similar to the ideas represented by the nascent Assamese middle class' (Sharma 2002:63). The 'nascent Assamese middle class' can be said to be those

## 134   *Protim Sharma*

educated Assamese who lived in the later part of the nineteenth century and in the early part of the twentieth century and were aptly represented by organisations like *Axomiā Bhāxar Unnati Xādhini Xobhā* (the body for the uplift of the Assamese language) of 1888 or Assam Association of 1903. The Assamese nationalism can also be termed as linguistic nationalism as Assamese language is the main binding force behind the formation of ethnic Assamese identity and solidarity. Earlier, the great cultural renaissance initiated by the saint Shankardev in the fifteenth century Assam through Vaishnavism had laid the foundation for development of a composite Assamese identity. Assamese language flourished during the Vaishnavite period as scores of texts, largely religious in nature, in the form of prose, poetry and drama were written by saint Shankardev and his followers. However, the situation had changed with the advent of colonialism into the region. From 1837 to 1873, Bengali was the language of the courts and government schools of Assam. It was a decision taken by the British authorities apparently for an efficient administration, but with it Assamese came to be regarded as a mere 'dialect' of Bengali. The American Baptist Missionaries must get credit for the regeneration of the Assamese language and literature which they started with the publication of *Arunodoi* as early as in 1846, just 20 years after the Treaty of Yandabo. The dominant educated Assamese middle class too took on the mantle for the uplift of the Assamese language per se. They were all set to establish Assamese as the language of the state, the language of power in the true sense of the term. In fact, 'the Bengali linguistic hegemony was perceived as the real threat to the burgeoning Assamese nationality. The Assamese students studying in Calcutta, who designed Assamese nationality in the late nineteenth century, took the language as the most important unifying factor for the formation of an Assamese nationality' (Dutta 2005). The trend continued and Assamese intelligentsia right from Anandaram Dhekial Phukan, Gunabhiram Barua, Hem Chandra Barua, Chandra Kumar Agarwalla, Hem Chandra Goswami and Lakhinath Bezborua in the turn of the century to Ambikagiri Roychoudhury, Nilomoni Phukan and others in the first half of the twentieth century jumped into the bandwagon of Assamese Nationalism. The Assamese language gave meaning to their endeavour. The Assamese language, they believed, 'was the umbilical cord of the Assamese culture' (Bora 1992:2). Appeal by the Assamese intelligentsia to different sections of people for making Assamese the state language at different points of pre- and post-independence time is noteworthy, as is the slogan 'Assam for Assamese' of the *Asom Jatiya Mahasabha* during the 1920s. In their support for the anti-imperialist movement, or for a mainstream Indian identity, the Assamese elite also remembered their 'Assamese identity which was to be upheld through the identity of Assamese literature, language

*Identity consciousness* 135

and culture' (Sharma 2002:59). A section of the Assamese elite 'did not want the Assamese nationalism to be completely submerged and lost in the Indian national movement' (Phukon 1996:64). Ambikagiri Roychoudhury in the Assamese weekly *Chetana* (No. 2, Vol. III, 1920) distinguished *Asomiya Swaraj* (Assamese Independence) and *Bharatiya Swaraj* (Indian Independence). Such a sentiment of a separate identity of the Assamese has been variously termed as 'Little Nationalism' (Guha 1977:274) or 'sub-nationalism' (Baruah 1999:5). All these led to the formation of a coherent Assamese identity, but it was at the cost of alienation of the tribal communities coexisting in this land for hundreds of years. The Assamese middle-class hegemony is seen as one of the main causes of their alienation. And this is the negative outcome of Assamese nationalism.

The caste Hindu Assamese elite and also the mainstream Muslim elite did not have sympathy for the tribal brethren, who were in fact 'more' indigenous than them. In this context the comment of Andrew Clow, the then governor of Assam (1942–46), is noteworthy: 'The Assamese, both caste Hindus and the Muslim, professed solicitude for the tribes, but neither had troubled to study the question nor had any real sympathy with the tribes' (Mansergh 1978 as cited in Bhuyan and De 1999:311). Echoing this feeling of deprivation and negligence, the conference of the leaders of tribal communities of Assam, which was held in Shillong in 1946, demanded a few privileges for them in the new constitution in their memorandum titled 'Demand of the Tribal Communities of Assam': 'These communities must be assured separate political existence in the new constitution by providing for them in the case of hill tribes, local autonomy and in the case of others, separate electorate. They must be allowed to live their own life with their own customs and culture without any encroachment either by the Hindus or by the Muslims' (Phukon 1996:134). The stratification in the Hindu society or the superiority complex of the caste Hindu–dominated Assamese society was somehow responsible for pushing the ethnic groups away from the larger Assamese society. The various ethnic groups in the Brahmaputra valley felt the pinch of the deprivation and the negligence of the dominant class. Various ethnic communities started to project their views and aspirations through organisations such as *Kachari Sanmilan, Koch-Rajbangshi Sanmilan, Chutia Sanmilan, Muttuck Association* etc. which led to the formation of (The Assam Plains) Tribal League in 1933. The motive behind the formation of this umbrella organisation of the mongoloid tribes and communities is to bring them together on a common platform and to exert political power for their all-round socio-economic uplift. The hill tribes also extended their support to the common cause of preservation of ethnic identity and joined hands to form the Assam Tribes and Races Federation in Shillong in 1945. All the ethnic tribes became apprehensive

## 136 Protim Sharma

about the land settlement policy of the government in the face of unabated influx of immigrants. The encroachment of land in tribal belt resulted in resentment among the ethnic tribal population. This is evident in Bhimbar Deuri's speech in the Assam Legislative Council (*ALC Proceedings*, Vol. I, 26 February 1940) in which he termed the immigration policy of the then Muslim League government as a 'policy of invitation'. The successive Assam governments in both pre- and post-independence India, which have mostly been ruled by the Assamese elite, could not do much to help protect the interests of the indigenous people and the tribal people have, from time to time, advocated the preservation of the 'line system' (the Line System was introduced in the 1920s by the government to impose restrictions on settlement in some areas so as to protect the interests of the indigenous people), a separate electorate and even autonomy or right to self-determination. The Gopinath Bordoloi government in 1947 added a new chapter called chapter 'X' to the Assam Land and Revenue Act, 1886, whereby buying and selling of land in the newly created tribal blocks and belts became restricted. But the restrictions could not protect the interests of the tribal people and many complaints about the illegal transfer of land of tribal belt or block poured in. In 1974 the Assam government constituted a sub-committee of the Advisory Council for Welfare of Scheduled Tribes (Plains) under the chairmanship of Malchandra Pegu, MLA, to study the implementation of the provisions of chapter X. The committee report says: 'The provisions of chapter X of the Assam Land and Revenue Regulations have nowhere been sincerely implemented. On the other hand, it appears to the committee that the officials responsible for the implementation of the said provisions have, instead of guarding the interests of the tribal people within such belts and blocks, for whom these were meant, frequently infringed the provisions by themselves by way of not only conniving the encroachers in *sarkari* (government) land but also allowing the illegal land alienation that have taken place from tribal to non eligible non-tribal. . . .' Backlog in reservation quotas in government jobs is another reason for the sense of alienation among the tribes. It is observed that 'there has never been a sincere attempt on the part of the Assamese to uplift the tribal brethren to their level through reservation and other available constitutional method. Since the state machinery is dominated by the Assamese caste-Hindu, reservation in job and educational institutions has been sabotaged through neglect and obstructionism, and what is worse, the tribal people are totally insecure. With rapid loss of land in areas reserved for them as tribal belts and blocks, there is no lack of evidence that this important safeguard has been hollow to begin with and has been made meaningless by the way it has been enforced' (Gohain as cited in *The Telegraph*, 8 February 1991). The Plains Tribal Council of Assam

*Identity consciousness* 137

submitted a memorandum to the then prime minister Indira Gandhi on 22 October 1972, where it said: 'The plains tribals have been systematically and in a planned way uprooted from their own soil, and the step-motherly treatment towards them by the administration dominated by the Assamese speaking people, has reduced them to the status of second class citizens of the state' (Phukon 1996:137). They insisted upon equal opportunities for all in the independent India. In 1991 the central government had to constitute an Expert Committee on the Plains Tribes of Assam headed by Dr Bhupinder Singh to submit a feasibility report on granting of autonomy to the Plains tribes of Assam.

The process of disintegration that started in pre-Independence period led to secessionist tendencies among the hill tribes also. After the passing of the Assam Official Language Bill in 1960, Nagaland got separated from the greater Assam in 1963, to be followed by other hill districts and provinces. In this context the deliberations made during the Assam Legislative Assembly Debates on the Bill by two prominent tribal leaders are noteworthy. A. Thanglura, the Scheduled Tribe Member from Ajal-West, said: '. . . Assamese might be a very beautiful language and the richest language, but I feel that we must think rather in terms of the integration of the state of Assam more than anything else. And this really is the challenge to the Assamese brethren. Sir, actually I have no ill feelings towards the Assamese brethren. I do respect their sentiment. But Sir, I feel that the Assamese brethren should have the wisdom and decency to realise the feeling of the minority. . . . But if the Assamese people insist by dint of their majority that Assamese should be the official language and press the passing of this Bill, then do not blame us. Personally I am not fascinated with the terms of separation. But when the aspirations of the Assamese people cannot be stopped, then we shall move for separation' (*ALA Debates*, 18 October 1960). The other Scheduled Tribe Member from Phulbari, William A. Sangma, had this to say: '. . . ever since 1948 when the move for declaring Assamese as the State language the Hill leaders including myself expressed our strong opposition to the proposal. Ever since that time the Hill leaders made it very clear that they were not prepared to accept Assamese as the State language of Assam. It was not because we disliked Assamese or we had ill-feeling against our Assamese brothers and sisters. But we are convinced that by accepting Assamese as the Official Language we shall be handicapped. . . . Shall we be placed on the same footing along with Assamese speaking people in case Assamese is declared the Official Language of the State? Is it the desire of our more advanced brothers and sisters who are the majority that we should be handicapped and that we always remain as second-grade or third-grade citizens? . . . I entirely subscribe to the view expressed by my friend, Shri Thanglura. He said that more importance

138   *Protim Sharma*

should be given to integration of the State than to language. We shall never accept the idea that the people of the Hills and other linguistic minorities should have the right to accept and thereby become second-grade or third-grade citizens. I, therefore, once again beg to submit that in case the Official Language Bill is passed the only solution is the separation of the Hills from Assam. . . . I would, therefore, earnestly request the honourable Members of the Brahmaputra Valley, through you, Sir, that since we shall have no more chance to stand against their Official Language Bill they should also give us an opportunity and a free hand to shape our destiny as we want' (*ALA Debates*, 18 October 1960). These statements are clear indication of the destiny that was to follow soon.

The hegemonic attitude of the middle-class Assamese elite was responsible for the segregation and disintegration of the composite Assamese society, and this typical middle-class mentality of the Assamese elite got reflected in the activities of the Assamese student community also. An apt example is the *Assam Chatra Sanmilan* (All Assam Students' Conference), the 'first national organization of Assam' (Bhattacharyya 1962 as cited in Baruah 2002:71). In 1926, it took a resolution to request the Raja of Manipur and the Khasi leaders to spread the Assamese language among the students of these communities. Starting with the *Asom Chatra Sanmilan*, the various mainstream non-political student organisations of the state such as the All Gauhati Students' Union (1958), All Assam Students' Association (1959) down to the AASU in 1967 have represented the middle-class ethos and aspirations. The 'Assamese Nationalism' per se is a notion well nourished in the collective consciousness of the Assamese middle class since the formation of the Assamese identity in the previous century; and this feeling got percolated in the plans and programmes of these student organisations. The middle-class ideology or the ideological predominance of the middle class over the subordinate class is referred to as 'hegemony of the dominant class' in the line of Gramsci by A. K. Baruah (Baruah 2002:16). The students are one of the most 'receptive members of the intelligentsia, and as persons constantly engaged in studies, are exposed to this hegemony' (Baruah 2002:16–17). In Assam from the end of the nineteenth century that hegemony came to be exercised by the Assamese middle class, and thus the students articulated the values of that class almost as their own values, regardless of what class they came from. The aims, aspirations, values and interests of the dominant class became the aims, aspirations, values and interests of the students (Sharma 2002:64). In post-independence period different agitations like Refinery Movement (1957), Language agitation (1960), Food agitation (1966), Agitation against reorganisation of Assam (1967–68), Second Oil Refinery Movement (1969), Medium of Instruction agitation (1972) and anti-foreigner agitation (1979–85) rocked the

*Identity consciousness* 139

state from time to time, which saw the involvement of the student community at large.

For an understanding of the Assamese nationalistic sentiment vis-à-vis the role of the AASU, the happenings of the post-independence period become important. Deka opines that 'Student movements in the post-independence period up to 1960 were developing more into social movements in a quest for identity and took issues to safeguard the interests of Assam. . . . The development of student movements into social movements is characteristic of the growth of regionalism, to protect the identity of the state' (Deka 1996:170). The student movements in Assam were '. . . borne out of a feeling of neglect by the Centre and out of the realisation that no change or development, whether social, economic or political, in the State, could be brought about without resorting to agitations and movements, of which the student class formed the nucleus. The significant development in the post-independence era was the gradual organisational maturity attained by the student movements particularly the formation of All Assam Students' Union (AASU) in 1967 with a regular constitution and a five-tier organisational network of its own. What may be traced as a legacy of the Indian National Movement were the non-violent methods of agitation, which continued to be popular and effective until recent times; the AASU agitation of 1979–85 is a manifestation of this' (Deka 1996:212–13).

The agitations mentioned earlier assume significance as they saw the participation of the masses, and a nationalistic fervour was seen in the collective action of the mass. This was true more particularly for the official language movement of 1960, Medium of Instruction agitation of 1972 and the anti-foreigners agitation (Assam Movement) of 1979. The newly formed AASA, considered to be the predecessor of the AASU, started the 1960 agitation for declaration of Assamese as the state language with non-violent means like processions, protest meetings, strike, Demand Day etc. The Gauhati Students Federation and the Dibrugarh chapter of *Asom Chatra Sanmilan* and a few other organisations too joined hands in the agitation. The killing of Ranjit Borpujari, a student of Cotton College, in police firing on 4 July 1960 was the climax of the agitation which ignited all the indigenous people across the state. Sporadic incidents of violence were reported, which was not uncommon during an agitation of such proportion. The Inspector General of Police issued circulars to all police officers of the districts to 'particularly keep watch over the students, the movements of students' leaders and agitators. . .' (Chakravarty 1984:51). However, the Official Language Bill was passed, marking the end of the language agitation.

The 1972 Medium of Instruction agitation too was full of Assamese nationalistic sentiment. It was the ultimate struggle for linguistic identity

140 *Protim Sharma*

by the educated Assamese, largely represented by the student community. The chief minister's statement on 2 June 1972 at the Cachar Political Conference advocating Bengali as one of the mediums of instruction in colleges under Gauhati University, and the Gauhati University Academic Council resolution that along with Assamese students could write their examinations in Bengali, Hindi or English sparked off opposition from the Assamese students which led to widespread protest. The AASU led the agitation from the front, with the result that Assamese would remain the medium of instruction in colleges in Brahmaputra valley along with English.

The six-year-long anti-foreigners agitation, also spearheaded by the AASU, was on the same line of the previous agitations. Assamese nationalistic sentiment reigned supreme in the minds of the Assamese students and youths as well as in the middle class. The presence of a large number of illegal foreigners in the state was a burning problem for all indigenous people of the state and so in the initial stage the agitation drew the indigenous ethnic groups of the state to the same platform with the 'mainstream' Assamese. But the ethnic groups were not taken into confidence by them. A pointer to the fact is the very first demand of the 22-point AASU memorandum to the chief minister before the start of the agitation in 1979, which was the scrapping of the special privileges enjoyed by the Scheduled Tribe and Scheduled Caste people of the state (Borbora 2007:107). Such an attitude towards the ethnic communities led to their dissociation from the agitation. The middle-class hegemonic role of the Assamese elite, which was full of nationalistic zeal, got reflected in the plans and programmes of the AASU, like in some other student-led organisations, which we have already observed. The chauvinistic attitude of the agitation leaders was severely criticised by many scholars. The following observation by Hiren Gohain is noteworthy in this regard: 'Chauvinism has since independence been the deadly enemy of all radical and genuinely democratic forces in Assam. The Assamese ruling elite lack both the economic resources and cultural strength to be able to integrate non-Assamese groups into Assamese society. . . . Hence it uses from time to time the cudgel of chauvinism to beat into submission non-Assamese groups who might resist the domination' (Gohain 2006:28). With the signing of the Assam Accord or the Memorandum of settlement between the central government, state government and the agitation leaders came a formal end to the anti-foreigners agitation in 1985.

Here it is interesting to note that the rise of Assamese nationalism was out of the Assamese people's fear of being swamped by the Bengali language in the late nineteenth century; and the same feeling of fear was later seen in the ethnic minorities of the state with respect to the Assamese language. Ahmed says, '. . . soon after independence the attempt to

*Identity consciousness* 141

impose the language on the unwilling minorities eventually proved to be self-defeating. Instead of making a larger space for the *Asamiya* (Assamese) nationalism to flourish, it circumscribed its wings. The unregulated chauvinism belittled the prospects of *Asamiya* little nationalism for natural growth and expansion. The blame for this retarded development undoubtedly goes to the *Asamiya* middle class' (Ahmed 2006:6). It is also noteworthy that the nationalism practised by the AASU with unprecedented support from the Assamese middle class during the anti-foreigners agitation to an extent found expression in militant nationalism of the United Liberation Front of Assam (ULFA). Born in Sivasagar of upper Assam in the same year the anti-foreigners agitation started, the ULFA showed its radical stance on the issues of the AASU-led agitation. The militant separatist group became more energised and consolidated its power after the formation of the so-called illegal government in the state in 1983, and more particularly after the student leaders formed the AGP government in 1985. The ULFA claimed that 'the mass movements of the past and especially the illegal elections of 1983 prove beyond dispute that there is no so-called moderate road available to the people of Assam' (Baruah 2006:143). The ULFA received some sympathy from the indigenous Assamese middle class in its initial years. The reason for such sympathy was largely, according to a critic, due to the 'structural deficiencies based on unequal power relations between the indigenous people of Assam and the Indian state' (Handique 2007:107). Treating Assam as a colonial hinterland by the successive governments in the Centre had angered a section of people, who in turn found an alternative in the ULFA. The non-implementation of the Assam Accord was also seen as an evidence of the central government's lack of interest in solving the perennial problem of illegal immigration and carrying out of developmental activities in the state.

Nationalism and nationalistic sentiment has been the driving force in the activities of the AASU, as it is observed in the three well-known protest movements. As a non-political student body dedicated 'for making the masses free from all sorts of exploitation' (AASU Constitution), the AASU has again stood up against the illegal foreigners residing in the state. This is because the implementation part of the Assam Accord has taken a backseat as the nodal agency for its implementation, the central Home Ministry in New Delhi has not shown much interest over the years. The present batch of AASU itself has recognised the six-year-long anti-foreigners agitation as a futile exercise as the central issue of detection and expulsion of foreigners from the state has not met with desired success, even after three decades of signing of the Accord. Of late, a new debate at various platforms has been initiated by the AASU over the question of 'indigenous' Assamese people

142   *Protim Sharma*

as per Clause Six of the Assam Accord. The Clause Six of the Assam Accord states that 'Constitutional, legislative and administrative safeguards, as may be appropriate, shall be provided to protect, preserve and promote the cultural, social, linguistic identity and heritage of the Assamese people'. An important signatory of the Assam Accord, the AASU, along with twenty-six other ethic student bodies, has come up with the position that people living in Assam before 1951 and their descendants are indigenous people of the state. The new-generation AASU leaders are conscious of their past mistakes and would not repeat the blunder of detachment with other ethnic bodies of the state. The AASU of today is more mature and proactive, equipped with reasoned justifications for its actions. In recent past, all the major decisions by the AASU, be it agitation against big dam over river Subansiri or regarding updating of the National Register of Citizens, are taken in consultation with other ethnic student bodies. It signifies a significant departure of the AASU from its old position of identity assertion to a more cohesive identity movement in the spirit of true Assamese nationalism in contemporary Assam.

## References

Ahmed, Abu Nasar Saied, ed. 2006. *Nationality Question in Assam: The EPW 1980–81 Debate.* New Delhi: Anakaha Publishing House.

Baruah, Apurba K. 1991. *Social Tensions in Assam: Middle Class Politics.* Guwahati: Purbanchal Prakash.

Baruah, Apurba K., ed. 2002. *Student Power in North-East India*, pp. 67–94. New Delhi: Regency Publications.

Baruah, Sanjib. 1999. *India against Itself: Assam and the Politics of Nationality.* New Delhi: Oxford University Press.

Bhattacharyya, G. S. 1962. 'Trends in Growth of the Assam Students' Federation', *Milon*, 40(1) as cited by Shiela Bora in A. K. Baruah, ed. 2002. *Student Power in North East India.* New Delhi: Regency Publications, pp. 67–94.

Bhuyan, A. C. and S. De, eds. 1999. *Political History of Assam*, Vol. III. Guwahati: Publication Board, Government of Assam.

Bora, Sheila. 1992. *Student Revolution in Assam.* New Delhi: Mittal Publications.

Borbora, Golap. 2007. 'Bideshi Bitaron Andolon Byartha Hoisil Kiyo: Etiau Bastab Xomadhan or Upai Ki?'. In Hiren Gohain and Dilip Bora (eds), *Axom Andolon: Pratishrutiaru Phalashruti.* Guwahati: Banalata, pp. 96–119.

Chakrabarty, Saroj. 1984. *The Upheaval Years in North East India.* Kolkata: Chakrabarty & Chakrabarty.

Deka, Meeta. 1996. *Student Movements in Assam.* New Delhi: Vikas Publishing House.

Deuri, Bhimbar. 1940. Speech in *Assam Legislative Council Debates.* Shillong: Government of Assam.

*Identity consciousness* 143

Dutta, Uddipan. 2005. 'The Growth of Print Journalism and the Formation of Assamese Identity in Two Early Magazines: Arunodoi and Jonaki'. Paper written for SARAI-Centre for the Study of Developing Societies, Kolkata.

Gohain, Hiren. 1991. 'Assamese Nationality and Tribal Anxieties', *The Telegraph*, 8 February.

Gohain, Hiren. 2006. 'Cudgel of Chauvinism'. In Abu Nasar Saied Ahmed (ed.), *Nationality Question in Assam: The EPW 1980–81 Debate*, New Delhi: Anakaha Publishing House.

Gokhale, Nitin. 2007. 'Insurgency in Northeast'. In Paramananda Sonowal (ed.), *Insurgency and Economic Development in NorthEast India*, pp. 57–69. Guwahati: DVS Publishers.

Guha, Amalendu. 1977. *Planter-Rajto Swaraj: Freedom Struggle and Electoral Politics in Assam, 1826–1947*. New Delhi: People's Publishing House.

Handique, Rajiv. 2007. 'Analyzing the ULFA Imbroglio'. In Paramananda Sonowal (ed.), *Insurgency and Economic Development in North-East India*, pp. 104–15. Guwahati: DVS Publishers.

Majumdar, Paramananda. 2007. 'Axomot Jatiotabad or Utthanaru Xongkotor Patbhumi'. In Hiren Gohain and Dilip Bora (eds), *Axom Andolon: Pratishrutiaru Phalashruti*, pp. 120–51. Guwahati: Banalata.

Mansergh, Nicholas, ed. 1978. *The Transfer of Power 1942–47*, Vol. 7, pp. 18–40, as cited in A. C. Bhuyan and S. De, eds. 1999. *Political History of Assam*, Vol. III. Guwahati: Publication Board, Government of Assam.

Phukon, Girin. 1996. *Politics of Regionalism in North-East India*. Guwahati: Spectrum.

Sharma, Manorama. 2002. 'Students and Nationalism: An Assessment of the Assam Chatra Sanmilan, 1916–1939' as cited in A. K. Baruah, ed. *Student Power in North-East India*. New Delhi: Regency Publications, pp. 55–66.

# 9 Assamese identity and the ethnic dissent

## *Asom Sahitya Sabha* at the crossroads

*Ivy Dhar*

The issue of language captured the minds of the people of Assam far earlier than the birth of the *Asom Sahitya Sabha*.[1] The colonial policy of giving language a significant status in deriving state and market relations gave enough reason for stretching language as an issue of great importance.[2] Language, since modern ages, has been considered an important means to participate in the market, seek employment avenues and gain economic prospects. Thereby any hindrance to its progress is seen as encumbrance to the development of the language group. The Sabha[3] took the task of development of Assamese-speaking people and talked of adequate representation of Assamese[4]; it tried to cast an influence towards developing a sense of identity and unity of Assamese. The social and territorial space of different language groups in Assam is very thinly demarcated, so the exclusivity of Assamese language was giving lack of breathing space for other identities to survive. Yet the Sabha went ahead with its agenda on the belief that it would be beneficial for the existence of a unified society, cutting across ethnic and even class inequalities. The chapter examines the language politics of the Asom Sahitya Sabha, largely in post-independence period and debates on how its dominance is threatened by the divergent identities of Assam. It analyses various issues raised by the Sabha in its assertion for a composite Assamese society and the countering debates raised against the idea of a unified Assamese society. It would focus on both, the influence of the Sabha on the people and the state, as well as the challenges that reduced its ambit of influence. There are some historical references of the Sabha's stand in the pre-independence period. The chapter illuminates debates of the Asom Sahitya Sabha as a middle-class organisation while analysing its assertion goals. It broadly takes up three themes, first looks at Sabha's view on Assamese identity and language and then moves on to discussing the ethnic dissent and the representation of plains tribal identity and finally it ends with a response to multi-cultural existence of Assam.

*Assamese identity and the ethnic dissent* 145

The relationship between different ethno-linguistic communities of Assam has been very complex and controversial. Difficulties arose between Assamese and other ethnic groups in reconciling over matters pertaining to the common habitat. Differences over land, language and share in legislature had been constantly infuriating the cultural and political climate of Assam. The spokesperson of the Assamese-speaking community had been trying to pacify the differences by calling for inclusion of all indigenous language groups[5] under the unified umbrella of Assamese society and featuring it as 'composite' or 'assimilated' society. The assurance of unification had been less likely a source of constellation between Assamese language group and tribal groups and acted more as the source of rift among them. The rift so widened that it went to the extent of demands for separate states and separate status of language by the minority linguistic-tribal groups. These cleavages often brought forth the basic weaknesses and challenges to the idea of a unified Assamese identity. The educated middle class of Assam, trying to represent masses, had spoken 'for' or 'against' the compositeness of Assamese society, in either way that defended their interest.

The interest of the middle class was though much beyond cultural interests; they had to pave their way into the heart of the masses without disturbing the trust and promise that were laid on them. It is often stated that cultural interests might have got inextricably mixed with the material progress because economic underdevelopment of Assam was a constant reminder to the educated Assamese middle class. The most feasible path that could be routed out was to make the concerns of its own class popular among the mass so that asserting voices could increase. In an effort to organise mass cultural interests, Assam experienced the birth of organisations that worked for the protection of cultural identity. The first remarkable achievement was the formation of *Axomiya Bhaxa Unnati Sadhini Sabha* in 1888.[6] As the meaning of this name signifies 'Association for the Development of the Assamese Language', its major concern was to see the progress of Assamese language. Though language-based cultural nationalism would have benefitted only a small section, it could generate a mass appeal. Following the same path of the *Axomiya Bhaxa Unnati Sadhini Sabha*; in the twentieth century, the Asom Sahitya Sabha took the torch of cultural nationalism. It held its first session in 1917 and its motto was 'My mother language-my eternal love'. It became the mouthpiece of the Brahmaputra valley by giving intellectuals a platform to express their vision. It is a product of the Assamese renaissance that swept across Assam during the colonial times. It has played an intensive role by keeping the issue of Assamese identity alive throughout decades by actively involving with the affairs of the state.

The identification of 'Assamese' has not seen the light of the day; there has been constant debate whether Assamese-speaking people and Assamese

146 *Ivy Dhar*

identity are one and same or could it be extended to some other definition. In 2015 in the Assam Assembly, the government admitted that there is no proper definition of the 'Assamese' people, in wake of fresh debates on the implementation of the Assam Accord and constitutional safeguard of the people.[7] The Sabha has been entrusted on several occasion to explain Assamese identity and its stand has changed over years but it has been constant that Assamese identity is about bringing homogeneity. The most recent explanation is 'all Indian citizens who live in Assam and speak Assamese language either as their mother tongue or as their second or third language, irrespective of places of their origin, ethnicity, caste or religion, are inseparable part of the greater Assamese society, hence they are Assamese' (*The Assam Tribune*, 14 March 2015). In response to such claim, there has been resistance from tribal communities that Assamese term should be replaced with 'indigenous' people, because Assamese term does not protect the identity of Bodo, Mising, Karbi, Rabha, Tiwa and other tribal groups, who have their own distinct language and culture (*The Assam Tribune*, 8 March 2014).

Language has been seen as a binding force for advocating and promoting the use of Assamese language as a principal and link language of Assam. Despite resistance, the Sabha maintained that language could be used to bring political and cultural cohesiveness. It had tried to maintain a collaborative tone towards all tribal ethnic communities, with some rough edges and patches, at times. The dreams were however short-lived; in trying to assert Assamese language salience, other identities were invigorated which in turn challenged the dominance of Assamese language identity. The voice for assimilation by Asom Sahitya Sabha echoed back to them with rejection, it polarised the various ethnic groups from Assamese heartland. It is important to begin discussion on issues on which Sabha has lived its existence.

## The representation of Assamese identity

When the Sabha began its journey, Assam already had a long history of apprehension, fear and revolt of losing the distinctness of Assamese language. On the positive front, it had also seen how Assamese language was becoming a symbol of collective unity transcending class inequalities.[8] It took upon itself its duty and right of representing Assamese identity and did not attempt to make any clarification on whether Assamese identity included other indigenous groups as well. The theme of identity was only projected along the lines of Assamese language. The situation was not in favour of making any such explanations because languages of tribal communities had not yet attained the level of assertion of marking its presence vis-à-vis the Assamese language. In the colonial times, the only difference

*Assamese identity and the ethnic dissent* 147

that the Asom Sahitya Sabha sought to make was marking a distinction of Assamese language with other advanced languages of India.

The discrete identity of Assamese found expressions in flamboyant speeches of Sabha leaders. Benudhar Rajkhowa, while showing consent towards maintaining smooth existence of India's distinct nationalities, stated in his presidential address at one of the annual sessions of Asom Sahitya Sabha, 'Let all nationalities (jati) of India follow their own path. The Brahmaputra, the Ganga, the Yamuna, the Kaveri, the Sind; let all of them go on and flow along their respective courses. Let there be no attempts to merge one with the other' (Nag 1990:131). Tarunram Phukan remarked in his presidential address at the Asom Sahitya Sabha session in Dhubri, 1927, that 'Assamese are a distinct nationality amongst Indians. Though its language is Sanskrit based, it stands as a distinct language' (Nag 1990:131).

These remarks strongly highlight the word 'Assamese', yet it is very difficult to judge whether the Sabha was only keen in keeping the identity of Assamese restricted exclusively to those whose mother tongue was Assamese. However, over a period of time it came to be judged that representation of Assamese identity was non-inclusive of other ethnic communities. It was viewed as hegemonic, chauvinist and elitist. It was felt that the Sabha, while trying to mobilise the Assamese community, and articulate Assamese nationalism, was rather expressing middle-class aspirations and terming them as mass appeal. The middle-class opinion reflected in all important developments in Assam. This trend of dominance is seen as the 'hegemonic disposition of the middle class' (Baruah 1994; Sharma 1990). The Sabha had its foundations on middle class, so it was very unlikely that it would not act hegemonic. Its inclination to mass appeal could be explained by the very characteristic of hegemony. Since hegemony is not possible without mobilising the consent of the subordinate classes, it becomes necessary for all dominant classes aspiring to exercise hegemony to articulate at least some of the interests of the strata below them. National interest is defined by their propagators as the interest of the entire community and the cultural, economic and political demands embraced by such interest are publicised as demands for the entire community (Baruah 1994:245).

Since post-independence, there was further hardening of the Sabha's stance and it was becoming more assertive on maintaining an exclusive status of Assamese language. It began its systematic campaign from 1950s onwards to secure recognition for Assamese as the official language of Assam. Its popular campaigns called for assimilation of all ethnic communities to claim the strength of Assamese language identity. Such assertions were considered to be diluting the existence of other ethnic communities. The popular struggles in which the Sabha played a leading role were confined mainly to demands directly linked with the Assamese-speaking

148    *Ivy Dhar*

population concentrated in the Brahmaputra valley. It was less sympathetic to give space to other ethnic identities and the issues raised had very little commonality with the peasantry. Contrary to the above, Sabha's role was interpreted as pro-peasants and aligning with concerns of the mass. It was never alienated from the peasants and extended its support on issues of economic backwardness and thereby could gather large momentum of support in its mass agitation (Misra 1988:121). Even when the Assamese middle class attained a degree of identity and leadership in its struggle for restoration of Assamese language, this class retained its ties with the peasantry. Even if the Sabha had shown distinct middle-class culture, after independence it was concerned about people in the surrounding areas of the Brahmaputra valley and talked about the security of the Assamese peasantry that was threatened by large-scale peasant immigration from the erstwhile Pakistan (Sharma 1988:432).

The Sabha members never accepted that by stressing on the use of Assamese language they intend to be chauvinist. Rather, they claim that their stand accommodates interests of other ethnic population of Assam, along with Assamese language group. They defended that they were in favour of bringing all communities into the Assamese fold because they believe Assamese as a modern independent language of India. The members had often synthesised their statements in favour of giving all languages respect and that they work for the development of other languages of Assam, while it does not intend to work for any imposition and dominance of Assamese language. Sitanath Brahmachoudhry, in his presidential address at of one of Sabha's annual sessions, stressed that though there is a need to accept Assamese as the state language of Assam, there is also need to develop tribal languages. There is no sense of feeling of Assamese as a dominant language (Misra 1988:115). The verdict of the Sabha on the status of the Assamese language vis-à-vis other languages of Assam brought forth further contradictions and challenges.

## The status of Assamese language

Since the pre-independence days, the Asom Sahitya Sabha advocated Assamese language as the language of the masses. At its Sixth Session in 1924, at Dibrugarh, the Sabha took the responsibility for making arrangements, in many ways, including financial, for girls and boys to pursue studies in Assamese keeping in mind the eagerness shown by their parents. It also decided in that session to request the government to use 'Assamese language in forms and notices issued in court, post office, railway station and steamer ghats' (Asom Sahitya Sabha 1977:55). In 1938, the Sabha decided

## Assamese identity and the ethnic dissent   149

to make an appeal to the government to introduce post-graduate course in Assamese language in Cotton College, an educational institute in Assam, so as to address the problem of the seclusion of the Assamese people from their own language.

The Sabha's efforts to bring out some sort of affinity of different languages of Assam with the Assamese language were being worked out. In 1940, it prepared a dictionary that consisted of translated words in Assamese language from different tribal languages. In the proposed lexicon, it also intended to highlight the similarities between Assamese language and other languages. This suggested that it was not blind in showing concern to foster an understanding between different cultures of Assam but somewhat maintained that the status of Assamese language would remain as that of Big Brother. In 1954, the Sabha expressed that Hindi could not be the link language in the Northeast; rather, it proposed that Assamese should be made the link language and should be introduced at all levels of education. Though it was conducive towards bringing all languages in common platform with Assamese language, its tone and actions guided towards revealing its desire of making Assamese language as 'first among equals'. The most concerted effort was the movement for establishing Assamese as the state language of Assam.

Proposals were put forward by the Sabha during 1950s to 1970s for establishing Assamese as the state language. Consequently, tribal communities of Assam were alienated from the mainstream Assamese people due to the imposition of Assamese language as the medium of instruction. In schools and state administration, Assamese language was arbitrarily imposed without taking the consent of local ethnic groups. Assam, before the implementation of the Federal Plan (1972), had within its territory many hill tribes like Khasi, Garo, Manipuri etc. whose locality, language and culture were different from the Assamese, so without considering their language needs, imposition of Assamese language was distasteful. The Sabha argued that the hill people had good economic and social relations with the plains people for centuries and the problem of isolationism of the hills was the result of British unmindful policies. It is important to work against the isolation of hill tribes by adopting a language that could be shared by the hills and the plains people. Assamese, which was spoken by more than 60 per cent of the total population and understood by a large section of hills and non-Assamese people, has been enriched through the process of assimilation of many ethnic groups. The Ahom rulers of Assam realised the importance of a common language for administrative facilities and cultural enrichment of the people, hence they adopted Assamese as court language. Some of the dialects of the tribe are very much similar to Assamese language like the Nagamese. Most of the tribal communities

## 150   *Ivy Dhar*

communicate in Assamese language in their intra-tribal communication (Goswami 1961:1–4).

The language issue became the mainstay of tribal dissent, though consciousness of language may not have been important to each and every tribe that dissented. Voices from different quarters raised protest against the imposition of Assamese language and considered the move as a strategic motive to dominate the tribal communities. Some had said, 'as long as tribals remained with Assam their destiny lay in the hands of the Assamese' (Nag 1990:19). The Assamese leadership, however, maintained their confidence on the influence of Assamese language. The Sabha while opposing the Centre's federal plan for Assam constantly warned the central government not to take any constitutional steps which would endanger the security and integration of the Northeast.

The Asom Sahitya Sabha's work during 1964–72 focused on matters for improving the status of Assamese language, culture and identity. It moved many resolutions, such as for implementation of Assamese as the language of the high court, concern over inadequate supply of Assamese typewriters, need for Assamese language training for non-Assamese officials, adoption of Assamese as the medium of education at all levels, concern about the availability of Assamese language text, inclusion of Assamese in the curriculum of non-Assamese institutions, introduction of Assamese language lessons through state-owned radio and celebration of birth anniversaries of major figures of Assamese cultural nationalism. Many of the Sabha's decisions were taken seriously by the state government. Such reliance on the Sabha portrayed its power and influence in Assam's politics. It was given due respect by the government as an intellectual body, and its meetings were attended even by state officials to the extent that even casual leaves were granted to government employees who wanted to attend the Sabha's annual meet. From the measures adopted by the Sabha it was apparent that it did not intend to silently work on the development of the Assamese language. Its active involvement in protest and hardliner opinion for the exclusive status of Assamese language shows its own political inclination, though its historical lineage was that of a non-political cultural and literary organisation.

The Sabha's tilt towards politics was largely encouraged by its close association and support of the Congress party. The government in 1950s and 1960s gave high patronage to the Sabha, with cabinet ministers and legislators of the ruling party attending its meetings. The state government's pro-active support for the Sabha shows its failure to become the balancing actor. It easily gave in to pressures mounting from the Assamese elite circle to pursue exclusionary language policy. The concept of broad Assamese identity and exclusive language policy was a total misfit. Their assurance of

## Assamese identity and the ethnic dissent 151

keeping the interest of all tribal communities while advocating for higher privilege for Assamese language was not received well; it rather spurt tensions not only between hill tribes and the Assamese but also between the plains tribal[9] and the Assamese. Even today, when the Asom Sahitya Sabha talks of Assamese to be used popularly, there is a common assumption that it only talks of promoting the interests of the Assamese-speaking population.

Language and cultural separation of the tribal from the Assamese became the most practical outlay for political separation of the hills. By 1960s, hill leaders had started a full-fledged movement uniting its different hill tribes under All Party Hill Leaders Conference (APHLC), strongly protested and took offense to the imposition of Assamese language in hill areas. The outcome of the movement, as we know, was separation of hill districts from the Brahmaputra valley in 1972. During the time of independence, language was not an important criterion among the plains tribes of Assam for distinguishing themselves from the non-tribal Assamese. Following independence, language consciousness among the Bodos had grown. The Bodos and other plains tribal started rallying behind the Bodo Sahitya Sabha (BSS).[10] The establishment of the BSS had ushered a new era for the Bodo community. It got the tribal masses associated with the assertion of Bodo language identity. It relentlessly made efforts for the protection of Bodo language. Among its various demands, the prime was to pressurise the state government to introduce Bodo medium in schools situated in Bodo-populated areas.

The administrative policies on language were also heavily loaded with an uncaring attitude towards minority language and this added further complexity to the situation. The plains tribal placed their interests forward based on two factors – language and tribal status. For instance, representatives of different tribal organisations[11] of both plains and hill tribes of Assam in 1986 had collaborated and held up resolution against language policy pursued by the state government. They objected to the language policy of the state as discriminatory to non-Assamese medium students and also a hindrance for employment. They rejected the proposal made by the central government in the National Policy on Education, 1986, of using tribal languages as a mere bridge to collaborate with the regional languages thereby putting hindrance to the development of the Indian tribal languages. They demanded that it was necessary to review the clause and provide provision for development of tribal languages as medium of instruction up to the secondary stage of education. The tribal organisations opposed the government's concessions being accorded to one-sided lobbying of a particular language group, which threatened minority language groups.

The state, at times, tried to mediate the difference and sometimes the mediation itself added fuel to the fire. In order to protect peace in the state,

## 152 *Ivy Dhar*

the Centre made territorial division of the hills. Such move provoked alarm among the Assamese political leaders that now they must harden their stand and try to keep their hold on the rest of the areas; interestingly this gave an easy passage for the Bodo leaders to carry forward similar claims of division. Pressure points were building up and masses were divided into segments of identities. There has been a sanguine urge among the plains tribal to give their language a rightful place and establish their cultural identity distinct to Assamese identity. Identities that struggle for recognition often inadvertently replicate the image of the other identities that are relatively better situated because they imagine their recognition will be attained if similar route of protests are followed. The hill tribal protests that began with asking for separate language identity was later routed towards territorial division and became a trendsetter for plains tribal.

## The representation of plains tribal identity

Some lessons were hopefully learnt from the territorial division of Assam and the Assamese leadership proposed to go slow in urge for representation of Assamese identity. After the constitutional division of Assam, the Sabha leaders seemed to have gone out of their way to assuage the feelings of the plains tribal people to win their confidence. The earlier nostalgia about an undivided Assam and a dominant Assamese language was absent and there seems to be a healthy acceptance of the fact that Assam is just one of the several constituents of the Northeast (Misra 1988:115). At times it shows that unlike its image of getting political benefits, the Sabha's motives were never very harsh. Its foundations in middle-class category, which included elites from all circles, had put a similar impression of middle-class chauvinism on the Sabha members. At the same, it is very difficult also to assume that they were innocent to the middle-class motives; rather, it could be interpreted that they joined hands with chauvinism to enlarge its sphere of influence.

The Sabha made several attempts to contribute to the tribal life and culture and tried to neutralise the influence of the BSS. On the other hand, the BSS had been trying to get a level playing field and challenge the dominance of the Asom Sahitya Sabha. The Bodos had already gained confidence and strength to be able to carry a separate identity all on their own. To some extent, the state had played the cards to set its own power backup upon the plains tribal of Assam. The distance between the Sabha and Congress evolved with the emergence of other civil and political organisations in the fray. The state led by the Congress party in the 1980s had become alarmingly conscious of a strong nexus that was growing up between the All Assam Students' Union (AASU), the Assam Gana Sangram Parishad

*Assamese identity and the ethnic dissent* 153

(AGSP) and the Asom Sahitya Sabha, the stakeholders of the Assamese community. The growing political role of the Sabha caught the attention of the government during the time of intense agitation of the Assam Movement.[12] The government suspected it of taking political leverage and deprived it of its earlier stature. The state refused to give the Sabha annual grants and started giving higher patronage to the BSS to which the Asom Sahitya Sabha reacted, asserting the right of the Assamese people to fight for their cultural and linguistic identity. The Sabha's president accused the government of trying to set up a new Sahitya Sabha. He declared that if necessary yet another agitation would be launched 'to give a rightful place to the Assamese language and also for its wider use' (Misra 1988:116).

History was being repeated, the Sabha went ahead with an attitude which polarised the various ethnic groups of Assam, mainly the plains tribal. The Bodo leaders, in older times, had easily interacted and mingled well with their Assamese counterpart. But the Sabha's rigid stand on Assamese language and identity and the emergence of middle class among the plains tribal speeded up the process of separation of a sizeable section of the plains tribals from the Assamese mainstream. The plains tribals of the Brahmaputra valley assembled behind the leadership of Bodo intellectuals who stopped identifying themselves with the Asom Sahitya Sabha. It was criticised by the Bodo leaders as an organisation that solely worked for the interest of Assamese-speaking people. The Bodo identity acquired the necessary strength to resist the expansionist view of Assamese identity, which is exemplified by the movement for autonomy.

The political movement for a separate state of 'Udayachal' led by Plains Tribal Council of Assam (PTCA) and the cultural movement for Roman script for Bodo language had been going on side by side in the 1970s. The Bodos rejected Assamese intellectuals' proposals for using Assamese script for Bodo language. The BSS gave arguments in favour of the Roman script as recommended by the Kothari Education Commission.[13] The Roman script was widely used by tribal communities of Northeast who don't have their own script; it has been widely recommended as the most appropriate for the Bodo language for easy adaptation and popularity of the script and also because Bodo textbooks were prepared in Roman script in 1904 to introduce primary education among the Bodos which they used up to 1936 (Bhattacharya 1996:102). The script movement involved the entire Bodo community and ultimately the Assam government had to seek Centre's intervention on this issue. The Centre proposed the use of Devanagari script for the Bodo language. The proposal was subsequently reviewed by the Executive Committee of the BSS and the All Bodo Students' Union (ABSU) and finally Devanagari script was accepted. The Government of

## 154  *Ivy Dhar*

Assam and the Asom Sahitya Sabha became helpless and their opinion was not taken into account, but the issue was amicably solved between the Centre and the Bodo community. Later on, the Bodos proposed to name their proposed state as 'Bodoland', which shows the ambit of influence of language on the people could be quite intense that they replaced 'Udayachal' with an English name.

In the wake of motivation amongst the plain tribes for a separate identity, the Sabha remained firm to its earlier sentiment of bringing cultural cohesiveness, but definitely with ego. In the 1985 issue of the *Asom Sahitya Sabha Patrika* its editor, Samsing Hanse, wrote that even at this critical juncture when Bodos, Karbis, Mishing etc. of Assam were not willing to live within the political boundaries of Assam, the Asom Sahitya Sabha's attempt to unite the various ethnic groups through goodwill and brotherhood was a laudable one (Nag 1990:435). With the emergence of new counter-hegemonic groups among ethnic communities of Assam, the Sabha had to some extent complicated the tensions by not comprehending the historical developments until they became explosive. The Sabha's attitude of overstretching the status of Assamese language and even sometimes overreacting over the issue of giving a separate space to tribal identity has resulted in severe backlash from the plains tribal.

The Bodo Sahitya Sabha, though, could not succeed fully in the script movement yet it did not let Bodo language to be sidelined as a minority language. Having secured the Bodo language as medium of instruction and as MIL in higher secondary and graduate level, it placed demand before the government of Assam to adopt Bodo language as the official language of Assam. The government found enough justification and also perhaps considered it a milder demand compared to demand for separate political unit and hence accorded the Bodo language the status of associate official language for Bodo-dominated district of Kokrajhar and Udalguri sub-division of Darrang district in 1984. In the recent times, another long-drawn battle by BSS that finally came to an end was inclusion of Bodo language in the Eighth Schedule of the Constitution of India. Bodo language was incorporated in 2003 as part of the Eighth Schedule. From the 1980s the BSS had sizeably cut down on the popularity of the Sabha and this had affected their relations with each other.

The Sabha had been playing a central role but after the BSS came into the fray, it had slightly lost its earlier pomp. It was not just the BSS but other Sahitya Sabhas like Mishing Sahitya Sabha and Tiwa Sahitya Sabha that had their respective share of public support in their own communities for representing language and other social causes. Several of them got government patronage and so it was much easier for them to restrict the influence or rather replace the Sabha in the plains tribal areas. The sessions

*Assamese identity and the ethnic dissent* 155

of the BSS also began to be graced by Cabinet members and had all the appearance like that of Asom Sahitya Sabha annual meet. The government did not have enough choice but to act as a balance to several identities that claim an equal importance in state politics along with Assamese identity; otherwise, the frictions may even lead to territorial break-up. The disintegration of hills from Assam was already lying as a lived experience. On the positive note it also made the Asom Sahitya Sabha realise its responsibility towards the plains tribals of Assam.

The Sabha earlier did not realise the gamut of consequences at several times; it showed unimaginativeness towards identities of smaller communities in order to pursue the promotion of Assamese language. On several occasions, it opposed the demands made by BSS like the demand for Bodo language to be accepted as the associate official language. Kamal Kr Brahma stated in his presidential address (Basugaon 4 March 1992) that the development of language and literature of smaller ethnic groups depended on the Sabha and its directions as it is the parent organisation. It was, therefore, imperative on the part of the Sabha to co-ordinate the activities of other Sahitya Sabhas like the BSS, Mishing Sahitya Sabha etc. The Sabha had not remarkably lived up to fulfilling this vital area of its activity and hence these organisations of the smaller ethnic groups felt alienated.

The threat of its declining popularity prompted the Sabha to adopt other tactics to entice the tribal populace. It tried to make over its image and change its approach not only towards the BSS but also towards other Sahitya Sabhas. It understood that it had been responsible to some extent for the estrangement between Assamese and other communities. However, the Sabha's vague generalisations about a composite Assamese society and culture encompassing all the tribal communities or speaking of greater Assamese identity could not conceal the fact that its sphere of influence had been severely narrowed down by organisations like the BSS. The expanding role of the Sahitya Sabhas in language politics brought forth challenges to test each other's ambit of influence on the people, state and government.

## Multi-cultural existence of Assam

The very idea of representation did not strike a chord with all alike; it became a subject of protests. The tribals began moving away from the Assamese-speaking populace because they saw no role assigned for them in the mainstream politics. The Sabha had always been in two minds; it did not want the tribals questioning the influence of the dominant community and also wanted to concentrate its efforts on integration. A major blunder

## 156   *Ivy Dhar*

committed was initiating the integration process through use of 'one state one language' formula, which was seen by the tribals as Assamese chauvinist politics. The state was pressurised to respond to overt identity claims based on language criterion. The state, at any given time, is constituted by the balance of the group pressures and the government is concerned with the establishment of regularised adjustment process for handling the struggle of various competing groups (Johari 1989:589–90). The state had to gradually reflect back and modify the language policy of Assam. However, it had been rather slow in responding to the demands of linguistic minorities. This was probably because representation of minorities in state politics tends to be low and their socio-economic development was slower. Even before independence, language has been the most sensitive issue of discord in Assam. Language became the most potent tool for elites to draw affiliation and distinction with its contemporary elite groups.

In the 1960s and 1970s the state could not effectively manage due to lack of experience and was unfamiliar to handling such controversial issues. Baruah raises arguments on federalism practised in India that if only the Indian federalism had space for inclusionary politics, instead of carving out states, if only cultural policies could be carved that was more in tune with the ethno-political realities of Assam, then division of a large state into several smaller states would have not happened (Baruah 1999:113). Arguments could be made on getting a different historical picture if blunders do not happen. Later on in the era after the 1980s, carving out new states was a discarded policy; the state tried to accommodate pressure by modifying the language policy and trying to formulate revised cultural policy. The government tried hard to address the language issue, which has been a bone of contention between the Assamese and other linguistic minorities of the state. The attitude of the government differed according to the exigencies of time. The state reviewed the needs of the linguistic minorities.

The development of minority languages is the responsibility of the state. The state government has provided financial aid to BSS, Nepali Sahitya Sabha and Tai Ahom Academy that are engaged in the development of their respective languages. The approach of the Asom Sahitya Sabha has changed over the years as it is trying to move ahead with a new perspective. In its formative years, it represented the youth of Assam and it could serve as a common platform beyond cultural distinction. But, in the period just after independence, the Sabha spoke its chauvinist mind loudly. It failed to remain a non-political organisation and kept on making political statements that affected the placid composition of the Assamese society. However, in the last 20 years, it has evolved a new role for itself.

*Assamese identity and the ethnic dissent* 157

It seems to have understood the fact that its presence in the society can remain intact only when it takes into consideration the challenges arising from other small ethnic communities of Assam and play an accommodative role. It stressed on addressing youth's involvement in keeping alive its cultural interest and giving platform to other ethnic communities. The Sabha members are also aware of the fact that these perspectives need to be worked upon. They were no more in a position to ignore the problem of cultural conflict and have been working for peace, harmony and integrity with tribal leaders.

Over the years they have also tried to accommodate the interest of inter-state Indian migrant population residing in Assam. The Sabha has developed many new projects in collaboration with the government for the promotion of cultural interests of the people of Assam. It wants to remain politically neutral on the issue of cultural identity. The Sabha, having patronage of political leaders, particularly in the 1960s throughout till mid-1980s, was greatly influenced by political parties. It has been trying to extend support and recognition to the cultural identity of other smaller ethnic groups of Assam.[14]

Language policy and tribal issues came to be seen from a new perspective in order to keep alive the cultural diversity and restrict further political fragmentation of Assam. Certain efforts made by the state government like instruction through minority languages both at primary and secondary level, maintenance of Advance Registers for registering linguistic preference of linguistic minority students both at primary and secondary stages of education, making textbooks available in minority languages and distributing them free of cost at the primary stage of education reflect the changes. The drawing up of cultural policy is a new endeavour to show the multicultural existence of the state of Assam.[15]

## Conclusion

Ethnic struggles have taken an explicit form of consciousness emerging from encounter with the dominant cultures. Power dynamics and economic interest are mostly present in these struggles, although these often get a vent through cultural assertion. The hill tribes put forward their ethnic claims for separation from the plains people stating that imposition of Assamese language was threat to their cultural identity. Since there is very limited space for expression, conflicts between identities are bound to arise and disintegrate any theme that wants to bind them together. There has been a continuing process of reinvention by various communities, tribals and non-tribals, by seeking a change in the status of their culture, language and identity as a part of the strategy for political advancement.

158 *Ivy Dhar*

The plains tribal assertion led by the Bodos for separate political and cultural identity germinated when they were not given benefits as tribal community in any form in the Constitution as compared to hills tribes. The dissent of the Bodos from the Assamese was such a challenge, which the Assamese middle class had never expected and such situation had put the Asom Sahitya Sabha in dilemma. In reality, it was not just the Sabha which gave opinion that the Bodos were completely assimilated with the Assamese but even the colonial and post-colonial political leaders' opinion was not different. Then if history could have placed the assimilation process in a different way, was it possible that the Bodos would have still remained within the protective shell of Assamese identity? This might not have been possible at all because the race for recognition grips one and all; the Bodos could not remain cocooned letting others reap the fruit of development. The Bodos, slowly and steadily, reached a certain stage of development from where several other factors were equally strong to reverse the process of distinction between the Assamese and the Bodos.

The Sabha remains at the crossroads; it has not been wholly successful in bringing the tribal emotionally close to its cause because there is still a gap between what the Sabha says and what it actually professes. It talks of larger Assamese identity but could not explain satisfactorily how it would accommodate other ethnic groups of Assam. Its leaders belong largely to the Assamese-speaking community. Unless it creates enough space for tribal leaders there will remain a gap between the ethnic communities of Assam. The distinction is still not so large enough that gaps cannot be filled in.

The Sabha's objectives of work have largely remained confined within the contours of development of language, literature and culture. It is nearing a century-old existence but has not digressed from its objective. A positive trend can be seen which will help the Sabha to take on its future role. It has been able to withstand many challenges because it has always been working as a democratic institution. It has also been resilient to changes and adopted its approach according to the needs of time. The Assamese intellectuals provide it direction taking into account the interest of the common mass. The Sabha cannot be said to be just an alliance or network among the people who are like-minded; rather, it is highly organised and formal in its presentation. It is truly an organisation that has well-defined objectives. Since its membership is voluntary and it assists as an intermediary link between the individual and the state, it falls within the broad contours of civil society. The image of the Sabha never remained alike; its attitude over many decades has been conservative and reactionary as well as liberal and modern. It has always tried to get the pulse of the people and has represented the Assamese society in its crisis, without much bothering about the composition of the Assamese society.

## Notes

1 The Asom Sahitya Sabha was born by the 'Act XXI of 1860' under the registration of Literary Scientific and Charitable Societies. The Constitution of the Sabha laid objectives for all-round improvement of Assamese language and literature, which includes revising and updating Assamese dictionary and grammar; encouraging research in the study of the ancient Assamese literature; encouraging the publications of works on subjects in which the Assamese literature is generally poor; assisting publications of useful works by authors who cannot afford to do so; preparing gramophone records of bona fide Assamese tunes; granting scholarships for encouraging the study and culture of music and arts and publishing periodicals of the Sabha and carrying out propaganda for the study and research in Assamese language and literature among the general public. To commemorate these objectives, it further states that the Sabha must collect subscriptions and donations from the public, hold and manage funds, purchase, sell, acquire on lease or by gift property of the Sabha and do all such things to the attainment of its objectives (Asom Sahitya Sabha 1977:18–20).

2 The British, after annexation of Assam in 1826, introduced new laws, brought significant change in market relations by introducing wage labour and started harnessing resources and all this required a cushion of a clerical force that would help in implementing the change. Having already established their rule in neighbouring Bengal, they found it more suitable to bring in Bengali clerks to Assam who were accustomed to colonial laws, as the Assamese people had not yet acquired the required competencies to give support to the British administration. Once the Bengali immigration to Assam flowed, their language too followed and since it was already being used in all transactions it did not take time for British to introduce Bengali as the official language of Assam. In 1836 Bengali was declared as the official language of Assam and it continued to remain so till 1873. These dates did not mean that Bengali was used only within this period; in reality it began to be used much before it was introduced officially and did not cease to be used much after Assamese was re-introduced officially. The fear of losing the exclusivity of Assamese language motivated leaders to launch a struggle for reinstatement of Assamese language and to secure its place and pride in Assam.

3 'Sabha' in the text will be used to refer to Asom Sahitya Sabha. Though in later parts, there are references of many other Sabhas like Bodo Sahitya Sabha, Tiwa Sahitya Sabha etc., they are written in full form or in abbreviation.

4 The word 'Assamese' when used in reference to a group of population denotes 'Assamese-speaking people'. In terms of population statistics they are the largest linguistic group of Assam.

5 The indigenous language groups, apart from Assamese, are the tribal groups. Though there are Bengali, Hindi and Nepali speakers in Assam, and are even larger groups than some of the tribal groups, they are not considered as indigenous to Assam as these speakers largely migrated during the colonial phase. The tribal groups are minorities and very few of them have more than 1 per cent of linguistic strength in Assam. Among the tribal language groups, Bodo language has the highest number of speakers.

160　*Ivy Dhar*

6 Important literary figures of Assam like Hemchandra Goswami, L. N. Bez-barua and Kanaklal Barua have been associated with *Assamiya Bhasa Unnati Sadhini Sabha*, which collected and published old Assamese manuscripts and undertook the task of developing a standardised Assamese grammar to be introduced in vernacular schools of Assam. It published a monthly journal named *Jonaki* that largely published materials on the problems of colonial dependence and tried to inspire people of Assam's glorious heritage.

7 Clause 6 of the Assam Accord, an agreement reached with the Government of India, says that the Centre will provide constitutional safeguard to the Assamese people. Detection and deportation of non-citizens of India was also part of the Accord.

8 The middle class and the peasant class both faced the difficulties, though for different reasons, of coping with the use of Bengali language in courts and schools. There had been an informal attraction for saving Assamese language. The sentiment of all classes was same – that they were facing immense hardship because they were not allowed to use their own language. This consciousness brought together the otherwise conflicting classes together (Nag 1987: 454).

9 Plains tribes are tribal communities that live in the Brahmaputra valley like Bodo, Mishing, Rabha etc. unlike hill tribes whose population (prior to 1972) had included Manipur, Meghalaya and Mizoram population and now the hill tribes of Assam live in the North Cachar hills and Karbi Anglong district of Assam.

10 Bodo Sahitya Sabha, known as *Boroni Tunlai Aphat* in Bodo language, was formed from the remnants of an organisation called 'Bodo Literary Club', which was formed after independence in 1950 by a handful of government officials in Dhubri. The Bodo Sahitya Sabha carried the originating ideas of the Club to work for the upliftment of Bodo language, develop the Bodo literature, preserve historical literary works in Bodo languages, publish books, support financially poor Bodo students, spread education among the rural youth and remain outside political activities. The first general convention of the Bodo Sahitya Sabha was held on 15–16 November 1952 at Basugaon.

11 All Assam Tribal Students Union, All Bodo Students' Union, All Rabha Students Union, All Assam Deuri Students Union, Ameri Karbi Students Union, All Cachar tribal Students Union, Karbi Anglong Students Union, Bodo Sahitya Sabha, All Mising Students Union, Mising Agom Ke'bang, Mising Bane Ke'bang, All Assam Tiwa Sonmilon, Bebak Rabha Krourang Runchum, All Assam Tribal Sangha and Tiwa Sahitya Sabha.

12 The Assam Movement that started in 1979 and continued till 1985 was led by Assam Gana Sangram Parishad and All Assam Students' Union (AAGSP–AASU) combined. The main agenda of the movement was the immigration issue; the problem of continuous flow of illegal migrants from Bangladesh were raised by AAGSP–AASU. The illegal migrants were arbitrarily included in the voters list as Indian citizens. The Assam Movement demanded that election be held only after thorough revision of the voters list and detecting names of foreign illegal migrants. The Sabha gave its intellectual input to the movement; in its annual session of 1975 and 1979 it demanded that the state government look into the census enumeration of Assamese-speaking population because illegal migrants were also listed as Assamese speakers.

*Assamese identity and the ethnic dissent*  161

13 Kothari Education Commission, 1964–66, which was the sixth commission in the history of commission in India was appointed under the provisions of a resolution of the Government of India, dated 14 July 1964. The commission included eminent educationists in diverse fields from India and abroad. It consisted of total 17 members, 14 members, 1 member secretary, 1 associate secretary and Dr D. S. Kothari, chairman of the UGC, was appointed as the chairman of the commission. Therefore, it is also known as the Kothari Commission. This commission focused its attention not to specific sectors or aspects of education, but to have a comprehensive review of the entire educational system. It discussed on Indian languages as the medium of education in India (www.kkhsou.in/main/education/edu_commission.html, accessed 29 April 2012).

14 These arguments are drawn from my PhD field experience based on interview with Asom Sahitya Sabha member in 2005. I acknowledge Sabha members who participated and answered my queries on the role of the Sabha in the present decade.

15 The Assam government proposed a cultural policy in 2001–02. The draft was prepared that defined culture of Assam as an amalgamation of various streams of thought. It also laid down several objectives that talk mainly of preservation of ethnic and indigenous tribes, preservation of historical monuments and promotion of cultural and emotional integration among the people across the state and universally across state borders.

# References

Agarwal, K. S. 1999. *Dynamics of Identity and Inter-Group Relations in North-East India*. Shimla: Indian Institute of Advanced Studies.

Asom Sahitya Sabha. 1958. *This Is Assam*. Jorhat: Asom Sahitya Sabha.

Asom Sahitya Sabha. 1977. *Abhilekh 1917–1977*. Jorhat: Asom Sahitya Sabha.

*The Assam Tribune*, 8 March 2015: 1. 'Replace Assamese with Indigenous People: BSS'.

*The Assam Tribune*, 14 March 2015: 4. 'It's Govt. Duty to Define Assamese People: Sabha'.

Barpujari, H. K. 1998. *North-East India: Problems, Policies and Prospects since Independence*. New Delhi: Spectrum Publications.

Barua, Indrani. 1990. *Pressure Groups in Assam*. New Delhi: Omsons Publications.

Baruah, Apurba K. 1964. *Social Tensions in Assam: Middle Class Politics*. New York: Orion Press.

Baruah, Apurba K. 1994. 'Middle Class Hegemony and the National Question in Assam'. In Milton S. Sangma (ed.), *Essays on the North-East India*, pp. 278–93. New Delhi: Indus Publishing House.

Baruah, Sanjib. 1999. *India against Itself: Assam and the Politics of Nationality*. New Delhi: Oxford University Press.

Bhattacharjee, Chandana. 1996. *Ethnicity and Autonomy Movement*. New Delhi: Vikas Publishing House.

Bhusan, Chandra. 2005. *Assam: Its Heritage and Culture*. New Delhi: Kalpaz Publications.

## 162 Ivy Dhar

Bodo Sahitya Sabha. 2002. *The Bodo: Mouthpiece of the Bodo Sahitya Sabha – 27th Issue*. Kokrajhar: Bodo Sahitya Sabha.

Bodo Sahitya Sabha. 2005. *The Bodo: Mouthpiece of the Bodo Sahitya Sabha – 30th Issue*. Kokrajhar: Bodo Sahitya Sabha.

Dasgupta, Jyotinrindra. 1970. *Language Conflict and National Development*. London: University of California Press.

Dash, J. N. 1989. 'Udayachal Movement in Assam: A Case of Socio-Political Identity for the Bodos', *The Indian Journal of Political Science*, 50(3): 335–42.

Datta, P. S., ed. 1990. *Ethnic Movements in Poly-Cultural Assam*. New Delhi: Har-Anand Publications.

Dhar, Ivy. 2007. *Cultural Organisations and Politics of Identity in Assam: The Role of Asom Sahitya Sabha and Bodo Sahitya Sabha*, Unpublished PhD Dissertation, Jawaharlal Nehru University.

Directorate of Cultural Affairs. 2004. *Draft Cultural Policy*. Guwahati: Government of Assam.

Goswami, Trailokyanath. 1961. 'Assamese, the Official Language of Assam'. In Maheshwar Neog (ed.), *Assam's Language Question: A Symposium*, pp. 1–4. Jorhat: Asom Sahitya Sabha.

Guha, Amalendu. 1980. 'Little Nationalism Turned Chauvinist: Assam's Anti-Foreigner Upsurge', *Economic and Political Weekly*, 15(41, 42 and 43): 1699–720.

Johari, J. C. 1989. *Principles of Modern Political Science*. New Delhi: Sterling Publishers Pvt Ltd.

Krishna Kanta Handique State Open University. 'Introduction to Education Commissions 1964–66', www.kkhsou.in/main/education/edu_commission. html (accessed 29 April 2012).

Misra, Udayon. 1988. *North-East India-Quest for Identity*. Guwahati and New Delhi: Omsons Publications.

Nag, Sajal. 1987. 'Language, Class and Superstructure: A Study in Aspects of Nationality Formation in the 19th Century Assam'. In J. B. Bhattacharya (ed.), *Proceedings of Northeast India History Association: Seventh Session, Passighati*. Shillong: Northeast India History Association.

Nag, Sajal. 1990. *Roots of Ethnic Conflict: Nationality Question in North-East*. New Delhi: Manohar Publications.

Neog, Maheshwar, ed. 1961. *Assam's Language Question: A Symposium*. Jorhat: Asom Sahitya Sabha, 1961.

Neog, Maheshwar. 1976. *Annals of Asom Sahitya Sabha, 1917–1975*. Jorhat: Asom Sahitya Sabha.

Sangma, Milton S., ed. 1994. *Essays on the North-East India*. New Delhi: Indus Publishing Company.

Sharma, Manorama. 1988. 'The Assamese Middle Class and Integration: The Role of the Asom Sahitya Sabha'. In J. B. Bhattacharjee (ed.), *Proceedings of Northeast India History Association: Ninth session, Guwahati*, pp. 430–37. Shillong: Northeast India History Association.

Sharma, Manorama. 1990. *Social and Economic Change in Assam: Middle Class Hegemony*. New Delhi: Ajanta Publications.

# Part V

# Civil society, Indian state and conflict resolution

# 10 Between state and the insurgents
## Violation of human rights in Assam

*Dilip Gogoi and Uddipan Dutta*

All human beings are born free and equal in dignity and rights (UDHR 1948). But there is a gap between principle and practice. Every man and woman possesses certain basic rights which are inherent and inalienable. This claim is articulated in the form of human rights in modern times and is very essential in realising the human dignity and to ensure equality and justice. It is fundamental to govern without any prejudice of race, religion, nationality, language, sex, place of birth etc. Human rights are above all form of rights and constitute the very source of all rights. While civil, political and economic and cultural rights are dependent on a person's legal status as citizen of a particular nation, his or her human rights are not determined by any such considerations. The value of human dignity and principle of equality of all members of the human community can be found in every culture and civilisation, philosophical roots and also in religious traditions. It is now regarded as the fundamental principle in democratic governance systems worldwide. However, the idea of human rights is relatively recent in origin and is closely linked with natural rights. It was the United Nations that took the initiative by declaring *Universal Declaration of Human Rights* 1948 and subsequently adopted two very significant covenants on civil and political and economic, social and cultural rights 1966 at its initial stage to universalise these human rights. The human right has been broadened further by recognising group rights like right to development, clean and peaceful environment, food and shelter. Now it becomes a part of human development and human security and wishes to share a common vision and goal of establishing a just and humane society everywhere.

However, human life and human dignity have been disregarded throughout the history and continue to be disregarded even today. Assam and Northeast India are no exception to it. Rather, the region has become a classic example of every form of gross violation of human rights – not only by non-state armed groups but also by the state security forces. In many cases, the state veers away from its defined responsibility in the Northeast

## 166  *Dilip Gogoi and Uddipan Dutta*

and assumes extra-constitutional responsibility to dispel perceived national security threat arising out of insurgency and its compulsion to maintain territorial integrity. The complexity of governance, economic backwardness and lack of effective activism on the part of the civil society to protect rights of the people further aggravate the situation. The region has a long history of insurgency ranging from seeking complete secession from the Indian Union to autonomy movements. This has helped to develop a popular perception – making the Northeast synonymous with insurgency. The region has a distinct identity in popular imagination in terms of origin, growth and history of the various communities and their integration with mainland India. These historical factors compounded with economic backwardness, misgovernance and sense of insecurity, real or imaginary of losing one's own identity in his or her own land at the hands of the outsiders, resulted in a prolonged insurgency. This creates a situation of turmoil where the human rights of the people are often ignored by both security forces and the insurgents. It is unfortunate and quite an irony that the Indian Union, which deeply adheres to the international human rights instruments[1] and formulates its constitutional as well domestic laws under global norms, often tends to violate not only the global human rights norms but also its own domestic standards while dealing with insurgency.

## Human rights in Indian Constitution

India has a right-based constitution, adopted in 1950, that follows international bill of human rights and recognises these rights at various levels. The value of human rights not only gets reflected in the Preamble of the Constitution but also extensively gets included in chapter III (from Articles 14 to 32 of the Indian Constitution) as Fundamental Rights which are basically civil and political in nature and in chapter IV (from Articles 36 to 51) as Directive Principles of State Policy dealing with economic, social and cultural rights which are also recognised as fundamental to the 'governance' of the country. Fundamental Rights and Directive Principles of State Policy together form the 'conscience of the constitution'. The main intention of the founding fathers of Indian Constitution is that civil and political freedom must combine with social and economic justice to establish a just social order for all. The Supreme Court of India is also helping the growth of human rights through its various judicial pronouncements. For example, the Supreme Court of India has recently interpreted Article 21 of the Indian Constitution and given a new meaning that the word 'life' means 'not merely animal existence or survival' but a 'life with dignity' (*Maneka Gandhi vs. Union of India* 1978) which also helps to transform the directive principles such as right to education, better living standard and clean

*Between state and the insurgents* 167

environment, non-exploitative working conditions into fundamental rights regime in India. Besides, under the Protection of Human Rights Act, 1993, which also defined human rights in the Indian context as 'rights relating to life, liberty, equality and dignity of individual guaranteed by the constitution or embodied in the international covenants and enforceable by the courts of India', a National Human Rights Commission was instituted. The main purpose of the Commission is to protect the legal and political foundation of human rights and to promote them as core values in public and private domain in India. The primary aim is to restore the faith of victims of human rights abuse in the court of law and initiate steps to see that such violations do not go unchecked and those responsible for human rights abuse are made responsible for their actions or inactions. Apart from the Constitution, human rights are also protected and guaranteed under various ordinary laws legislated by the Indian Parliament.[2]

In spite of all protection and regulating mechanism at global and domestic levels, India is indifferent towards insurgency-prone areas of the Northeast. People of the Northeast frequently witness gross violations of human rights in the form of violation of the right to life, violation of the right to human dignity and physical security and violation of the right to equal protection of laws and violation of the right to freedom of expression. It is primarily due to the imposition of draconian laws such as the National Security Act, 1980, the Armed Forces (Special Powers) Act 1958, the Terrorist and Disruptive Activities (Prevention) Act 1987 etc. which transgresses the provisions of the Human Rights embedded in the Constitution. The right to life, the right to live with dignity, the right to equal treatment and not to be discriminated against, the right to freedom from fear and torture and wrongful arrest, the right to a fair trial and right to free speech are often being ignored in this part of the country. The Northeast is a classic case of state failure in addressing the question of human rights while dealing with insurgency. The state apparatus is often found indulging in violence in the name of maintaining territorial integrity and sovereignty. This, it often does at the cost of civilian lives and gross violation of human rights of its own people. It is also essentially a state duty to protect the rights and lives of the innocent civilians from the insurgents. Instead, the state itself involves in gross violation of human rights in the name of tackling insurgency by imposing frequent non-productive armed interventions.

It is in this context that the chapter tries to examine the plight of the people of Assam caught between the state and the insurgent group whose proposed ideology seeks to establish a 'sovereign independent Assam through armed struggle'. Although the ULFA was established in 1979, its ideology started acquiring political space only after the AGP ministry assumed power in 1985. It is generally acknowledged that the ULFA got no substantial

## 168  *Dilip Gogoi and Uddipan Dutta*

opposition from the ruling state government during the period and slowly it established a very strong organisational base. By 1988, the organisation had a strong presence in the state. Following its manifested ideology of violence, the organisation engaged itself in the killings of the people it deemed its enemies. The Centre placed Assam under President's rule and declared the whole state as disturbed area by a Presidential Notification issued on the night of 27 November 1990. The state assembly, whose term would have expired one month after, was kept in suspended animation. The United Liberation Front of Assam (ULFA) and the National Socialist Council of Nagaland (NSCN) were declared as unlawful associations. The army operation was named Operation *Bajrang*. It is widely acknowledged now that the ULFA got wind of the army operation, deserted their camps and took refuge in safer places. This decision on the part of the government gave a new direction to the politics of Assam. It also marks the end of the first phase of the activities of ULFA. The ULFA operated almost unopposed and unchecked before the declaration of President's rule and was not a banned organisation before 28 November 1990 in spite of its avowed aim of a 'sovereign independent Assam'. The news was unexpected and came as a shock to the people of Assam. After this, a series of operations were carried out by the Indian Army under different umbrella terms like Operation Bajrang and Operation Rhino. Later on the strategy was changed a bit and a unified command structure[3] was put in the place incorporating the help of the state police and the paramilitary forces.

### Counter-insurgency operations and violation of human rights

No sooner President's rule was declared, massive search and arrest operations were conducted in thousands of villages and major towns in Assam. From that period onwards, Assam was put virtually under the military rule, although a democratically elected state government was in place. Assam was brought under Disturbed Areas Act, Armed Forces Special Powers Act, TADA and National Security Act to counter and wipe out the militancy but people had to pay the price of the draconian provisions of these laws which take away basic rights of the people. People were picked up by the army indiscriminately and arbitrarily. The most ominous fact for the people of Assam at that time was the collapse of civil administration and the Indian Army usurping its power. In the name of searching ULFA cadres, innocent males were picked up, taken to the army camps and subjected to brutal torture. People still remember how electric shocks were administered on the private parts of the bodies, nails were pulled out from the victims' body and often kicked and beaten mercilessly. The females in the villages

*Between state and the insurgents*   169

bore the brunt of the cruelty of the men in uniform. In the local media extensive stories were carried out how females left out in the villages were molested, raped and treated shabbily by the Indian Army that was supposed to protect the honour of the citizens at the time of external aggression. It is commonly acknowledged that the ULFA got wind of Operation Bajrang and fled to safe places and it was mostly the common villagers who had to face the wrath of the Indian Army in its most barbaric form. It must also be mentioned here that the ULFA was not a banned organisation before 27 November 1990 and mere association with the organisation should not have been taken as a crime by the law enforcing agencies. But that common sense was not applied at that period and innocent civilians were subjected to torture of the most brutal shape.

Operation Bajrang was called off on 20 April 1991 on the eve of the state assembly election, but the army was redeployed due to rapid escalation of ULFA-related violence, under the code name Operation Rhino. During this operation, once again the state was virtually placed under army rule in spite of the existence of an elected state government. The grim state of affairs and lack of basic human rights are apparent from the fact that US Department of State enumerated 40 custodial deaths between 1991 and early 1992.[4] The killings of Babul Baruah, Dibakar Hangique, Khireswar Bora, Nitu Rajbanshi, Kiran Saikia[5] and many other innocent civilians bear the testimony of glaring violation of human rights by the Indian state through its security forces.

During the operations under the *Unified Command*, there were also reports of gross violations of human rights. It arose primarily as a form of extrajudicial killing – fake and deliberate encounters and custodial deaths. More than hundred cases of such nature of crime were reported. The most heinous crimes against the common civilians were perpetrated during the phase when unknown killers unleashed a reign of terror with the help of security forces on the close relatives of the ULFA leaders, the phenomenon popularly known as 'secret killings' which is mentioned in the later part of the chapter separately. The security forces under unified command picked up innocent civilians mistakenly as ULFA members and subjected them to brutal treatment. Ajit Mahanta, a resident of Kakopathar, Tinsukia, was picked up by the army on 5 February 2006 on suspicion of being an ULFA linkman. His body was recovered from a gunny bag in Assam Medical College, Dibrugarh, the next day. The army said he died while trying to escape from their custody. His death caused widespread resentment in Tinsukia which has been a stronghold of the rebel group. On 10 February 2006 people from around a hundred villages near Kakopathar area gathered to protest Mahanta's death because people believed he was innocent and the sole bread earner of the family. In order to disperse the mob the local

## 170  Dilip Gogoi and Uddipan Dutta

police opened fire upon them in the name of self-defence, which resulted in the death of eight people and a CRPF *jawan* was also stoned to death by the angry protestors. It was a complete failure of the unified command structure as S. Kabilan, the chief secretary who also headed the command, openly blamed the army for not following the instruction of the *unified command*. Later the army extended an apology to the victim's family by the visit of the General Officer Commanding in Chief, Eastern Command, Lt Gen. Arvind Sharma on 12 February 2006, who handed over a cheque of Rs one lakh and five thousand cash to Ajit Mahanta's widow. He also informed her that the army would adopt her two children and assured another one lakh to be given to them soon.

The killing of Dulen Baruah, 55, the *namgharia*,[6] on the eve of Rangali Bihu, the most important festival of Assamese people, on 14 April 2008 exposed the insensitivity of the security forces under the unified command. As reported, a group of 149 CRPF battalion had gone to Himpora village of Moranhat police station of Sivasagar district, in search of ULFA militants, but as the militants had left the place much before the arrival of the forces, the forces vented their ire on a helpless Baruah. This case came to the light only when the villagers protested vehemently and resorted to road blockade with the other civil society organisations.[7] The protesters demanded that the culprits be brought to book but so far no one has been put to trial and convicted. Incidents like this have caused people's loss of faith on the *unified command*. There is a popular demand from all quarters against security forces and repeal of the coercive laws operating in Assam. It needs to be mentioned that the K. N. Saikia Commission has also recommended the disbanding of the unified command structure as it is viewed as an extra-constitutional authority.

The Royal Bhutanese Army also conducted a massive operation in 2003 against the militants to flush out the militants taking shelter in their land with the tacit and logistic support of the Indian Army. Although the operation was relatively successful, there was a massive violation of human rights. This came into light when wives of top level ULFA cadres protested and launched an indefinite hunger strike on 21 March 2007 demanding to know the whereabouts of their missing husbands. All the top militants, namely Ashanta Baghphukan, Robin Neog, Benning Rabha, Nilu Chakrabarty, Ponaram Dihingia and Naba Changmai, were missing soon after the Bhutan operation against the militants. They were allegedly arrested by the Royal Bhutan Army and handed over to their Indian counterpart. Even, Shyamoli Gogoi, wife of a missing ULFA leader, had moved the Guwahati High Court (Prabhakar 2007) to find out the whereabouts of her husband since Operation All Clear. Later, the court was also not satisfied with the affidavit filed by the government and directed to provide all

*Between state and the insurgents* 171

necessary information about the missing ULFA cadres. So far no authentic information has been provided and this apathy on the part of the state has pushed the missing cadres' wives and children to an uncertain future by denying right to information. As the cadres of the banned organisation do not cease to be the citizens of the country by virtue of their association with the organisation, their rights to life cannot be transgressed by the state agencies.

## Kangaroo courts of ULFA and mass graves

One of the foremost gross violations of human rights that Assam had witnessed which was never seen in the history of post-colonial Assam was the discovery of sixteen highly decomposed human bodies (popularly called the mass graves) from Lakhipathar camp of ULFA near Digboi on 3, 4 and 5 December 1990.[8] The discovery of mass graves throws light on a unique aspect of the modus operandi of ULFA during its early phase. There were the reports of the organisation establishing kangaroo courts[9] to punish the local criminals and the people it branded as 'spies'. The activities of these courts remained mostly unknown to the general populace and the whereabouts of many people disappeared at that period are still unknown. A glimpse of the torture meted out to the people came to the light from the description of an eye witness who visited the camp after the discovery of the dead bodies to claim the body of Sri Dimbeswar Gogoi, a Tai Ahom student activist of Rahan Pathar near Sapekhati. According to this description, some of the bodies were blindfolded while others had their hands tied. These dead bodies bore the testimony of the cruelty with which the ULFA punished the people it held guilty. The torture committed on Dimbeswar Gogoi before he was killed bore the testimony of the barbarous torture perpetrated on the victims by the cadres of the ULFA at their Lakhipathar camp. Chaw Puspadhar Saikia cites post-mortem report and gives a small description of the torture meted to Dimbeswar Gogoi. According to him the mouth, hands and feet of the victim were tied very tightly from the behind, the teeth were broken with a hammer, many parts of the body were chopped off and acid was poured all over the body before he was killed (Saikia 2005:75). Dimbeswar Gogoi was not the only victim; the other fifteen people whose bodies were recovered from the mass graves had received similar treatment in the hand of the ULFA cadres. According to media reports, Rana Goswami, Radhesyam Lahoti and Debu Chowdhuri were some of the people whose dead bodies were identified by the family members along with Dimbeswar Gogoi's. Although the discovery of the mass graves and the existence of the highly decomposed bodies were reported in the media, in the face of the pouring reports of the reign of

## 172    Dilip Gogoi and Uddipan Dutta

terror let loose by the Indian Army on the innocent civilians of Assam during Operation Bajrang, the stories of the cruelties meted out to the victims who were kidnapped and whose bodies were found in the mass graves remained largely untold.

The members of all major political parties in Assam had to bear the brunt of the armed insurgency, although in the early part of it Congress workers were especially targeted. Apart from Congress workers, leaders of the United Minorities Front (UMF), formed after the Assam Accord to protect the rights of the minorities in Assam, also came under the attack of the ULFA. The United Revolution Movement Council of Assam (URMCA), a conglomeration of different ethnic organisations under the leadership of CPI (ML),[10] gave resistance to the ULFA in many places at the grassroots and came under brutal attacks from the ULFA before the starting of army operations. It may be mentioned that Congress (I) became very unpopular in Assam after 1983 and there was a general resentment prevailing against the Congress leaders at that time in Assam.[11] The attack on Congress workers continued for a long time chiefly due the reason that the party was instrumental in the declaration of President's rule in 1990 and it was under its aegis that Operation Rhino and the division in ULFA were executed. But as Prafulla Kumar Mahanta toughened his stand on ULFA in his second term as chief minister in 1996 and a unified command structure was mooted to fight the insurgents, the AGP leaders and workers became targets of the insurgent group. To provide a vignette of the terror tactics of ULFA, a few cases are mentioned here. On 19 February 1986, Tankeswar Dihingiya, an ex-minister in the Hiteswar Saikia ministry, was shot at by ULFA cadres in Sivasagar and he succumbed to his bullet injuries on 20 February 1986.[12] In the same year, Sri Kalipada Sen, the president of United Minorities Front and president of Citizen's Rights Preservation Committee (CRPC), was shot dead in his residence on 17 September.[13] On the night of 8 January 1987, Sri Rajib Rajkhowa, the vice president of the Jorhat District Youth Congress (I) and son of former forest minister Shri Dinanath Rajkhowa, and Ranjit Barua, a Congress worker and a friend of Rajib Rajkhowa, were killed on the spot when ULFA cadres sprayed them with bullets from automatic weapons near Eeli cinema at Jorhat.[14] On 16 September 1987, unidentified gunmen shot dead Sonitpur District Congress (I) Committee president Shri Dulal Bhuyan on Dandiram Road in Tezpur town. Lekhan Lahon, then president of District Congress of Lakhimpur, was shot dead during the early period of ULFA's insurgency. According to the report, the assailants were suspected to be the members of the ULFA.[15] On 23 July 1990, Rohiteswar Saikia, younger brother of Hiteswar Saikia, the former chief minister of Assam, fell to the bullets of the suspected ULFA militants.

*Between state and the insurgents* 173

But it was only after the killing of Manabendra Sarma, the son of a prominent freedom fighter and a man of impeccable political career, that the state witnessed unprecedented protests against the insurgents. Nagen Neog, then a cabinet minister of Hiteswar Saikia ministry, was also killed along with his bodyguards at Golaghat on the eve of the 1996 assembly election.

The biggest blow to the AGP came when Nagen Sarma, the then PWD and forest minister, and four others were killed in a bomb blast detonated by the banned ULFA with a remote-controlled device at around 1.55 p.m. near Nalbari on 28 February 2000.[16] During this period, the liberation wing of CPI (ML) that extended its ideological support to the cause of the ULFA in the initial phase also came under the latter's attack when the party decided to contest the Lok Sabha poll of 1998, boycotted by the ULFA. As a result, Anil Baruah, its candidate from Dibrugarh constituency, was shot dead on 11 February 1998. In a similar poll-related violence, Jayanta Dutta, the BJP candidate from Dibrugarh assembly constituency, was killed by the ULFA on 1 May 2001. During AGP's second term, there were attacks on the lives of many of its ministers like Chandra Mohan Patowari, Hiranya Konwar, Joinath Sarma and Biraj Sarma.

There are many other acts of violence which went unreported but are still fresh in popular memory. Above instances show complete disrespect to right to life, human dignity and political freedom which is very much required in a democratic country like India. Although the ULFA was held responsible for such killings, the state also cannot abdicate its responsibility to protect the human rights.

## Denial of rights to the lives of the men in uniform

As ULFA had strengthened its position during the late 1980s, it started targeting the police. The ULFA emerged as a parallel law enforcing agency, resulting in demoralising the state's police forces. The ULFA carried out a series of attacks on the police officials against whom its cadres harboured a grouse and it was quite successful in breaking the confidence of the police in that period. Three brutal attacks on the security personnel and their families are analysed here.

On 10 September 1989 at about 8.30 p.m., the ULFA shot dead the wife of the Superintendent of Police, Dibrugarh, A. K. Mullick. The personal security officer, Sri Ramnath Singh, and the driver, Banikanta Handique, also died in the attack. Mullick was not in the car. His two children, who were also in the car, however had a narrow escape. According to the report Mullick's wife and the other two were brutally killed by the miscreants when they were coming back from Tinsukia to Dibrugarh.[17]

174  *Dilip Gogoi and Uddipan Dutta*

Similarly, on 29 July 1990, Daulat Singh Negi, Superintendent of Police, Dibrugarh District, his PSO and the driver were gunned down by the ULFA activists at Lahoal in Dibrugarh district at around 3 p.m. He had earlier held the posts of Special Superintendent, CID, at Guwahati and SP (City) Guwahati. It may be mentioned here that by this time the situation had changed completely and there was an all-pervading influence of the ULFA in Assam. As obvious from the reports it was an act of revenge on the part of the ULFA and Negi's dealings with the 'people' was described as 'tyrannical' in a statement issued by its 'Publicity Secretary' of the ULFA, Siddhartha Phukan, on 10 August 1990. It was alleged that he had tortured Hirokjyoti Mahanta, one of the top leaders of the ULFA, in police custody and Mahanta vowed revenge[18] as reported across the media. The ULFA kidnapped H K L Das, the General Manager of IOC, his son and the driver on 16 July 1990 and bargained the release of Mahanta and two of his accomplices. On 28 July 1990 the hostage drama came to an end with the release of the three ULFA leaders, Hirakjyoti Mahanta, Anadar Thakuriya and Amrit Rabha, by the state government. On 29 July, the hostages were released by the ULFA and within minutes after the release of the hostages the SP was shot dead in Dibrugarh. Home Minister Bhrigu Kumar Phukan gave his resignation the same day owning his moral responsibility of the killing of Negi.[19]

On 3 September 1990, the in-charge of Laluk Police Outpost, Sub-Inspector, Sri Atul Sarma, was gunned down at Laluk Tiniali in Lakhimpur District around 4 p.m. According to reports, the assailants had come in a blue Maruti car.[20] Similarly, Nitya Dutta (SP Fire Service, Guwahati) was killed on 27 October 1991 while having food in a restaurant with family members. The militants also gunned down Lt Col. Devendar Tyagi while he was making a private visit to the Kamakhya Temple in Guwahati on 28 April 1996. Rabikant Singh, S.P. Tinsukia, also laid his life at the hands of militants on 18 May 1996. There are many other victims from the men in uniform who had to lay their lives either directly fighting the militants or while not in duties.

## Suppression of freedom of expression and attack on media

The media, the fourth estate of democracy, is also not free from suppression and is constantly under attack from both the militant and the state apparatus in Assam for the last three decades. Both the state and the non-state actors tried to gag the media and upon resistance from the journalists both acted rather violently. Way back in 1990, ULFA for the first time tried to suppress the freedom of expression. In a notice issued on 25 July 1990,

*Between state and the insurgents* 175

ULFA warned the press and the audio-visual communication media not to publish any news in connection with the organisation, without its prior written permission from its Central Publicity Wing. The notice was signed by Hiren Pathak, the Commander of the ULFA of Kamrup district. It warned that violation of the directive by any journalist, interviewer, commentator or anyone connected with the news will be considered as the enemy of the people of Assam and would be awarded the death penalty. The warning should come into effect with the receipt of the statement, the ULFA said.[21] However the ULFA partially lifted the ban on 10 August 1990. According to the report, the ULFA had clarified that it had not imposed any ban on the publication of objective or relevant news item concerning the organisation, but prior permission has to be taken only for publication of analytical articles about the ULFA. A statement dated 10 August by the Central Publicity Secretary Siddhartha Phukan said that the organisation regretted the misunderstanding created by the 25 July 1990 statement of the organisation on the issue. Elaborating on the policy of the ULFA towards newspapers and magazines, Phukan said that the ULFA had observed that a section of the newspapers and magazines of the state had been indulging in a planned 'counter revolutionary' propaganda under the cover of dissemination of news. In the statement, the Publicity Secretary of the ULFA categorically accused the magazine *Sutradhar* of spreading canards against the organisation in the name of journalism. Moreover, Phukan said pessimistic observations of a section of intellectuals in their analytical writings about the ULFA were affecting the 'revolutionary spirit' of the people. He said that the primary obligation of the ULFA was towards 'revolution' and all democratic values would be guided by the 'revolution' only. So, he stressed that they would not allow the 'revolution' to be affected by 'counter revolutionary propaganda'.[22]

Although the publicity secretary withdrew the diktat later on, the manifestation of this intolerant mindset was found in the killing of Kamala Saikia, a 65-year-old journalist who wrote regular columns in most of the leading newspapers of Assam. He was brutally killed by ULFA cadres on the night of 9 August 1991 after being dragged out from his residence at Melachawk, Sivsagar. ULFA leaders were miffed with late Saikia for a series of articles he had written condemning ULFA and its ideology.[23]

Media in Assam, particularly the radical faction of the print media often engaging in the making of anti-establishment public opinions, also came under sharp attack from the state law enforcing agencies.[24] The state often engaged in suppressing such voices through the use of coercive laws. Such instances can be drawn from the case involving Parag Kumar Das, Ajit Kumar Bhuyan, Prakash Mahanta, Manjit Mahanta, Atanu Bhuyan and some other *mofussil* journalists. Most glaring example of the state violation

176   *Dilip Gogoi and Uddipan Dutta*

of human rights and freedom of expression is manifested in the ill treatment meted out to Parag Kumar Das for his radical views against the state and his ideological support to the cause of a sovereign Assam. Subsequently he had to lay his life at the hands of SULFA[25] assailants on 17 May 1996 for airing his views openly in the print media. Before the tragic incident, he was booked several times under draconian laws, namely TADA and NSA, along with his colleague Ajit Kumar Bhuyan and was given inhuman treatment during their detention.[26] But the government failed to prove the charges and had to release them.

## Gender dimension of human rights violations

In Assam, women and children – the most vulnerable groups in the conflict situation – are the worst sufferers particularly in the insurgency-affected areas. Due to insurgency and subsequent operations by security forces, women of Assam often have to live in a state of insecurity and anxiety. It is widely acknowledged that violence against women is an oft-used weapon of the security forces to break the morale of the insurgents and Assam was not an exception when operations were started against the ULFA by the Indian Army. Cases of rape and molestation poured in from all across the states during the army operations. Not only that, caught between the state and the insurgents, the women members became the victims of the circumstances when they had to lose their children, siblings or spouses and the responsibility of the family fall upon them. Such acts of violations and denial of rights often go unreported and unaddressed. The Guwahati High Court had to intervene on one such occasion to protect the rights of the spouses and children of the ULFA cadres who went missing during Operation All Clear in Bhutan.[27] Two early cases of army brutality are narrated here to explore the intensity of violence perpetrated against women by the state security forces.

Raju Baruah, a 20-year-old college student of Sutargaon near Gohpur in Sonitpur district, was brutally raped and killed by a group of seven army personnel on 6 October 1991. According to one report, after raping her repeatedly, the army men threw her senseless body into a pond and went away. It was her brother-in-law Kamal Barua who came to the spot and pulled her out from the pond and took her to Dhalpur hospital, where she was declared dead. The post-mortem report testified this barbarous act of the men in the uniform. In another incident of 16 October 1991 at Khowdang village near Naoboisha of Lakhimpur District, Bhanimai Dutta, a 14-year-old girl, was gang raped and killed by a group of the Indian Army. According to one report, on that day, the army suddenly cordoned of the residence of Mukuta Dutta, father of Bhanimai Dutta, and picked

*Between state and the insurgents* 177

his son Babul Dutta up to their vehicle by beating him mercilessly. Seeing that, Mukuta Dutta and his wife rushed to the gate to bar the army personnel from taking Babul away. At that very moment, three army personnel entered the house and barbarously raped 14-year-old Bhanimai repeatedly one after another. When Mukuta and his wife returned back from the army vehicle where Babul was kept, they saw the army personnel leaving their house in a hurry, then both entered the house and surprisingly discovered the dress-less body of Bhanimai on the bed wet with blood. After a while she died. The army men even blocked the post-mortem of Bhanimai up to three days. The army used force upon the doctor, who did post-mortem and forcefully took his signature in a blank paper before performing the post-mortem. Later on, after three days the raping was proved only by counting the barbarous marks on her left cheek and other private parts of the body (MASS 1998:4–5).

But the ULFA also drew public wrath when the killing of Rashmi Bora, a 16-year-old Bihu exponent, by its cadres hit the headlines on 9 June 1998. By 24 June, the ULFA came out with the statement that the organisation had awarded her death sentence. The explanation given by the ULFA was that she was physically involved with an army officer and that she acted as a spy for the army and took 30,000 rupees for providing information about the organisation. The hollowness of the claim of ULFA was exposed when the incident was dredged out by the journalists. According to one account, Rashmi, who was a very good Bihu exponent, was requested by an army major to teach his daughter Bihu dance and accordingly she had given her classes in his residence. This infuriated Govinda Das alias 'Fifty', a local ULFA cadre, who was attracted to her beauty. He threatened her and asked her not to continue her classes. Upon non-compliance, he along with his fellow cadre Deep Das kidnapped her and first claimed that the army had raped and killed her (Aditya 2002:83–84). But, when their role in kidnapping came out in open, they used the old tactic and charged Rashmi of spying against the organisation and tried to smother the public outrage. Her body was never returned back and people suspect that the kidnappers might have put her under inhuman treatment before her killing.

## Kidnappings

Kidnapping of innocent civilians taken as hostages and their subsequent killing speaks a volume about the insurgent group's complete denial of right to life and dignity. As soon as Hiteswar Saikia assumed power, several important officials working in government and public sectors were taken as hostages on 1 July 1991. Among them was Sergei Gritsenko, a Russian

## 178  *Dilip Gogoi and Uddipan Dutta*

engineer working with the Coal India Limited at Ledo in Tinsukia district. Later on, the publicity secretary of the ULFA claimed on 9 July that he got killed while trying to escape from their captivity (Deka 1998:165). Similarly, Oil and Natural Gas Corporation Limited (ONGC) engineer T. S. Raju who was also abducted along with others also got killed by the militants under mysterious circumstances.

Another victim of such act of violence was Sanjoy Ghosh, a social worker with a credible repute, who was kidnapped from the river island of Majuli and was subsequently killed on 4 July 1997.[28] It is mentionable here that AVARD-NE of which he was the secretary tried to save Majuli, the biggest river island in the world, from the danger of soil erosion, which in the course of time may lead to its extinction, with the active support of the local populace. According to one version, the local contractors, irked at his efforts to save the island with the local people, hatched a conspiracy with the local ULFA cadres to eliminate him. Accordingly, he was abducted with one of his aides and later on he was killed, although his body was never returned. This particular incident would always remain as a black spot to the credibility of the ULFA. The organisation tried to cover up the incident in the beginning and later on tried to legitimise the killing by branding him as a RAW agent. But this effort on the part of the ULFA came under severe criticism from the people of Assam.

What surfaced instead, in the two months after the abduction and killing of Ghose – secretary of the voluntary agency AVARD-NE – was a plot that was hatched months in advance; the subsequent attempts by the banned ULFA to confuse the public about the circumstances of Ghose's death in order to avert a public relations disaster and the inadvertent aid it got from the establishment in this pursuit. The Jorhat police said though the ULFA kept claiming for long that Ghose was alive and well – they were convinced that Ghose was dead by 7 July. And in the next few days, they also realised that his body would never be recovered, for between 8 and 12 July, the Brahmaputra swelled and the site where Ghose's body was dropped was under 5 feet of water. 'The currents would have swept the body away in no time', said Jorhat SP G. P. Singh.

Meanwhile, the police arrested Amrit Dutta, one of the six persons involved in Ghose's abduction. During interrogation, he confessed that Chandan Doley, a colleague of Ghose, was used by the ULFA to trap Ghose. Doley claimed that he too had been 'abducted' by the ULFA, but had 'escaped' by jumping off the boat and battling the currents to reach land. But the police rebutted his version. The police arrested 16 persons in the case, including a journalist advising the ULFA on how to launch a public relations campaign after Ghose's killing. Ghose's body has not been recovered till date and justice has been denied to his family.

*Between state and the insurgents* 179

The abduction of P. C. Ram, the executive director of the Food Corporation of India's Northeast office, on 17 April 2007 was another example of gross violation of human rights. Later he got trapped in a gun battle between the security forces and the insurgents on 12 July 2007 and subsequently got killed. This particular incident reflects the insensitivity, inefficiency and lack of professionalism in handling of the cases of abduction by the state. As reported across the local media, when the police team surrounded the house of Govinda Deka where the ULFA militants had taken shelter along with P. C. Ram, he had shouted *Mein Ram hoon, Mujhe Mat Maro* (I am Ram. Don't kill me.). Although this version of the sequence of the event is contested, still nobody can deny the fact that P. C. Ram had to lay his life in at the hands of the security forces. Unfortunately, the government has not owned moral responsibility for this act of utter negligence.

## Secret killing: a worse form of human rights violation

One of the darkest chapters in the history of human rights violation in Assam is the killing of the relatives and sympathisers of ULFA with the full state patronage, popularly known as 'Secret Killings'. There were many commonalities between the different killings that took place in the period between 1998 and 2001, and in most of the cases, the identities of the assailants were not known.

There were series of cases of killing, primarily directed against relatives of ULFA cadres by unidentified assailants to demoralise ULFA. This is popularly known as secret killing. Before occurrence of such incidents, there were some political as well as public appeal to shun the path of violence and sit in the negotiation table. Then chief minister Prafulla Mahanta publicly appealed to the ULFA and tried to persuade it through Assam *Sahitya Sabha* and *Bodo Sahitya Sabha*. Pressure was also mounted on the family members of the banned ULFA leaders to persuade them to come to the mainstream, but it did not yield in any positive outcome and subsequently a series of brutal killings took place in various parts of Assam. As evidence suggests, the government machinery, especially police forces with the help of SULFAs, executed them, which later become part of revenge against former colleagues as SULFA people were living in a state of insecurity after leaving the organisation and facing threat to their lives. This situation was exploited by some of top police officials and they designed a strategy in a similar line of Punjab by executing relatives and sympathisers of ULFA without thinking about the consequence and constitutional obligations. This state of affairs was officially confirmed when the Justice K. N. Saikia Commission Report,[29] submitted to the government of Assam, described

180   *Dilip Gogoi and Uddipan Dutta*

it as 'darkest chapter in the history of Assam'.[30] In his report Saikia Commission categorically mentions role of Prafulla Mahanta, then chief minister who was in charge of Home Department, and SULFA after examination of a series of cases, referred to the Commission. By and large, the Commission came to the conclusion with some common points of reference. The Commission observed that *each killing involved a ULFA family or ULFA related family, no charge sheet was submitted in any of the cases, executed at the dead of night except few and invariably spoke in Assamese to awaken the inmates for killing victims, the assailants were invariably armed with prohibited bores normally found with police or the militaries, the identities of the assassins were masked with black wrappers or caps, although there were police patrolling prior and posterior to the crime it did not exist at the time of the crimes reported, that the government did not pursue the cases with the seriousness these crimes entail and that no condolence message was sent or any ex-gratia payment was made by the government.* The commission coins the term 'Ulfocide' to describe the killings and infers from the nature of some crimes committed with 'remote orchestration' and the principle of 'kill and get killed'. Two important cases of extrajudicial killing of the relatives of the ULFA leaders and one attempted murder of a student wing member are cited here to comprehend the gross misuse of state power and absence of constitutional, legal and human rights of the citizens in the state at that period.

The killing of Dimba Rajkonwar, an employee of ASTC (Assam State Transport Corporation), who happened to be the elder brother of Rajib Rajkonwar alias Arabinda Rajkhowa, the chairman of the ULFA, reveals the state's policy of liquidating the close relatives of the ULFA in order to mount pressure on the leaders to come back to the 'mainstream'. Rajkonwar, an amiable personality, loved by the people of his locality, was shot dead inside the Chowkidinghee Bus Station compound of the ASTC, Dibrugarh, by unknown assassins on 11 August 1998 while he was on duty. Both police inaction and the fact that there was no reference of any other reason except being the elder brother of ULFA's chairman make it clear that the police were hand in groves with the assailants and his killing was remotely controlled by the people in power during that period.

The state barbarity against the family members of the ULFA leaders got its most cruel expression when the entire family of Dr Dharanidhar Das, the elder brother of Dipak Das alias Mithinga Doimary, the central publicity secretary, was wiped out on 11 August 1998. That day, unknown assailants killed Dr Das, his wife Rupjyoti Das, his sister Latika Das Kachari and mother Phuleswari Das. His younger brother Nitul Kachari and his son Bhaskar escaped the bullets. The circumstances leading to their killing exposes the SULFA–police nexus and the complicity of the government in power.

*Between state and the insurgents* 181

The kidnapping of Ananta Kalita from Hajo on 17 September 1999, his attempted murder and his miraculous escape in Guwahati bears the testimony of the state of affairs in Assam at that period. According to the version of Kalita, who was a member of AJYCP, was coerced by the police to join Yubo Parishad, the youth wing of AGP, the party in power. As he declined the offer, there were planned attacks on him prior to his kidnapping. His testimony that after he was kidnapped, he was taken to various police stations and reserves and that he was tortured in these places before being shot point blank below his ear, made the Commission to comment that the role of Assam Police has been akin to that of Gestapo, the secret police during the Nazi regime. Fortunately, Ananta Kalita survived as he fell down from the top of the hill where he was shot at and he reached with efforts of the AJYCP office of Maligaon to disclose his horrific tale. The identities of the 'secret killers' can be well inferred from the account of Kalita and most importantly the accusing fingers are pointed towards the state police and the surrendered ULFA militants.[31]

## Civilians as victims: ULFA's war against the state

The desperation of the ULFA to show its existence in the face of a dwindling support base got its expression when it adopted the terror tactic of killing non-political innocent civilians by planting exploded devices in the public places. In one such incident, sixteen school children, including nine girls, were killed and forty others got injured when suspected militants of the ULFA triggered a powerful blast on 15 August 2004. The children had gathered at the Dhemaji College ground in order to celebrate the Independence Day when the cadres from the banned organisation triggered off the blast.[32] The small children had to lay their lives due to the insurgent group's desperate attempt of sending the message to New Delhi about its powerful military existence. The ULFA owned the responsibility of this blast and the state security forces are yet to apprehend the culprits, thus showing their failure. The outfit also launched coordinated attacks on the Hindi-speaking Bihari community in order to incite the sentiment of the natives. In the process, around sixty-two people got killed in 2007 by the ULFA cadres. Most of the victims were daily labourers and workers of brick kiln, petty traders and roadside vendors. The string of attacks took place in Dibrugarh, Tinsukia and Sibsagar districts of Upper Assam. Similar attacks were carried out against the migrant Bihari labourers in 2002, when the ULFA tried to cash on the public upsurge towards some Bihari goons who had allegedly molested many female passengers from the region and publicly stripped off a female passenger from Mizoram. The militant

182  *Dilip Gogoi and Uddipan Dutta*

organisation carried out a series of blasts in public places, particularly the business hubs like Fancy Bazar in Guwahati where the non-Assamese traders have a major share in the business. The other town which witnessed similar attacks is Tinsukia where the connectivity through rail lines has converted the town into a business centre. But in most of the attacks the common civilians, daily wage earners and petty traders got killed and injured. In one such significant incident eleven people got killed and forty-one injured in twin blasts triggered by the ULFA in the busy Fancy Bazar and Narengi area in the year 2006.[33] The blatant attacks on the innocent civilians have created a sense of insecurity and there persists a psychological trauma among people and the state has failed completely to remove it.

## Conclusion

From the above select study of human rights abuses, one can argue that there is a gross violation of human rights perpetuated by both the state and the militants in Assam since the very inception of insurgent movement. There is no doubt that many such cases went unreported and were never properly addressed by the state agencies and civil societies. Assam police record stated that between 1991 and 2006, relating to insurgent violence in Assam, the total civilians killed were 3,076, total persons kidnapped 1,397, total security forces killed 799, total militants killed 2,146 and total detained militants 15,894.[34] Even there are a growing number of human rights violation cases in Assam registered in National Human Rights Commission. For instance, between 2001 and 2004 the total number of cases registered in the Commission was 564, revealing the disturbing trend (Lal 2005). The figures are pointers to the sense of insecurity prevailing in the state and reveal how the citizens of this part of the country are subjected to a perpetual violence acted upon both by the state and the non-state actors. But the state cannot be equated with the insurgent groups. The primary responsibility of the state is to protect and preserve the basic rights of its citizens and the basic responsibility of the state often get undermined during the counter-insurgency operations. In many cases, state actions lead to gross violation of rights in Assam and it becomes counterproductive and even multiplies the problem. During military operations, there occurs gross transgression of basic rights of the citizens, often leading to the alienation of the people. The state security forces often undermine the fact that they deal with their own people. In the name of maintaining national security, the draconian laws, which are discriminatory and inconsistent with the basic provisions of the Indian Constitution and against the international covenant on civil and political rights adopted by the UN in 1966, are invoked. These laws permit extrajudicial power to the armed forces and allow taking away

*Between state and the insurgents*   183

the rights embedded in Articles 20 and 21 which cannot be suspended even during the time of emergency. The specific clause for preventive detention under coercive laws operating in Assam reveals maximum number of violations which goes completely against the rule of law. Hence, these laws need to be repealed immediately to suit the common human rights norms to uphold human dignity and bring transparency and respect for rule of law. It is also mentionable that the violators of human rights often escape and there is no significant evidence of conviction against the offenders. Thus justice is denied to the victim families and the state cannot abdicate its responsibility. Due to ignorance and lack of effective national and international media coverage and proper vigilance and activism among civil society organisations, the state often tends to violate human rights in the name of national security by using coercive laws, unregulated use of force and occasional use of vigilante groups like SULFA. Therefore, independent and neutral institutions like Human Rights Commission need to be strengthened with sufficient power to investigate and monitor the human rights norms in conflict zones. The Indian state must adopt a democratic strategy, instead of a militaristic, move along with masses, and engage itself with the root causes of the problem and respect and preserve the rights and dignity of its own citizens.

## Notes

1 India has signed and ratified two main Covenants on Human Rights – the International Covenant on Economic, Social and Cultural Rights (ICESCR) and the International Covenant on Civil and Political Rights (ICCPR), adopted by the UN General Assembly on 16 December 1966. The other major international conventions that India has signed and ratified include International Conventions on the Elimination of All Forms of Racial Discriminations (ICERD) 1969, Convention against the Elimination of All Forms of Discrimination against Women (CEDAW) 1981 and Convention on Rights of the Child (CRC) 1990. In 1997, India signed the Convention against Torture and Other Cruel, Inhuman or Degrading Treatment or Punishment (CAT) but it is yet to be ratified.
2 Such as Civil Rights Act 1955, Dowry Prohibition Act 1961, Bonded Labour System (Abolition) Act 1976, Child Labour (Prohibition and Regulation) Act 1986, Schedule Castes and Schedule Tribes (Prevention of Atrocities) Act 1989, Right to Information Act 2005 etc.
3 In 1997, this structure was created by the government of Assam by a notification on 24 January 1997 in order to co-ordinate among the civil administration, state police department, paramilitary forces and the army in the operations against the militant group.
4 US Department of State, *Country Reports on Human Rights Practices for 1992, p. 1136*, mentioned in *Asia Watch*, Vol. 5, Issue 7 (18 April), 1993.
5 For detail see *Asia Watch*, Vol. 5, Issue 7 (18 April), 1993.

184 *Dilip Gogoi and Uddipan Dutta*

6 *Namgharia* is the person who takes care of Namghar, the worship place of the Vaishnavite Faith. He is often revered by the villagers for his holy duty.

7 *The Telegraph*, 15 April 2008.

8 'Lakhipatharot Puti Thuwa Pundhorota Mritodeh Uddhar'. *Dainik Asom*, 5 December 1990.

9 An illegal court of law that punishes people unfairly. ULFA built its public image instituting Kangaroo courts in its initial phase.

10 The group under the leadership of Bhaskar Nandi.

11 The 1983 election was boycotted by AASU as a part of the campaign against the influx of illegal migrants and it was held against the will of a large section of the people in the Brahmaputra valley to avert a constitutional crisis.

12 'Gulibiddho Prakton Manti Dihingiyar Mrityu' (Bullet-ridden Ex-Minister Dihingiya Died). *Dainik Asom*, 21 February 1986.

13 *Dainik Asom*, 19 September 1986.

14 'Durbrittor Hatot Prakton Mantrir Putra Nihot' (The Son of the Former Minister Killed by the Miscreants). *Dainik Asom*, 10 January 1987.

15 'Sonitpuror Congress Sabhapatik Hatya' (Sonitpur Congress President Shot Dead). *Dainik Asom*, 17 September 1987.

16 'ULFA Kills Assam Minister'. *The Tribune*, 28 February 2000.

17 *Ajir Asom*, 12 September 1989, on front page as 'Atotayir Guli Salonat Police Bixoyar Patnike Dahri Nihoto Tini' (Three, Including the Wife of the Police Officer, Killed by the Assailants).

18 Editorial *Dainik Asom*, 31 July 1990.

19 For details see *Dainik Asom*, 30 July 1990.

20 *Dainik Asom* on 4 November 1990 as 'Police Bixoyak Guliyai Hotya' (Police Official Shot Dead).

21 'Prasar Madhyamor Lokoloi ULFAr Nirdex' (ULFA's Directive to Media). *Dainik Asom*, 27 July 1990.

22 'Niropekkhyo' Batori Paribexonot Nixedhagya Arop Kora Nai – ULFAr Bibritti' (No Ban on 'Objective' Reporting – ULFA's Statement). *Dainik Asom*, 13 August 1990.

23 To cover up its brutality, ULFA engaged itself in a malign campaign calling Kamala Saikia a spy of Indian government. The official position of the ULFA was cleared in *Freedom* (1 February 2006 issue), the mouthpiece of ULFA, that termed Kamala Saikia as an informer for security forces and also accused him of being corrupt. This claim of ULFA was vehemently opposed by the journalist fraternity of Assam.

24 There was a rise of radical vernacular print media during the 1990s, often exposing the corruption in public life.

25 In spite of a CBI inquiry into the case, the accused of his killings are yet to be brought before the court of law.

26 'No end in sight: Human rights violations in Assam'. 18 April, Vol. 5 Issue 7, *Asia Watch*, 1993.

27 A two-member bench of the Gauhati High Court of Justice A.H. Saikia and Justice Hrishikesh Roy had on 12 April 2007 directed the Centre to file the affidavit on 2 May. The court intervention came when the wife of an ULFA leader, Shyamoli Gogoi, had moved the court, demanding the whereabouts of her husband and the other ULFA and NDFB cadres, untraced since 'Operation All Clear' by the Royal Bhutan Army on its soil in December 2003.

*Between state and the insurgents* 185

28 *India Today*, 22 September 1997.
29 The Justice (retd) K. N. Saikia Commission of Inquiry was constituted in 2003 by the government of Assam to investigate select cases of Secret Killings.
30 *The Hindu*, 18 November 2007.
31 For more details see *K. N. Saikia Commission Report*, 2006/2007.
32 *The Hindu*, 16 August 2004.
33 *The Hindu*, 6 November 2006.
34 As presented by Khagen Sarma, IGP, SB, Assam, in the seminar *Terrorism: Emerging Trends and Need for Strategies* held in Guwahati on 7–8 November 2006 organised by Assam Police in collaboration with MHA and BPR&D.

## References

Aditya, Paragmoni. 2002. *Swadhinata: Saponaru Dithak*. Guwahati: Niyor Prakashan.
Asia Watch. 1993. 'No End in Sight: Human Rights Violations in Assam', 5(7).
Basu, D. D. 2002. (Reprint) *Introduction to the Constitution of India*. Nagpur: Wadhwa and Company.
Chaman, Lal. 2005. 'Human Rights Situation in the North-East', *Dialogue*, 5(4).
Deka, Kanaksen. 1998. *ULFAr Swadhin Asom*. Guwahati: Dispur Print House.
Justice (retd) K. N. Saikia Commission of Enquiry Report on *Secret Killings*, submitted to the Government of Assam, 2006/2007.
MASS. 1998. *Rape: The Hatred Weapon of Indian Armed Forces*.
Prabhakar, M. S. 2007. 'ULFA and Politics of Separatism', *The Hindu*, April 17.
Saikia, Chaw P. 2005. '*Napahoru Tumak Dimbeswar*'. In Krishnakanta Gogoi and Dimbeswar Bora (eds), *Tai Ahomar Pratham Jatiya Swahid, Chaw Dimbeswar Gogoi*.
South Asia Human Rights Documentation Centre. 2006. *Introducing Human Rights: An Overview Including Issues of Gender Justice, Environmental and Consumer Law*. New Delhi: Oxford University Press.
Terrorist and Disruptive Activities (Prevention) Act (TADA), 1987, Government of India.
The Arms Forces (Special Powers) Act, 1958, Government of India.
The National Security Act (NSA), 1980, Government of India.
*Universal Declaration of Human Rights* (UDHR) adopted by UN General Assembly, 10 December 1948.

# 11 The ULFA and Indian state

## Role of civil society in conflict resolution

*Akhil Ranjan Dutta*

Ethnically polarised state of Assam, a constituent unit of Indian federalism, has both ethnically defined civil societies as well as a trans-ethnic civil society which may be called the civil society of Assam. Historically, the civil society in Assam evolved in the domain of literature and education, and not in the economic domain to counterpose the state as is the case with the Western world. In the post-colonial era the civil society played a significant role as a rallying point in asserting voices and manifesting grievances on issues like language, medium of instructions and also control over resources and very particularly on the issue of illegal migration to the state of Assam. The civil society in Assam in most instances was overtaken by collective passion and therefore it has not been a domain of free exchange of ideas and critical thinking in many instances. In more than three decades of United Liberation Front of Assam (ULFA) and Government of India (GoI) conflict, the civil society has undergone different experiences – from being overtaken by collective passion for the cause raised by ULFA to complete subjugation and marginalisation under coercion both by the Indian state and the ULFA and to that of gradual revival as a critical domain to question both the state and ULFA.

The chapter is an attempt to explore the role of trans-ethnic civil society in Assam as a broker of peace in case of the three-decade-long conflict between the ULFA and GoI.

## Civil society in Assam

It is important to argue that a domain of civil society in liberal sense, supposedly independent of the state, entrepreneurial in nature and secular and universal in approach, does not exist in post-colonial societies. These societies do have a domain called civil society, which are, however, unique in nature. Claiming to be non-political, however, the civil societies in such contexts are mostly engaged in political projects as is the case with

# The ULFA and Indian state   187

Northeast India today. Sanjib Baruah, therefore, argues that Assamese sub-nationalist politics 'originates in and is sustained by civil society and not by political society' (Baruah 2005:134). The civil societies in the post-colonial situations may not have parallel presence to that of the state. Here, whereas the state with its institutional apparatuses – both political and representational as well as coercive apparatuses – may acquire more or less a uniform character, the civil societies, however, may be fragmented. These fragmentations, in a situation like India, may be on diverse fronts – regional, ethnic, cultural, linguistic as well as religious. In other words, the civil society here may be sectarian in nature compared to the relatively universal and secular nature of the state. Civil society in such a situation acts as the domain of collective expression of dissent, mostly against the state which has political implications in the long term.

Being a multi-ethnic society, Assam has number of civil societies across ethnic lines. However, when one refers to civil society in Assam it means the trans-ethnic domain which represents the broader and composite society in Assam. However, it is now mostly confined to the Brahmaputra valley and its presence in the ethically concentrated areas within the valley too is marginal. For example, in the present-day BTAD, it is the Bodo civil society which has its dominance. Same may be the case in Karbi Anglong. But the unique thing about the trans-ethnic civil society in Assam is that it has the potential to give representation to a number of ethnic communities too, which is not the case with the ethnically defined civil societies. It is in this sense that we are using the term 'trans-ethnic civil society' in Assam. It is not dominated by a particular ethnic community, although historically it has been dominated by the caste Hindu Assamese. Assamese is the dominant language in Assam and it is also the lingua franca in the state.

The ULFA also represents a trans-ethnic struggle in the state of Assam against the Indian state. However, apart from the ULFA, almost all ethnic communities have their own militant outfits engaged in fighting against the Indian state. The claim of the ULFA to liberate Assam from the occupation of the Indian state, therefore, is contested by those ethnic outfits who have also been struggling for liberation of their territories across ethnic lines.

These two issues are relevant when one discusses the role of civil society in Assam in the context of ULFA–GoI conflict.

Historically the civil society in Assam also acted as a domain of manifestation of grievances against the state, particularly against the Union Government. That is how, the civil society in Assam was almost overtaken both by the wave of the AASU-steered anti-foreigners movement and ULFA-steered armed struggle for Assam's independence. Although the

188  *Akhil Ranjan Dutta*

civil society did not endorse the path of violence pursued by ULFA for its proclaimed goal of Assam's independence, a comprehensive critical voice against the militancy and violence pursued by them has been almost absent. While discussing the role of the civil society in Assam as a broker of peace in ULFA–GoI conflict, these inherent limitations and contradictions need to be focused on.

The ULFA has been both regimented and crude in its approach to the critics even from within the Assamese society. It almost believed that it is through barrel of guns that the revolution will take place and therefore did not bother for a revolutionary mass culture. It even considered assassinations as means of campaign of revolution. In the long run such a regimented nature of ULFA marginalised the voice of the civil society. This in the long run also caused the decay of ULFA, its vulnerability to state repression and manipulation, division within the rank and file of ULFA and erosion of peoples' sympathy even for the 'sacrifices' made by it. It is in this context of ULFA's growing vulnerability and fragmentation that the civil society either was allowed to or it carved out a space and endeavoured to play a role for facilitating negotiation between ULFA and GoI for peace.

## Debating ULFA in the domain of civil society: a short sketch

Parag Das (1961–96) was one of the leading ideologues of *Swadhin Asom*. A master's degree holder in Economics from the Delhi School of Economics, Delhi University, Das was the editor of *Budhbar* (a weekly published on Wednesday) since its inception in 1989 and also edited and published a magazine called *Aagan* since 1994, joined as an Executive editor of a popular vernacular daily *Asomiya Pratidin* in 1995 and was assassinated in May 1996. During the very short span of his active public life, particularly as a columnist and a journalist, which was not even a decade, Parag Das emerged as the most influencing ideologue of ULFA's armed struggle for independence. Detained under the National Security Act in 1991 and again under TADA in 1993, Parag Das wrote and published *Swadhinatar Prastab* (Proposal of Independence) in 1993, the most significant book that forcefully argues the legitimacy behind ULFA's *Swadhin Asom*. His other books like *Nishiddha Kalam Aru Ananya* (Banned Pen and Others), *Rashtradruhir Dinalipi* (The Traitor's Diary), *Mok Swadhinata Lage* (I Ask for Independence) and *Swadhin Asomor Arthaniti* (Economy of Independent Assam) etc. also forcefully justified the cause for independence. He, however, became critical about ULFA's activities once ULFA started indulging in indiscriminate killing etc. in the name of 'struggle'.

*The ULFA and Indian state* 189

In *Swadhinatar Prasab* (1993), Parag Das legitimised Assam's right to independence primarily on four counts: the provisions of UN Charters, Covenants and Declarations from time to time which categorically justifies the rights of nationalities for self-determination; cultural and ethnic uniqueness of the people of Northeast India justified by anthropological exploration; illegality both in Yandabo Treaty, 1826, and Transfer of Power, 1947 through which Assam was made a part of British India and Independent India respectively and finally the persistence of colonial interest in Independent India.

Das argues that Assam fulfils all requirements identified by international covenants and declarations to constitute itself into an independent state. He also refers to various resolutions of the United Nations to show how the Indian state has violated those resolutions by forcibly suppressing the inalienable rights of self-determination of the people of Assam. He time and again referred to certain provisions of the UN Charter to bring legitimacy to his proposal for independence of Assam. He referred to the resolution No 2625 (XXV) of the United Nations General Assembly accepted unanimously on 24 October 1970 which states: 'by virtue of the principle of equal rights and self-determination of peoples enshrined in the charter, all peoples have the right freely to determine, without external interference, social and cultural development, and every state has the duty to respect the right in accordance with the provisions of the charter' (Das 1993:15). Das has pointed out that the Indian state, which has also formally agreed upon to abide by the provisions of right to self-determination as per international laws, however, provides distorted interpretation of it. According to the Indian state, the UN provisions on right to self-determination is applicable only in case of independent states, i.e. a state can be accused of violating UN provisions on right to self-determination if it violates the right to self-determination of another independent state. Das argues that as per the position of the Indian state the subjugated nationalities of an independent state cannot demand the UN-approved right to self-determination. 'Therefore, the Indian state has always been declaring the justified right to self-determination raised by the common people of Kashmir, Nagaland, Assam or Punjab as illegal' (Das 1993:15).

Parag Das also pointed out that the Part Eleven of the UN Charter recognises the demand for right to self-determination of the non-self-governing regions and nationalities as fundamental rights. Under different provisions of this Part of the UN Charter any non-self-governing nationalities legally may demand the right to self-determination and can appeal for intervention of the UN towards fulfilment of this demand. There are two critical issues here: first, the definition of a non-self-governing nationality and second, can Assam claim itself to be a non-self-governing nationality

190 *Akhil Ranjan Dutta*

and demand the rights recognised under Part Eleven of the UN Charter? It is here Das refers to the UN General Assembly Resolution No 1541 (XV) as adopted on 15 December 1960 which defines non-self-governing areas as 'A territory is prima facie non self governing if it is both geographically separate and ethnically distinct from the country administering it' (Das 1993:17). Parag Das asserted that the Indian state also voted in favour of this resolution in the UN General Assembly. It was on the basis of this resolution that India advocated for the independence of East Pakistan in the 1602nd meeting of the UN Security Council held on 4 December 1971. Based on this position of Indian state, Das argues: 'As India has practically recognised the theory of non self governing territory, therefore there should not be any problem in considering the applicability of this resolution in case of Assam' (Das 1993:17).

Assam is both geographically separate and ethnically distinct from rest of India which the UN resolution emphasised upon while defining a non-self-governing territory. Till 1826 Assam had no relation at all with India. Although Assam was forcibly made a part of British India through the Yandabo Treaty, the nationalist movement did not recognise the existence of Assam till 1920. Although the Transfer of Power Act, 1947, made Assam a constituent unit of the Indian state, geographically it still continues to be separate from rest of India. It is only through a 60-kilometre width corridor that a geographically separate Assam is artificially connected with India (Das 1993:18).

Nibaran Borah, an ideologue of Assam's anti-foreigners movement, also justified the cause for Assam's independence. In one of his articles published in 1998 titled *Swadhin Asom: Sambhab Ne* (Independent Assam: Is it possible?), Borah had provided a sketch of independent Assam to be called Federal Republic of Assam and asserted: 'We have to place our demand for secession before the government of India or Indian Parliament on the same logic which Mrs Gandhi and her government placed before the world for the creation of Independent Bangladesh. The logic applies to Assam and the North-Eastern State more appropriately.'

Hiren Gohain, the leading intellectual and a reputed columnist in Assam, has been very critical about ULFA's demand for sovereignty since ULFA's emergence as a visible force in the state particularly since the late 1980s onwards. Gohain has provided the most consistent and comprehensive critique of ULFA's demand for sovereignty. Gohain has been so critical of ULFA that he called the ULFA episode in Assam as *Andhajugar Agamon* – Coming of a Dark Age (Gohain 2011:183–209).

Gohain's critique of ULFA is centred on a wide range of issues – political ideology, strategy, leadership and mass base of ULFA. Gohain was one of the leading figures behind the platform called *Asom Gantantrik Nagarik*

*The ULFA and Indian state*  191

*Sanstha* (Assam Democratic Citizens' Association) in the early 1990s and *Sanmilita Jatiya Abhibarttan* (United National Convention) in 2010, which came into being to critically engage with ULFA. On the first occasion it was indiscriminate killing, atrocities, kidnapping and extortion of the ULFA that brought a number of concerned citizens together to take a collective stand against the ULFA's unjust methods and atrocities. On the second occasion it aimed at facilitating a dialogue between the pro-talk ULFA leadership led by its president (but, opposed by the C-in-C) and that of GoI in the backdrop of the ULFA's growing fragmentation, erosion of support base and arrest of the top ULFA leadership.

## Civil society's engagement with ULFA vis-à-vis Indian state

The role of civil society in Assam has received a boost in the recent years with its visible role in facilitating a process of dialogue between the rebel leaders of ULFA and the GoI. Although the initiative by People's Consultative Group (PCG) during 2005–06 did not yield into a process of negotiation between the parties in conflict, i.e. ULFA and the GoI, it opened up a channel of communication. The recent initiative by *Sanmilita Jatiya Abhibarttan* (SJA) to bring the rebel leaders of ULFA to the negotiating table with the GoI for resolving the fundamental issues raised by ULFA has yielded to a significant outcome with the Government of India releasing the top jailed leaders of the ULFA under bail, which in turn facilitated the initiation of a dialogue between the pro-talk ULFA section led by its Chairman Arabinda Rajkhowa and that of the GoI, whereas the hardliner faction of ULFA led by its Commander in Chief (C-in-C) Paresh Baruah denounces the talk initiatives calling them to surrender to the Indian state. However, the ongoing dialogue brought about some peace to the violence-prone state of Assam. These apparent successes on the part of the civil society as a broker of peace, however, need to be critically debated as the civil society in Assam in three decades of ULFA–GoI conflict has not comprehensively and critically debated the core issue of *Swadhin Asom* (Independent Assam) raised by the ULFA.

Organised response of the civil society to ULFA–GoI conflict has passed through different phases during the last two decades or so. These may be divided into three phases:

a  The initiative of *Asom Ganatrantik Nagarik Sangstha* – Early 1990s
b  Initiative by People's Consultative Group (PCG) – 2005–06
c  Initiative by *Sanmilita Jatiya Abhibarttan* (SJA) – 2010 onwards

## 192 *Akhil Ranjan Dutta*

## The initiative of *Asom ganatrantik nagarik sangstha*: early 1990s

The first organised challenge to the ULFA came from the URMCA (United Reservation Movement Council of Assam). The URMCA stood against the de-tribalisation theory of the ULFA, which the URMCA perceived as a threat to the rights of self-determination of the tribal and indigenous people of Assam and also a reflection of Assamese chauvinism. The URMCA organised a series of meetings and also took out processions. The ULFA retaliated by killing Dimbeswar Gogoi of Tai Ahom Students Union. It did not really make the URMCA weak, but more steadfast against ULFA (Gohain 2011:189–90).

It was at this juncture that the platform called *Asom Ganatrantik Nagarik Sangstha* (Assam Democratic Citizens' Association) came into being. Hiren Gohain and *Anwesha*, Guwahati, a socio-cultural organisation which was also publishing a magazine called *Deuka*, were instrumental behind this platform. The aim was to bring all democratic people who opposed both the anarchic activities and the political objective of ULFA. The initiative resulted in convening a state-level convention against the indiscriminate atrocities of ULFA. It was amidst these developments that President's rule was imposed in Assam on 28 November 1990 and the AGP government in the state led by Prafulla Kumar Mahanta was dismissed. The army also launched an operation called Operation Bajrang to flush out ULFA ultras. Operation Bajrang led to the arrest of around 500 suspected to be ULFA activists and it continued until April 1991 when fresh elections were announced to the state assembly. Gohain has pointed out that the people being killed were not members of the ULFA, although some had connection with ULFA with past acquaintances.

The atrocities and coercion by the army put new challenges to the organisers of the convention. It almost had turned peoples' attention from ULFA's indiscriminate killing and atrocities to that of the Indian state's coercion. Coercion by the army had also appeared to have brought some legitimacy to the ULFA's cause. However, the human grave of 15 persons found in the Lakhipathar camp of ULFA on 5 December 1990 and a few others in other places of Assam during the operation by the army equally exposed the inhumanity in ULFA. Therefore, it was a critical moment and the convention, originally aimed to address the anarchism and indiscriminate atrocities of ULFA, also had to address the coercion by the army.

The convention took place on 16 December 1990 in the District Library, Guwahati. A number of prominent political leaders, including former chief ministers of the state Sarat Chandra Sinha and Golap Borbora and veteran freedom fighter Bijay Chandra Bhagabati, participated in the convention.

*The ULFA and Indian state* 193

Hiren Gohain pointed out that all participants condemned the violation of rights of the citizens by the powerful armed forces in conflicts (particularly between the army and the insurgents); however, there were differences on who need to be blamed at the first instance for the whole situation in Assam. The important resolutions adopted in the convention were the following:

a   The problem confronted by Assam be solved by the Government of India by dialogue rather than only by military means
b   An appeal be issued to identify and defeat the communal forces engaged in creating division among the people in the state
c   An appeal be issued to the newspapers not to be biased on reporting and to abide by the ethics of journalism
d   A committee be constituted by the convention to enquire into the controversial issues in a comprehensive manner. (Gohain 2011:196)

It is clear from the resolutions that the convention did not singlehandedly condemn the atrocities by the ULFA, although it was the growing atrocities of the ULFA which brought into being the convention.

The speakers had raised a variety of issues and suggested to look into multiple dimensions while addressing the present stalemate. For example, eminent journalist M. S. Prabhakar raised the issue of continuance of TADA and AFSPA; Prabinchandra Kalita from Rongyia pointed out the all-pervasive corruption and asked: 'why the youths victimized by corruption should not be revolutionary?' Some speakers also raised the issue of nationality question in Assam and suggested that without a solution to this question violence will not end. It was also asserted that to defeat terrorism the black laws in Northeast India must be scrapped. Some speakers also suggested that the state will never surrender to the armed struggle and therefore, insurgency only subjects the common masses to a variety of atrocities. One of the conveners of the convention, Dhiren Bezbarua, commented that the ULFA was only the symptom and not the disease. The disease lies in 3,000 bureaucrats acquiring the power to point their fingers against three crore population. It is these bureaucrats who are responsible for the violation of rights of the crores of population. For Bezbaruah, presidential rule cannot be a cure to this disease (Gohain 2011:196–98).

The political scenario in the state was also changing fast. On 1 July 1991 the new Congress government led by Hiteswar Saikia was sworn in. On the same day the ULFA kidnapped 15 people, including officials of the ONGC (Oil and Natural Gas Commission), an Additional Secretary in the Assam government's General Administration Department, A. S. Srivastava, and a Russian national Sergei Gritsenko, an engineer working for the state-owned

194 *Akhil Ranjan Dutta*

Coal India. ULFA offered to release the hostages only if twenty-four hardcore ULFA members were set free. Hiteswar Saikia invited the representatives of the civil society to explore the possible way out to end the crisis. And it is through the consultation with the civil society representatives that the state government declared 'general amnesty' and initially released eleven of the hardcore militants along with a total of nearly 400 ULFA suspects who did not have serious cases pending against them. Amidst the crises ULFA killed two of the hostages, the Russian national and an ONGC engineer, T.S. Raju. The state government released twenty-one of the twenty-four militants whose release was sought by the ULFA. But ULFA refused to reciprocate it by releasing all the hostages. It was at this juncture that Operation Rhino was launched in the state on 15 September 1991. The operation continued till January 1992 when it was temporarily suspended following the prospect of talks between the ULFA and the Union Government. On 11 January five ULFA leaders, Siddhartha Phukan, Anup Chetia, Kalpajyoti Neog, Robin Neog and Pradip Gogoi, met Prime Minister Narasimha Rao in New Delhi with written direction from the ULFA president Arabinda Rajkhowa. These leaders assured the government that they will abide by the constitution and shun violence once the dialogue process moved in a positive direction. In the meeting where the Chief Minister Hiteswar Saikia was also present, the Union Government gave a green signal to start the preliminary preparation for a dialogue. Accordingly, the Union Government declared its decision of ceasefire from 14 January to 1 February. On 15 February the ULFA General Secretary Golap Baruah assured that if the government could ensure a peaceful solution his organisation would shun violence (Talukdar and Kalita 2011:112). Two meetings of ULFA General Council were held after this meeting between ULFA leadership and the prime minister where majority of the members supported the move for a dialogue. Both the meetings, the crucial one being held on 20 February held in Assam–Arunachal border, were avoided by Commander in Chief Paresh Baruah. Through his representative, he, however, opposed any move for a dialogue. The political wing led by the President Arabinda Rajkhowa, although, was in favour of moving ahead with the dialogue, but Rajkhowa restrained himself due to the opposition of the chief of the military wing. The move for dialogue collapsed prematurely and the army operations were resumed in April 1992 in six districts of Assam.

It is at this juncture that ULFA became a divided house with some sections favouring dialogue and some sections opposed to it. The government played with this division within the ULFA and offered rehabilitation packages to those who opted to come out of ULFA's fold. On 31 March 1992 15 leaders of ULFA, including the Publicity Secretary Siddhartha Phukan, issued a press release declaring the formal division in ULFA. This resulted

The ULFA and Indian state  195

in the birth of SULFA (Surrendered ULFA), a phenomenon that created a new phase of terror in the history of troubled politics in the state. These surrendered cadres were used by the security forces for counter operations and with no time another dark phase of history descended in the state and witnessed the phenomena of secret killings.

Once ULFA became a divided house, the clash and conflict between the two factions, i.e. ULFA and SULFA, also intensified. The state started using SULFA in its game plan to wipe out the ULFA. A dark phase descended in the history of Assam known as the age of secret killings. Although through the 1996 Assembly election the AGP under the leadership of Prafulla Kumar Mahanta came to power, the situation did not improve, rather deteriorated. Secret killings continued till 2001. During this period the relatives of ULFA as well as human rights activists were targeted. Many people disappeared, whose dead and decomposed bodies were discovered in paddy fields, banks of rivers and forests etc. The worst of the secret killings occurred at night on 11 August 1998 in which the mother, brother, sister-in law and the sister of ULFA's central Publicity Secretary Mithinga Daimary were killed by the secret killers in the residence at Barama. On the same day brother of the ULFA's chairman was also gunned down in Dibrugarh. The government also used TADA in an indiscriminate way to send the critical voices to the jail. Estimate suggests that between 1991 and 1998 a total 1,237 of cases were registered under TADA in session courts. Out of the 296 resolved cases only 14 persons were convicted in 4 cases (Talukdar and Kalita 2011:143).

Both Operation Bajrang and Operation Rhino forced the ULFA to shift its bases to the neighbouring country of Bhutan. Under the pressure of the GoI, Bhutanese authorities repeatedly appealed to the militant outfits to close their camps. It was reported that by 2003 there were around 30 militant camps with around 3,500 militants inside Bhutan. The militant outfits refused to shift their camps, which resulted in the launching of Operation All Clear by the Bhutanese Army against ULFA, KLO and NDFB in December 2003. The blueprint of the operation, of course, was prepared by the Indian Army, which provided the necessary logistics. Although the top brass of ULFA had escaped themselves and fled from Bhutan, two of its leaders – the ideologue and adviser of ULFA Bhimkanta Buragohain and its Publicity Secretary Mithinga Daimary – were arrested during the course of the operation. Although Operation All Clear was a severe setback to the ULFA, it could not write ULFA's epitaph. It was at this juncture that the ULFA committed another barbaric act by carrying out a deadly bomb blast in Dhemaji town in Assam on 15 August 2004, in which at least sixteen schoolchildren were killed and forty others were injured. This incident, which was played out both by national and regional press and electronic

196 *Akhil Ranjan Dutta*

media, invited condemnation from across all sections of the society. The ULFA was also alleged to have committed another act of violence on 25 and 26 August 2004 by setting off a chain of bomb blasts at different places all over Assam, killing seven persons and wounding ninety.

It was amidst these developments that on 20–21 September 2004 a two-day *Jatiya Mahasabha* was organised in Guwahati under the auspices of the Asom Jatiyatabadi Yuba Chatra Parishad (AJYCP). The *Mahasabha* adopted two major resolutions. The first called for the initiation of talks between the ULFA and the central and state governments, while the second called upon the ULFA to rein in its armed activities, and enter into a dialogue for the greater good of the state's people. During this period itself, it was reported that the top leadership of ULFA, including the Commander in Chief Paresh Baruah, contacted the Jnanpith awardee Mamoni Roysom Goswami and expressed its willingness for resolution of the ULFA–GoI conflict through dialogue. Goswami was urged upon to take an initiative. Accordingly, Mamoni Roysom Goswami met Prime Minister Manmohan Singh on 16 November 2004 and handed over a memorandum to him. The ULFA indicated that it was willing to sit for talks provided the Government of India did not have any preconditions and wanted the issue of sovereignty to be the core issue of the talks.

Mamoni Roysom Goswami also took the burden of carrying a formal letter of ULFA leadership addressed to the prime minister of India dated 2 February 2005 expressing its willingness to come forward for a dialogue with the GoI. The letter was handed over to the National Security Adviser Mr M. K. Narayanan by Goswami herself. In reply to the letter, the NSA, on behalf of the prime minister, wrote to Arabinda Rajkhowa, chairman, ULFA, dated 24 May 2005 that 'The Government of India is prepared to discuss core issues if the Group is willing to abjure violence'. The letter further emphasised that 'An acceptable solution can only emerge in a frank exchange of views through discussions' (PMO letter 2005: No H-4(1)/2005-NGO).

## People's Consultative Group (PCG) and peace initiative

It is against this background that the ULFA came forward for a civil society–driven approach to Indo-Assam conflict raised by the ULFA for almost three decades now. It declared the formation of a nine-member group called People's Consultative Group (PCG) on 7 September 2005 along with two Coordinators. Elaborating the rationale behind the formation of the Group, one of the members of PCG and also its Spokesperson, Arup Borbora, wrote: 'Three decades of armed conflict between the ULFA and

*The ULFA and Indian state*  197

the Government machineries have at the end of the day, left a trail of blood-bath resulting in killing of several thousands of lives. Apart from the two casualty lists of persons belonging to the parties in conflict and one list pointing a finger at the other, it has been the non-combatant civilian population that suffered the most' (Borbora 2010:9).

PCG was a nine-member group. In addition, the ULFA also officially pronounced the names of Indira Goswami (popularly known as Mamoni Raisom Goswami), Jnanpith Award winner novelist/litterateur, as the chief co-ordinator and Rebati Phukan as the co-ordinator for the PCG. The members of PCG were: Mukul Mahanta (engineer and human rights activist); Arup Borbora (senior advocate at the Gauhati High Court); Brojen Gogoi (senior corporate officer); Ajit Kumar Bhuyan (senior journalist); Haidar Hussain (editor in chief of *Asomiya Pratidin*); Hiranya Saikia (sportsperson and human rights defender); Dilip Patgiri (advisor to Asom Jatiyatabadi Yuva Chatra Parishad); Lachit Bordoloi (human rights defender and advisor to MASS) and Diganta Konwer (social activist).

PCG as a civil society entity, however, did not have the ability to debate the issue of independence sought by ULFA. It was nominated by ULFA only to prepare the ground for a possible direct negotiation between the GoI and ULFA for the resolution of three-decades-old Indo-Assam conflict. PCG on its own part neither supported, nor was opposed to, the core demand of ULFA and it was left to be argued and counter-argued in the negotiation table between the GoI and the ULFA.

The Government of India, particularly the armed establishment, did not appear to have taken the initiative of ULFA for peace through the PCG in good spirit. This was evident from the fact that within a week of the formation of the PCG, a massive counter-insurgency was launched by the Indian Army all over the Dibru-Saikhowa Reserve Forest in Tinsukia District. The incident evoked reaction from the PCG, forcing it to caution the Government of India on 14 September 2005 that 'talks and such operations cannot run simultaneously and hence the Government of India should choose either of the two'. Under PCG's initiative and with the intervention of the chief minister of Assam, who was urged upon by the PCG to do so, the army was finally withdrawn from the Dibru-Saikhowa Reserve Forest areas. It was only a month after the formation of the PCG that the GoI responded to the ULFA's initiative for peace and the PCG was invited to Delhi for a formal dialogue scheduled on 26 October 2005. The PCG appeared to have been overwhelmed to receive the invitation from the GoI. The invitation was perceived as recognition of the role of the civil society to broker peace in Assam.

The PCG had three rounds of discussion with the GoI during 2005–06. The first round was held on 26 October 2005; second Round on

198 *Akhil Ranjan Dutta*

7 February 2006 and the third round on 22 June 2006. Whereas the first round was attended by the prime minister of India, the third Round was attended by the home minister of India. National Security Adviser M. K. Narayanan was a key player in all three rounds of discussion. The PCG attempted to present a strong case for a direct dialogue between the ULFA and the GoI, putting ULFA's armed struggle in perspective. So far the PCG's initiative was at the highest level of the GoI where it appeared to have succeeded to present before the GoI the genuineness of ULFA's movement to an extent and also certain demands that needed to be fulfilled to facilitate a direct talk between the ULFA and the GoI.

In the first round of discussion, which was attended by the prime minister of India, the chief minister of Assam and the national security adviser apart from others, the PCG emphasised the fact that the ULFA's conflict with the GoI had to be resolved politically, the military means adopted by the GoI to solve the problem of insurgency in Northeast India had evidently failed, and in case of any direct dialogue with the ULFA, the GoI must not shy away from discussing the core issue raised by ULFA, i.e. the issue of sovereignty (Borbora 2010:39). Responding to the PCG, the prime minister stated that 'the Government of India is not scared of discussing any issue with the ULFA. We are prepared to discuss any or all issues with the ULFA'. The Prime minister, of course, reminded that he is a 'servant of the Nation and the Constitution' and believes in 'political resolution of any conflict or problem' (Borbora 2010:39–40).

The PCG suggested two positive steps to be adopted by the government to facilitate a direct dialogue with ULFA: first, to release the five jailed leaders of ULFA, which included the Political Advisor Bhimkanta Buragohain, Vice Chairman Pradip Gogoi, the Publicity Secretary Mr Mithinga Daimary, and two Central Committee members, Mrs Pranati Deka and Ramu Mech. The second demand was a white paper on whereabouts and status of the missing ULFA leaders and its cadres during the army operation in Bhutan in 2003. The response of the government appeared to be positive; however, it did not yield positive outcomes.

The second round of discussion which was expected within weeks by the PCG was, however, convened much later, on 7 February 2006. In this discussion too, the PCG emphasised upon addressing the core issue raised by the ULFA in the discussion table. The second round of discussion ended with the issuing of a joint statement by the PCG and the GoI. The statement, while appreciating the important role played so far by the PCG, said: 'The Government of India has agreed to examine and initiate a series of confidence building measures with regard to instances of human rights violations and to examine the issue of release of certain detainees in consultation with the State Government. Both sides agreed that maintenance

The ULFA and Indian state    199

of peaceful atmosphere in the State to create a conducive environment for a dialogue is a pre-requisite and agree to work towards creating such an environment.' The joint statement also declared that another round of talks with the PCG would be held as early as possible before the commencement of talks with the ULFA (Borbora 2010:56–57).

The confidence building measure assured by the GoI proved to be futile with gunning down of nine people by the CRPF on 10 February 2006 at Kakopathar in Tinsukia district of Assam. This incident occurred in connection with the brutal killing of Ajit Mahanta on 3 February 2006 by the Indian Army. On February 2006 several thousand people came on the streets to protest against the brutal killing of Mahanta. The CRPF jawans indiscriminately fired on the protesters without any provocation from their end. The PCG issued a warning that such act on the part of the government, which was contrary to that of assured confidence building measures in the second round of discussions with the PCG by the GoI, would force the PCG to withdraw from the peace process. It was amidst these developments that the election to the Assam Legislative Assembly took place in May 2006. The election, however, was almost free from violence. The election returned the Congress-led coalition to power with Tarun Gogoi as its chief minister for the second consecutive term. The PCG spokesperson Arup Borbora pointed out that although the holding of the next round of discussion had taken a backseat, the PCG continued to work on modalities 'to be adopted and agreed upon in the event of direct talks between ULFA leaders and GoI' (Borbora 2010:60). The third round of discussion finally took place on 22 June 2006, which was also attended by the Union Home Minister Sri Shivraj Patil. While from the end of the GoI, Home Minister Patil enquired whether the top leadership of ULFA, including its President Arabinda Rajkhowa and Commander in Chief Paresh, would participate in the event of a direct dialogue with the GoI, the PCG responded that it was the prerogative of the respective parties to decide who should take part in the discussion. The PCG submitted a few suggestions to facilitate the dialogue between the ULFA and the GoI. The joint declaration issued at the end of the discussion reflected the suggestions put forward by PCG. The declaration said: 'Responding to the points made by the People's Consultative Group (PCG), the Union home Minister stated that their request for the release of the five ULFA detainees would be considered favourably in consultation with the Government of Assam. Simultaneously he urged the PCG to impress upon ULFA to ensure a peaceful and conducive environment so that direct talks with the Government of India are held at the earliest. The PCG expressed satisfactions over the Home Minister's approach to negotiation that will help usher lasting peace in Assam. . . . Further, modalities for holding these talks between the ULFA

200  *Akhil Ranjan Dutta*

and the Government of India in a fixed time frame, would be worked out through mutual consultations' (Borbora 2010:77). The government, however, failed to maintain restraint. Security forces killed six persons in July 2006. With reaction from the PCG, the GoI declared the temporary suspension of army operation against ULFA on 13 August 2006. ULFA also reciprocated by declaring temporary ceasefire. However, the agreed-upon decisions in the three rounds of discussions were not moving in a positive direction for fulfilment. Arup Borbora writes: 'The highly responsive 22 June 2006 mutual postulations thus gradually slipped away and got diluted amidst day to day contradictions and lack of implementation of the declared assurances given by the Government of India' (Borbora 2010:87).

The top officials of the GoI in the meantime started asking for fresh letters from ULFA leadership expressing willingness for direct dialogue with the GoI. The PCG was of the view that this was absolutely absurd because the formal letter expressing willingness for dialogue with the GoI was sent by the ULFA way back in February 2005 and it was only on the basis of that expressed willingness that three rounds of discussions between the ULFA and the GoI were held in 2005–06. Being disappointed, the PCG members wrote both to the National Security Adviser M.K. Narayanan (dated 25 July 2006) and to the prime minister (dated 4 September 2006) regarding non-fulfilment of the agreed-upon decisions in three rounds of discussions between the PCG and the GoI. The PCG, however, did not receive any response either from the NSA or from the prime minister. The assurance of releasing five jailed leaders to facilitate the dialogue remained unfulfilled. Amidst all these, on 24 September 2006, the GoI unilaterally announced resumption of army operations in the state. Such deceptive attitude of the government forced the PCG to withdraw from the talk process which was made public through a press conference in Guwahati on 28 September 2006. The members of the PCG urged the ULFA to dissolve the group in the pretext that the existence of the group would do no help in carrying out the peace process, ULFA, however, refused to oblige and the PCG continued to exist.

After the PCG had withdrawn from the dialogue process, there was another attempt steered by People's Committee for Peace Initiatives in Assam (PCPIA), an umbrella organisation representing various civil society groups in Assam and sympathetic to the cause of the ULFA, which convened a two-day-long *Jatiya Mahasabha* on 22–23 March 2007 to put pressure on the GoI for dialogue with the ULFA towards the political resolution of Indo-Assam conflict. The convention demanded that sovereignty should be the core issue in future talks between the banned group and the government. It also asserted that sovereignty should be a 'pre-condition'

The ULFA and Indian state 201

for discussion with the government. The convention reminded the GoI that failure on the part of the government to address the issue of sovereignty would necessitate 'a plebiscite' that has to be held to ascertain public opinion on the demand for sovereign Assam. While blaming the GoI for the deadlock in the peace process, the *Mahasabha* also reminded the GoI that the ULFA issue should not be taken as an 'insurgency problem' but as a 'political problem', and so there can be no military solution (Bureau Report, Zee News 24 March 2007).

The *Mahasabha* raised two other demands which were already demanded by the PCG in the three rounds of discussion with the GoI. The first one was the release of five top ULFA leaders who were in jail so as to create a conducive environment and to facilitate the talks. The second one was to provide information about the whereabouts of missing ULFA leaders after Bhutan's crackdown in 2003.

The government, however, had chosen not to respond to these resolutions and demands of the *Jatiya Mahasabha*.

## Post-PCG developments: revolt in ULFA and arrest of top ULFA leadership

There were setbacks to ULFA in June 2008 with two companies (A&C) of the 28th Battalion of ULFA declaring cessation of war. These factions were now led by Mrinal Hazarika and Jiten Dutta that were later on joined by another cadre, Prabal Neog. They had chosen to be in designated camps established by the government of Assam and started propagating total autonomy instead of sovereign Assam. These leaders also came out openly against the top ULFA leadership with an allegation that the top ULFA leadership had come under the grip of communal forces in Bangladesh. This faction took up the issue of illegal migration to the state, which they perceive as a severe threat to the very existence of Assam.

There were developments at other fronts too. First, after the 26/11 Mumbai attack Shivraj Patil was dropped from the Union cabinet and he was replaced by the then finance minister P. Chidambaram. Chidambaram showed no regard for the three rounds of discussions already held between the PCG and the GoI and insisted that for such a talk the ULFA had to adjure violence, deposit their arms with the government as well as agree to talk within the framework of Indian Constitution. On the international front, the replacement of Khaleda Zia government by a more India-friendly Sheikh Hasina government in Bangladesh in early 2009 also brought about changes in the ground. It is to be mentioned that after the Bhutan operation in 2003 the top leadership of the ULFA shifted to and settled in Bangladesh. Among them were ULFA Chairman Arabinda

## 202 *Akhil Ranjan Dutta*

Rajkhowa and his wife Kaberi Kachari, Finance Secretary Chitraban Hazarika and Foreign Secretary Shasha Choudhury. These leaders were also alleged to have received patronage from the Khaleda Zia government and developed nexus with fundamentalist forces. The Sheikh Hasina government was determined not to allow the soil of Bangladesh to be used by insurgent forces, particularly from India, for their operations. In fast moving developments in November and December 2010, all top leaders of the ULFA, including the chairman, finance and foreign secretaries as well as Deputy Commander in Chief Raju Barua, were arrested by Bangladesh authorities and handed over to Indian authority. With these arrests and the developments that followed, ULFA got vertically divided into two houses, one led by its Chairman Arabinda Rajkhowa and other by the Commander in Chief Paresh Baruah. The Arabinda faction is now engaged in dialogue with the GoI facilitated by SJA, to which the commander in chief is completely opposed to and continue to assert for *Swadhin Asom*. All the arrested leaders were finally shifted to central jail Guwahati. In February 2010 two jailed leaders of ULFA, the Vice Chairman Pradip Gogoi and Publicity Secretary Mithinga Daimary, were granted bail by appropriate court of law, which resulted in a new initiative for peace through the platform of SJA.

### New initiative for peace: the *sanmilita jatiya abhibarttan*

Hiren Gohain has always been a critique of ULFA from its inception. Gohain, however, kept on asserting that the context in which ULFA had emerged cannot be ignored. Continued negligence on the part of Union Government towards Northeast India in general and Assam in particular that resulted in marginalisation of indigenous people in many ways provided the ground for emergence of a force like ULFA.

It will be worthwhile to mention one important interview given to a vernacular magazine in 1990 by Gohain on the issue 'What is the future of ULFA?' Gohain pointed out that the negligence on the part of the central government and the ruling class of India towards the demands of the people of Assam which manifested through the Assam Movement provided the much needed ground for the emergence of an outfit like ULFA. Asserting this position Gohain wrote in 2011: 'The ULFA found public support in Assam in the first phase of their armed struggle because under the Indian state the legitimate hopes and aspirations of indigenous people were not only not fulfilled since independence, but they were aggravated by certain deliberate policies of the Centre that took advantage of their weak socio-economic basis. Instead of making adequate and well-conceived investments to rescue Assam from colonial stagnation and

The ULFA and Indian state   203

backwardness, her natural resources were ruthlessly exploited with little benefit for the indigenous peoples of the state.' It is this approach of the Centre which has forced the 'desperate sections of the youth harassed by unemployment, economic stagnation in which unscrupulous businessmen alone thrived, and massive political corruption and misrule, took arms to wage a war against the Indian state' (Gohain 2011:The Press note dated 7/5/2011).

After the PCG initiative had failed and top ULFA leadership was arrested in November–December 2009, the leaders in jail explored the possibility of reviving the dialogue with the GoI for political resolution of the conflict. The two ULFA leaders released in bail in February 2010, Vice-Chairman Prodip Gogoi and Publicity Secretary Mithinga Daimary, who were arrested in 2003 during Operation All Clear, took the lead in this exploration. It is against this background that Hiren Gohain was approached, to which he responded positively and the SJA came into being. Led by Gohain the steering committee had total eleven members, none of whom subscribed to the ULFA's demand for sovereignty. Hiren Gohain is the chairperson of the committee. The other members were Indira Goswami (noted novelist and Jnanpith awardee who was instrumental behind the formation of the PCG); Nirmal Choudhury (former vice chancellor, Gauhati University); Rohini Kumar Baruah (retired IAS officer); Harekrishna Deka (noted poet, novelist, columnist and former DGP, Assam); Hiranya Kumar Bhattacharyya (former IGP, Assam, an ideologue of the Assam Movement 1979–85, who was also a member of the BJP and contested election on a party ticket); Indibar Deuri (retired postmaster general, Assam, and columnist); Ratneswar Basumatari (noted cultural and literary personality from the Bodo community) and K. Alom (former professor in economics, Gauhati University). Dilip Patgiri (Advisor of AJYCP) and Lachit Bordoloi (former secretary general of Manab Adhikar Sangram Samitee) who were members of PCG were appointed as secretaries to the steering committee of the SJA. Gohain pointed out that there were two main hindrances towards the dialogue between the ULFA and the GoI – the issue of sovereignty raised by ULFA and unwillingness on the part of government to release the jailed ULFA leaders. Realising that ULFA is not in a position to defeat the Indian Army in the battleground and there is a rare possibility of transforming peoples' sympathy for ULFA into sustainable people's revolt, the SJA decided to drop the issue of 'sovereignty' as the first and foremost demand. On the other hand SJA remained steadfast to its demand for the release of jailed ULFA leaders on the ground that the decision on the part of the ULFA for talks with the GoI cannot be taken under the vigilance of the government, but needs a free environment.

204   *Akhil Ranjan Dutta*

It was under the banner of the SJA that the state-level convention to find out solutions to all fundamental issues raised by the ULFA was convened on 24 April 2010. The convention was marked by lot of debates and controversies. The whole initiative was criticised and condemned by ULFA commander in chief Paresh Baruah and those who explicitly or implicitly expressed their allegiance and sympathy to Baruah. The debates between Paresh Baruah and Hiren Gohain were very intensive and it informs the positions of civil society initiative like the SJA's on the ULFA's demand for sovereignty. Gohain was personally targeted by Baruah, Gohain responded on almost all occasions and refused to buy Baruah's arguments on sovereignty.

The 24 April 2010 SJA convention organised in Pragjyoti Cultural Complex, Guwahati, was attended by around 2,000, people including representatives of more than 100 organisations. Political parties, except for the ruling Congress, also attended the convention and presented their views.

The draft resolutions of the convention had the following points:

1   Appeal to both the ULFA and the GoI for a negotiated settlement of the problems without any precondition
2   The talks be held at the highest level of ULFA leadership and that of GoI
3   Calling upon the government to give free passage to the ULFA leaders and demanded that the jailed leaders of the militant outfit be released to facilitate holding of meeting of the Central Committee of the ULFA to take decision regarding talks with the government
4   Appeal to the people concerned to give suggestions and opinions in writing within seven days which will be considered by the steering committee while finalising the resolutions
5   Formation of expert committees for studying basic issues like right of the indigenous people over the natural resources and other issues creating hindrances for the true development of the state
6   Sending a delegation to New Delhi to approach and apprise the Union Government about the resolutions and to press for an immediate start of a dialogue
7   Calling the public to organise conventions at district level to create public opinion in favour of negotiated settlement of the ULFA-raised primary issues.

The SJA immediately constituted a few expert committees to prepare reports on various burning issues of the state of Assam. The basic approach of SJA towards a negotiated settlement of the issues raised by ULFA may be found in the basic guidelines put forward by Gohain to the Expert

The ULFA and Indian state   205

Committee on Constitutional and Political matters. Gohain suggested the following measures at the minimum for sustaining peace in the state.

i. Special constitutional measures for the state of Assam to prevent the arbitrary power of the Union Government to transfer subjects from State list to the Concurrent list

ii. Amendment to the National Citizenship Act

iii. Full-fledged State Planning Commission for the state of Assam with the capacity to generate resources and employment

iv. Special constitutional protection for the state of Assam to prevent the arbitrary power of the Union Government to change the boundaries of the state, rename the state or to constitute new state from within the state

v. Local peoples' control and voice over the natural resources

vi. Channelisation of any investment from outside the state through state planning commission

vii. Restriction on neo-liberal privatisation and protection of local industrialists and traditional/cottage industries and farmers

viii. Local peoples' stake over patenting bio-resources

ix. Formation of Upper House to protect the rights of various ethnic groups.

This was further elaborated by Gohain through a press release while submitting the Reports and Charter of Demands prepared by the SJA to the ULFA leadership on 7 May 2011 which stated: 'The Charter demands constitutional amendments to give the state of Assam (and thereby its peoples) greater control over its own future through strengthening the state's power to control the revenues generated here, the natural resources, and the planning process, and a secure demographic situation as well as accelerated balanced development. If the Government of India and the ULFA honour the Charter in letter and spirit and do not undersell it, we may look forward to untroubled peace, true development and vigorous growth of democracy in the region. The SJA is formally handing over this Charter to the ULFA today.'

On 21 June 2010 a six-member delegation of SJA met Prime Minister Manmohan Singh at his residence. It was a 45-minute discussion, which the delegation described as cordial and inspiring. The delegation presented the political context of rise of ULFA and pointed out that ULFA continued to draw some sympathy from the people of Assam. Making their position clear that none of them had ever been supporter of ULFA, the SJA team said that the problem of ULFA cannot be solved by military suppression. Therefore, the whole situation, not merely the armed struggle, needed to be solved politically. Only then it will bring permanent and satisfactory resolution to the problem. They also apprised that a conducive environment brought about by new thinking among majority

206 *Akhil Ranjan Dutta*

of ULFA leaders and goodwill of the government needed to be used to resolve the conflict. Then they submitted the SJA Convention resolution to the prime minister and urged upon him for initiating dialogue without any pre-condition and to release the jailed ULFA leaders to facilitate a conducive environment to take decision on the part of ULFA leaders by convening the meeting of the Central Committee for a discussion with the GoI. The prime minister assured of positive steps. On 23 June the SJA team met the UPA chairperson Sonia Gandhi. On the same day the SJA team also met the Union home minister, who expressed his apprehension over ULFA's sincerity for talks and also the problems associated with having talks with an outlawed organisation. He also informed that the responsibility of dialogue with ULFA had been delegated to the state government (Gohain 2010:158–60).

On 15 July 2010 the Centre appointed P.C. Halder, former director (IB), as interlocutor to take forward the process of initiating peace with the ULFA.

ULFA leaders were released from jail in the last part of 2010 and early part of 2011. Arabinda Rajkhowa was released on 1 January 2011. On his release Rajkhowa said, 'We are committed to peace in Assam and take the peace process forward. We are ready for unconditional peace talks.' Other two leaders, Chitraban Hazarika and Sasadhar Choudhury, were granted bail on 10 January 2011 (*The Indian Express* online, January 2011, 12.55 hrs, accessed 3 June 2012). With this the central government fulfilled SJA's and earlier PCG's demand for the release of the jailed leaders of ULFA to facilitate the talks with the GoI.

ULFA's Central Committee meeting was held after eight years on 31 January 2011 in Nalbari to discuss the proposed peace talks with the GoI. The meeting was attended by ULFA Chairman Arabinda Rajkhowa, Vice Chairman Pradip Gogoi, Foreign Secretary Sasadhar Choudhury, Finance Secretary Chitraban Hazarika, Political Adviser Bhim Kanta Burhagohain and other Central Committee leaders.

ULFA formally met the Union home minister on 10 February 2011. Ahead of the Centre's meeting with the outlawed ULFA, Home Minister P. Chidambaram said that 'the Constitution of India is flexible and resilient enough to accommodate the aspirations of the people of Northeastern Region' (*The Assam Tribune*, 9 February 2011). The talks between the Government of India and the ULFA started on 10 February in a tripartite meeting chaired by the Union Home Secretary G.K. Pillai, while on the same day the ULFA leaders called on the Home Minister P. Chidambaram. On 14 February 2011, the ULFA leaders led by its Chairman Arabinda Rajkhowa met the prime minister at his residence and held talks for about 10 minutes in the presence of the National Security Adviser Shivshankar

*The ULFA and Indian state* 207

Menon and Centre's interlocutor for talks, P. C. Halder (*The Assam Tribune*, 14 February 2011).

With these developments, the ULFA faction led by its chairperson is now engaged with the GoI for a negotiated settlement and a series of discussions are under way. Facilitating such a direct dialogue, although with only a fraction of the vertically divided ULFA by the initiatives of the civil society in Assam, cannot entirely be ignored as it has paved a way for peace, which in the long run may be temporary if the Centre continues to be deceptive in its approach.

## References

Baruah, Sanjib. 2005. *Durable Disorder: Understanding the Politics of Northeast India*. New Delhi: Oxford University Press.

Borah, Dhrubajyoti. 1993. *Jatiya Prasnaaru Atmaniyantran*. Guwahati: Radiant Impression.

Borah, Nibaran. 1998. 'Swadhin Asom: Sanbhab Ne?' *Sadin*, 5 June.

Borbora, Arup. 2010. *All About PCG & Talks*. Guwahati: Aank-Baak.

Castro, Fidel. 2006. *My Life: Fidel Castro & Ignacio Ramonet (A Spoken Autobiography)*. London: Scribner.

Chandhoke, Neera. 2007. 'Civil Society', *Development in Practice*, 17(4/5): 607–14, http://www.jstor.org/stable/25548259 (accessed 7 June 2012).

Colvin, Christopher J. 2007. 'Civil Society and Reconciliation in Southern Africa', *Development in Practice*, 7(3): 322–37, http://www.jstor.org/stable/25548219 (accessed 6 June 2012).

Das, Parag. 1993. *Swadhinatar Prastab*. Guwahati: Author.

Elliot, Carolyn M., ed. 2008. *Civil Society and Democracy: A Reader*. New Delhi: Oxford University Press.

Fernandes, Walter and Gita Bharali. 2011. *Uprooted for Whose Benefit? Development-Induced Displacement in Assam 1947–2000*. Guwahati: NESRC.

Gogoi, Manoram. 2005. *Paragdaar Sannidhyat*. Guwahati: Prapti Prakash.

Gohain, Hiren. 1985. *Assam: A Burning Question*. Guwahati: Spectrum.

Gohain, Hiren. 1991. *Swadhinatar Sapon Aru Dithak*. Guwahati: Journal Emporium.

Gohain, Hiren. 2010. *Agnigarbha Asomaru Subha Uttaranar Prachesta*. Guwahati: Ashok Book Stall.

Gohain, Hiren. 2011. *Iman Tita Sagarar Pani* (Fourth Volume of the Author's Autobiography), Guwahati: Author.

Hussain, Wasbir, ed. 2012. *Peace Tools & Conflict Nuances in India's Northeast*. Guwahati: Word Weaves.

Kamrava, Mehran and Frank O. Mora. 2008. 'Civil Society and Democratization in Comparative Perspective: Latin America and the Middle East'. In Carolyn M. Elliot (ed.), *Civil Society and Democracy: A Reader*, pp. 324–55. New Delhi: Oxford University Press.

208   *Akhil Ranjan Dutta*

Kaviraj, Sudipta and Sunil Khilnani, eds. 2002. *Civil Society: History and Possibilities.* First South Asian edition. New Delhi: Cambridge University Press.

Khilnani, Sunil. 2002. 'The Development of Civil Society'. In Sudipta Kaviraj and Sunil Khilnani (eds), *Civil Society: History and Possibilities*, pp. 11–32. First South Asian Edition. New Delhi: Cambridge University Press.

Mandela, Nelson. 1994. *Long Walk to Freedom.* London: Abacus.

Persell, Caroline H. 1997. 'The Interdependence of Social Justice and Civil Society'. *Sociological Forum*, 12(2): 149–72, http://www.jstor.org/stable/684742 (accessed 6 June 2012).

Press note issued by SJA on Charter of Demands for Discussion between GoI and the ULFA dated 7 May 2011 and signed by Hiren Gohain, chief spokesperson, SJA Steering Committee.

Robinson, Mark. 2008. 'Civil Society and Ideological Contestation in India'. In Carolyn M. Elliot (ed.), *Civil Society and Democracy: A Reader*, pp. 356–76. Third Impression. New Delhi: Oxford University Press.

Talukdar, Mrinal and Kishor Kalita Kumar. 2011. *ULFA.* Guwahati: Nanda Talukdar Foundation.

# 12 Accommodating differences

## The Indian democracy and Assamese nationalism

*Rubi Devi*

Assamese nationalism, or *jatiotabad*, has found overt expression since the Assam Movement (1979–86) and afterwards armed movement by the United Liberation Front of Assam (ULFA). While the Assam Movement was more like a protest movement within the democratic framework of the Indian state, the ULFA has given Assamese nationalism a more radical and militaristic turn for nearly three decades. Prior to 1979, there were events or occurrences which can also be seen as expressions of nationalistic fervour such as the 1960s uprising demanding Assamese as the official language, most commonly known as *bhaxa aandolan*. But none of these happenings have ever challenged Indian democracy so strongly and consistently than the radical armed movement by the ULFA.

Since its emergence, the ULFA has been able to consistently challenge the Indian state for nearly three decades by upholding its demand for a sovereign state of Assam. It is not the first time that Indian democracy has ever faced such challenge of ethnic nationalism. Rather, India has been consistently facing numerous ethnic conflicts; many of them are radical and militaristic in nature. The first challenge to Indian democracy came from the Nagas, who have been fighting for a sovereign Nagalim for the Naga people since 1948. Another significant challenge was posed by the Sikh nationalists during the 1980s and the ongoing Kashmiri Liberation movement, demanding separation from India. Apart from such strong militaristic movements upholding their demands for sovereign states, there are other notable self-determination movements with demands for greater autonomy, separate state such as Tamil nationalists during 1950s, the Mizo revolt of the 1960s and the 1970s or the most recent demand for a separate state of Telangana by the Telugu people within the greater boundary of Indian state. The existence of such militaristic or non-militaristic cases of self-determination movements makes one to wonder why Indian democracy has faced so many ethnic identity crises from different groups just 60 years since independence. Democracy means power to the people,

210  *Rubi Devi*

freedom of choice, equal rights and opportunity for all people, majority as well as minority groups. Has Indian democracy failed to adhere to the basic principles of democracy when it comes to sharing equal political, economic and social rights and opportunities with its varied groups? Or can it provide space for the dissenting voices and create pathways for accommodating ethnic mobilisation within its democratic framework.

Taking into account the case of Assamese nationalism, the upsurge of ULFA and other armed radicals with their demands for sovereignty or greater autonomy, this chapter ponders the possibility of accommodation within the democratic structure of the Indian state. The chapter looks into the theoretical understanding of democracy and ethnic nationalism and the link between the two and focuses on Assamese nationalism in the Indian context to see if it can be accommodated within the greater democratic structure of the Indian state.

## Democracy and ethnic nationalism: theoretical understanding

Democracy as a political institution has been a subject of scrutiny especially since the Second World War. The development of democracy as a political governance system in the Western world has evolved over the centuries, since the signing of the Magna Carta, through the ideals of French and American Revolutions, to the establishment of parliamentary and presidential democracies in Europe and the United States. However, the celebration of democracy began only in the later part of twentieth century when it was adopted as the most viable form of political governance by the numerous newly independent states of Asia, Africa and Eastern Europe. The collapse of Soviet Union led to believe that democracy has no serious ideological competitor: it was 'the end point of mankind's ideological evolution' and 'the final form of government' (Fukuyama 1992:xi–xii; Dahl 2000). A democratic state founded on the premise of egalitarian law protects civil liberty and personal property, respects the rule of law and freedom of speech, maintains a representative government, reduces the risk of war and conflicts and a peaceful order is thought to be in progress (Diamond 1999; Dahl 2000).

However, democracy as political governance in the developing countries such as India has been rather challenging as these countries have experienced numerous political conflicts. Such happenings are often criticised with greater austerity since the success of democracy is assessed in comparison to those of Western nations. From the Western experience, democracy is a solution to the existing power struggle and an end to the class struggle where the power centred around a few. In contrast, democracy in the newly

*Accommodating differences* 211

independent nations or developing nations is still an ongoing experience. In the West, democracy evolved over a long time and is a framework of centralised authority at the top and the popular pressures at the bottom shaped up through a period of suffrage and political competition. The questions of group identity, which groups will constitute the nation or which areas would be considered within specific state boundary or national territory, were often resolved much prior to the introduction of democracy as a political structure. Thus, democracy in the West came as a solution after a long, continued power struggle between groups and social subdivisions. By contrast, democracy in countries like India came as an imported idea which is being translated into democratic institutions and these institutions provide new incentives for political actors to organise and mobilise.

The imported model of democratic systems in most developing countries does not readily fit with the inherent cultural structures of society. As Huntington discusses, the difference in the culture and religion create differences over political ideologies and also polity issues (Huntington 1993:72). As democracy is introduced and the power striving elite groups compete for power, the older identities clash with the imposed egalitarian identities and a feeling of fear and loss takes place. Lack of representation also adds towards progression of an identity threat. In the face of such perceived threats the older identities are revived, groups are formed and the mobilisation takes place. The process of group mobilisation is further strengthened due to the technological innovations of the present century and the collusion with different identities becomes obvious. The spread of democratic norm also threatens the traditional elite groups who in turn join or reorganise the conservative groups who view the development of democratic elements such as individualism as an eroding influence in the traditional culture.

A close look at the development of political culture also reveals that a considerable state intervention is a natural course of action for a developing nation, especially at the initial stage. State intervention as seen by many is inherent in the process of 'late development' (Kohli 1991). Unlike developed democracies, the differentiation mark between the public and the private spheres in the newly democratic countries is thin, and the accumulation and distribution of resources are mostly entrusted on the governments. Accumulation and distribution of resources generate competition and this often leads to the politicisation of issues. Also the different economic, social policies implemented by the state into the socio-economic life may create numerous political cleavages adding to the problems of developing democracies. As for example, India initiated family planning at the same time with China. While Chinese government was largely successful to implement the one-child policy by rule and force, India didn't yield much result in its two-child policy as it is considered undemocratic to forcefully implement law

212   *Rubi Devi*

against the socio-cultural beliefs and practices of the people and thus met with considerable opposition from various groups (Sen 2000). Another aspect of developing democracy is the weak institutional structure. Since democracy in most of the developing countries is introduced within a short time period, most institutions that serve as the backbone to democracy as a norm of electoral politics, parliaments, power sharing and political parties, are not fully developed. Competition for power often leads to concentration of power in the hands of a few leaders and such centralisation of power shared by few weakens the institutional structure. As seen in many developing democracies, ruling elites also confront a variety of oppositional elite groups. Such power competition results in group mobilisation and formation of ethnic identities and group boundaries. Another condition of developing democracies which differs significantly from the Western democracies is the emergence of new political pressure groups. Introduction of new electoral process, mass suffrage and weak institutions give space for the development of new political pressure towards a more equal distribution of power. Such trends to establish equilibrium in newer democracies would generate pressure leading to two track polities – a democratic polity and another not so democratic polity (Kohli 1993:671–89). Thus, the political society of many newly democratic countries on one hand can be characterised as 'too much democracy' in terms of presence of numerous conflicts and oppositions, and on the other hand it can also be seen as 'not-enough-democracy' because the state intervention is greater than liberal democracies and also the state protects itself against rising conflicts and demands.

The collective effect of such distinctive traits in the political landscape of the developing democracies partly, if not fully, explains why such countries experience increasing power conflicts. In other words, developing democracies seem to harbour more conflicts than to offer the solution to such power struggle. More than economic or social classes, ethnic and regional groups often express their demands for more power sharing and also stand for greater autonomy. Such groups within their respective cultural or regional or ethnic boundaries imagine themselves as total societies and in their demand for more power stand for 'self-determination'. Here the question emerges, why some groups demand for greater power and control and why such demands are accommodated in a more peaceful manner while others move towards a more militaristic stance, repression cycle, threatening the territorial integrity of the state?

## Ethnic nationalism and institutionalisation

Theories of ethnic mobilisation propose different approaches to explain why ethnic groups mobilise and become involved in conflicts (Gurr and

*Accommodating differences* 213

Harff 2004; Varshney 2003:85–99). The political mobilisation of the ethnic groups occurs due to the perceived differences in power sharing, ideologies, economic and cultural identities. The prevailing theories of primordialism, instrumentalism and constructivism all emphasise different but complementary aspects of ethnic mobilisation and conflict (Taras and Ganguly 2008). The primordial approach helps explain the intensity and persistence of ethnic political mobilisation based on shared identity deeply rooted in historical memories, cultural attributes such as customs, language, religion, common origin, dress, food and music. The instrumentalist approach stresses the importance of group identity to obtain material and political interest. Donald Horowitz and Arend Lijphart have explained how ethnic mobilisers strategically use shared identities to maximise their access to power and resources (Horowitz 1985; Lijphart 1977).

The constructivist approach rejects the primordialist notion of ethnic identity as a natural phenomenon; it also rejects the instrumentalist approach of ethnic identity simply as a tool towards achieving individual or group political gains. Rather, they look at ethnic identity as social construction – 'product of human actions and choices' rather than biologically given or strategic use (Taras and Ganguly 2008:15). It focuses on how the interests are defined and over a period of time, how the importance of ethnic identities changes depending on human actions and choices (Gurr and Harff 2004:97; Taras and Ganguly 2008). It is evident that certain characteristics such as strong sense of group identity, social, religious or cultural attachments as well as imposed or restricted identities play crucial role towards setting the stage for ethno-political mobilisation. Among many other important ethnic groups, ethno-nationalism, as pointed out by Gurr and Harff, coexists directly with modern state building. The 'Minorities at Risk' (MAR) project reveals that the ethno-nationalists are the most numerous among all other ethnic groups consisting of 85 per cent of the total (Gurr and Harff 2004).

The ethno-nationalist groups which mostly exist within the boundary of the state are often driven by the motivation towards achieving greater autonomy or statehood. Most of the ethno-nationalist groups exist in the developing world and although many have fought for self-determination only a few internationally recognised states have so far been born as a result of ethno-nationalist movements. Most of the ethnically based self-determination movements have either failed or resolved with negotiations of greater autonomy within the existing state boundary. Ethno-nationalist groups usually follow group leadership, demand greater autonomy and power sharing and in most cases adopt non-violent political means to demand their share from the existing central authority of the state. However, the use of militaristic means against the existing state is also not very uncommon.

214　*Rubi Devi*

To understand the trajectory of self-determination movements in the developing democracies is to examine the institutionalisation features of the central state authority. The degree to which the central state authority is institutionalised influences the level to which central authorities can impose their visions of political order on the society. The vision may not be initially more accommodative in nature but when the demand for autonomy and power sharing becomes stronger, the leadership strategy may be more willing to share power in the broader political context. The central argument of this study is that the more the central authority is institutionalised, the more accommodative the ruling strategy becomes. In the context of developing democracies the ethnic nationalism will emerge at the initial stage and over a prolonged period of time after negotiations of power with the central authority such ethnic nationalism will follow a declining pathway. A well-institutionalised state strongly affirms its boundaries within which political movements occur and an accommodative leadership makes provisions for such movements to arrive at certain negotiations and achieve certain level of power sharing. The reason for this is that the developing democracies themselves provide room for the rise of such self-determination movements and also at the same time possess a far greater amount of coercive power to repress such movements. When the leaders are non-accommodative, the central state authority denies concession to the ethnic nationalists and it often result in repression pushing the ethno-nationalist groups to turn into secessionist, separatist militant groups. However, if the leadership harbours accommodative polity, such situations may be avoided and a middle way can be sought for peaceful resolution.

Thus to say, the institutionalisation of central authority and the leadership strategy in developing democracies influences the course of self-determination movements. If the institutionalisation of central authority is weak, the self-determination movements may either result in peaceful breakup of individual territories or further turn into tumultuous ethnic conflicts leading to violent repression by the state authority. Such cases demand international assistance and mediation between the un-accommodative leadership of the weak states and the self-determination groups.

## Indian democracy: success or failure

India is one of the largest constitutional democracies in the world. From the time of its independence it has experienced a variety of political conflicts based on power cleavages of language, religion, regions, caste and class. While some of the ethnic conflicts have been accommodated much easily by some kind of power sharing, there are still many upholding their demand for

*Accommodating differences* 215

sovereign states. However, in comparison to other developing democracies such as Nigeria, Sri Lanka and Pakistan, India has fared well as an institutionalised democracy with a functioning parliament, an independent judiciary, free press and relatively free and fair election process. During the freedom movement as well as the formative years of the Indian state, the 'one nation' identity seemed to work well. However, the bond of national identity during the independence movement was short-lived as the nation-state faced with numerous threats from various ethnic groups claiming for separation of power and separate state (Khilnani 1997). India began its democratic journey with a well-functioning civil service and a strong ruling party. Though its democratic institutions were still weak, the leadership strategy was more accommodative. India under Nehru's leadership was successful to promote the notion of 'unity in diversity' by accepting and accommodating the ethnic and religious divergences. The administrative reorganisation of the states in 1950s was often discussed as an important step by the Indian state to respect the ethnic plurality and diversity within the framework of one nation. In 1950, with the adoption of the constitution, the line between state power and citizen's rights and practices were marked. At this stage there was not much political mobilisation among groups except for a few examples.

During the 1970s and 1980s under Indira Gandhi's leadership, the central state authority slowly became more powerful and authoritarian while the political institutions became weaker (Kohli 2001). The nationalist legacy declined and power politics centred around the family inheritance; erosion of institutional democracy was in place. The emergence of multiple parties at both regional and national levels indicates a different picture of political mobilisation constrained by competition, bargain and populism. The un-accommodative and authoritarian strategy of central leadership breeds discontent and dissatisfaction. The rise of numerous armed insurgencies during this period is an indication. Unlike the first few decades, political mobilisation at this phase took a definite shape as citizens, at the local levels as individual, community and groups, began to experiment the ideas of individual rights, power-sharing and autonomy. Use of various repressive measures such as imposing President's rule in Assam, Nagaland and Punjab at this era exacerbated the conflict between the state and the citizens. The citizens interpreted it in terms of violation and abuses of their constitutional rights. On one hand, the newly independent state faced the challenge to fulfil the growing aspirations – economic, political and social – of its vast population; on the other hand, it also faced tremendous pressures from the society based on its religious, social, ethnic divergences – all led to a different power politics in post-independence India. In the process certain groups and regions strived towards betterment while some felt humiliated, alienated and deprived.

## 216 *Rubi Devi*

One reason for this shift is that India's central state authority slowly became more powerful and authoritarian while the political institutions became, weaker especially during 1970s and 1980s under the leadership of then prime minister Mrs Indira Gandhi. As the nationalist legacy declined and power politics centred around the family inheritance, erosion of institutional democracy was in place. A close look at the leadership strategies during a span of five decades of Indian democracy reveals how an un-accommodative leadership worsened the political scenario of the country during 1970s–80s, leading to the rise of many insurgencies. The most notable ones are the Sikh insurgency during the 1980s, the Naga insurgency under the NSCN during the 1980s, insurgency in Jammu and Kashmir and so on. The personalisation of power, politicisation of parliamentary power, use of military for political privilege and reduction of autonomy for judiciary all contributed towards the meshed up political condition of Indian democracy during those decades. Three decades after Indira Gandhi was assassinated, there have been many changes in the central leadership. Compared to Indira Gandhi, subsequent prime ministers – Rajiv Gandhi and Narasimha Rao – had shown flexibility in accommodating differences (Kohli 2001), leading to further changes in the central polity and administrative stance. But whether or not there is a change in the policy and practices of the central government towards accommodating ethnic groups is subject of scrutiny.

### The Assamese nationalism

Assamese nationalism which Sanjib Baruah categorised as 'sub-nationalism' came into forefront since the 1970s and the 1980s (Baruah 1999). There had been various outbursts of Assamese nationalist sentiment prior to the 1970s, the most famous being the demand for Assamese as the official language in the 1960s. But nothing generated so much support from the Assamese civil society than the six-year-long Assam Movement by All Assam Students' Union (AASU) and the subsequent armed movement by the ULFA. An in-depth inquiry reveals that the advocates of Assam Movement and the ULFA were able to muster such support because their socio-political agenda was based on the historic and socio-cultural ethnic identity of the Assamese people.

Assamese nationalism is based on the ethnic identity of Assamese as a nation popularly known as *Axomiya Jaati*. This ethnic identity, like any others, has also evolved as a result of the historic, cultural processes of ethnic identity formation. Its claim of an ethnic Assamese identity is based on historic, cultural and social roots of Assamese society. Following Anthony D Smith's reference of the six 'bases' of ethnic identity formation

*Accommodating differences* 217

(Smith 1986, 1993), we examined the case of Assamese identity formation (Assamese *Jatiyotabad*). The concept of 'ethnie', as explained by Smith, is central to any ethnic nationalism. Formation of an 'ethnie', as Smith points out, rests on a few attributes: a collective group name to gain recognition as a distinctive community both from group members and outsiders; a common myth or belief in common origin or ancestry; a shared history; an attachment to a specific territory; shared cultural attributes in terms of dress, language, food, music and religion; and a feeling of common solidarity among group members.

A few of these characteristics can be useful in explaining the case of Assamese nationalism. In the historical context, Assam under the Ahom kingdom (1228–1826) had a distinct geographical entity separate from the Indian mainland. Even during the heyday of Mughal rules, the Mughals were not successful to extend their territorial border much beyond Guwahati. The legendary battle of Saraighat by Lachit Borphukan against the Mughals is a historic memory cherished by every Assamese. Although the state boundary of present-day Assam is not exactly synonymous with the territorial boundary of Ahom kingdom (Baruah 1999), the separate territorial identity of Ahom kingdom does contribute towards formulating the claim of ethnic Assamese identity based on a specific territorial land. In the same way the reference to the state of Kamrup and Pragjyotishpur in pre-Ahom period also lends support for the claim of a specific territory as homeland. The community-based political structure developed by the Ahom kings was unique to shape up a community-based identity. The name 'Assam' itself is said to be associated with the 'Ahom' kingdom.

In the cultural aspect, the socio-cultural and religious reform movement by Srimanta Sankardev contributed towards building a cohesive cultural identity for the Assamese people since the sixteenth century. The role of *naamghor* is crucial in creating a socio-cultural space for both religious and cultural discourse in Assamese society which has contributed towards shaping up and solidifying Assamese ethnic identity over centuries. The distinctive cultural affinity also grew around the celebrations of Bihu festival, Bihu dance and music alongside dress patterns such as *gamocha, mekhelachador* and food habits especially the *khar* – a traditional food item that has become the marker of identity.

The patriotic nationalist fervour of Lachit Borphukan's expression *dexotkoi momai dangor nohoy* is an example of the historic memory shared by the whole Assamese community. During the British rule, the early rebellion of Gomdhar Konwar against the British rule in 1828 is another example. The lack of recognition of Gomdhar Konwar in the Indian nationalist history which recognises Mongol Pandey episode as the first anti-British freedom struggle is still a matter of discontent among the Assamese. The

218 *Rubi Devi*

anti-British sentiment came out of imperial exploitative policies in the region, at the hands of Peoples Assemblies, popularly known as *Raij Mels*, followed by nationalist freedom fighters Moniram Dewan and Kanaklata and others who also contributed towards the growth of a united Assamese identity. Sanjib Baruah has also pointed out the role of *Xonrokhwini Xobha* headed by Ambikagiri Roychoudhury in articulating the 'notion of the Assamese as a *Jati* (nation) within the Indian *Mohajati* (great nation)' (Baruah 1999:69). The distinctiveness of Assamese identity is also centred around the Assamese language and literature. Every time the Assamese language was constrained by the dominant Bengali language, it created a sense of cultural consciousness among the Assamese people. In 1836, the colonial rulers accepted Bengali instead of Assamese as the language of state. Although Assamese was later adopted as the language of schools and judicial procedures, it created a language consciousness among the then Assamese public figures and intellectuals. The establishment of *Axomiya Bhaxa Unnati Xadhini Xobha* in 1888 was one of the earliest attempts to preserve and develop the unique identity of Assamese language and literature. The *Axom Xahitya Xobha* is another example which since its inception in 1917 has been playing its crucial role to promote and preserve the cultural identity of Assamese people through Assamese language and literature.

## Assamese nationalism, Assam Movement and ULFA

In the post-independence period, several factors contributed towards the strengthening of the ethnic nationalism, which in course of time culminated in the Assam Movement and radical insurgencies. The famous *bhaxa andolan* of 1961 to declare Assamese as the state official language has greater connotations in the nationalist politics of Assam. On one hand it consolidated the language-based identity of the Assamese population mostly living in the Brahmaputra valley. On the other hand it also marked a distinction between the mainstream Assamese and the tribal communities living in the hill districts of Naga Hills, Meghalaya, Manipur and NEFA which were part of the then greater Assam. The consolidation of Assamese identity further took place as these hill districts were given separate statehood and officially separated from Assam. The political reorganisation of the states left Assam with a much smaller geographic boundary and limited landmass and natural resources, which created a feeling of resentment among the Assamese elites and educated masses against the central government in Delhi.

The Assam Movement led by AASU during 1979–85 was centred around the illegal immigration. At the centre of the illegal immigration issue was the resource politics which was acutely felt by the mainstream

*Accommodating differences* 219

Assamese population in the post-independence period. The large influx of immigrant population from the then East Pakistan to Assam following the 1947 partition of British India and later during the Bangladesh liberation movement was perceived to be a major threat to the demographic stability of the state. The issue was raised as a socio-political concern by the AASU which soon gained support from other socio-political organisations. Supports from the civil society groups strengthened the mobilisation process. During the course of the Assam Movement, the illegal immigration issue was linked with other burning problems faced by the state such as the economic backwardness and the soaring unemployment problems. Resonance of such issues in the overall agenda of the Assam Movement further strengthened the ethnic nationalist voice against the pan-Indian nationalism. The already flowing sentiment of a distinct Assamese identity was crucial for the leaders of the AASU to successfully mobilise greater support towards the illegal immigration issues. The AASU and later the ULFA also brought the issue of economic exploitation of Assam's tea, oil and natural gas industry by the central authority by denying the state its larger share of profit and royalty (Gogoi 2007).

The songs of cultural icons such as Jyoti Prasad, Bishnu Rabha and Bhupen Hazarika were also useful to disseminate the nationalist fervour. The harsh, misinterpreted political moves by the central government to suppress the ethnic concerns further consolidated the ethnic nationalist fervour against the pan-Indian nationalism. Certain measures such as imposition of President's rule, armed laws and holding state election against the wishes of the people during the Assam Movement were also responsible for an anti-India sentiment among the ethnic Assamese which was later exposed in extreme form under the ULFA; the ULFA opposed the authority of the Indian state over Assam. As Sanjib Baruah has pointed out, the political tendency that expressed through the ULFA is 'the radical fringe of Assamese sub nationalist politics of the 1980s' (Baruah 2005). Against the coercive central authority, the ULFA's proposition of a separate homeland, or *swadhin Asom* (independent Assam), for the people living in Assam was alluring to many of its supporters. The ULFA enjoyed considerable mass support first, because its stated agenda was set in the nationalist sentiment already aroused by the Assam Movement, and second because of its social reformation agenda alongside the political rhetoric such as warning and punishing corrupt officials, prohibiting prostitution, drug, offering flood relief in rural areas, putting a ban on Hindi movies and song etc. Both the leaders of Assam Movement and the ULFA successfully used the limited economic resource scenario to garner public concerns and hence support for their causes. The exploitative nature of the central state over the oil and tea industry of Assam was brought to the forefront alongside the

220   *Rubi Devi*

other pressing issues. Using simple but powerful slogans such as *tej dim tel nidiu* (We'll give blood instead of oil), *desh bulile nelage adesh* (I/We don't need an order when it comes to the cause of the country), *joi aai Axom* (Success to my motherland Assam) during the Assam Movement and also afterwards, they made an impact on the minds of the Assamese multitudes.

From another perspective, the political mobilisation of Assamese society during the Assam Movement and afterwards can also be explained in terms of the democratic experimentation of the civil society groups. At the pan-Indian scenario, after the humble beginning of the early independence era, the democratic deepening of the state has begun to take shape at this period after the modest beginning of early independence years. The Assamese civil society groups also became familiar with the democratic practices of elections, voting rights, power sharing along with the fundamental rights to equality, free speech, freedom from exploitation, cultural and educational rights and so on. As the state of Assam struggled through economic sluggishness and immigration influx, the civil society became increasingly aware of the democratic rights and practices. The interplay of such factors creates political consciousness, leading to ethnic group mobilisation for greater power sharing. In the Assamese case, the civil society under AASU's leadership campaigned for power sharing to redress grievances. The public demonstrations of mass rally, picketing or sit-in can also be interpreted as democratic practices. However, the repressive measure adopted by the central authority to suppress such efforts shifted the course of such mobilisation into a more radical and violent path. On the positive side, the rise of a regional party, i.e. AGP and its success in the elections following the Assam Movement also points at the grievance and power sharing politics of developing democracies.

## Disintegration of Assamese nationalism and emergence of smaller nationalities

After the downfall of the ULFA, Assam has entered into a new phase of political upheaval along the narrow lines of tribal ethnic cleavages, which has resulted in the fragmentation of Assamese society. Many of the tribal groups such as Bodos and Karbis, Dimasa, Koch-Rajbanshi, Adivasi and others following the same ethnic nationalist agenda have uplifted their demand for greater autonomy and even separate states. The demand for a separate state of 'Bodoland' in 1987 came along with the demand for the recognition of Bodo language and culture as well as economic and social development of the Bodo people. Similarly the Koch-Rajbanshis are posing their demand for 'Kamatapur' based on their linguistic and historic identity. The emergence of such demands by various groups reveals the recurring

*Accommodating differences*  221

politics of ethnicity and power sharing. Most notably, these movements share ideological and tactical similarities with that of the Assam Movement. It indicates a failure on part of the Assamese nationalist groups to recognise the ethnic identity of these groups within the greater identity of Assamese nation. In the same way the radical militaristic turn of ULFA was also followed by these ethnic groups and militarised the ethnic societies, especially the BLT and NDFB in Bodoland, KNLF in Karbi Anglong and DHD in North Cachar Hills. The emergence of such radical militarism has resulted in endless numbers of killings, violent massacres alongside political unrest which severely constrained the socio-economic and cultural life of the people in Assam.

The crisis of ethnic identity since 1979, thus, has been at the centre stage of state politics in Assam. A close look would reveal that the successful mobilisation of the Assamese nationalist sentiment reached its peak during the Assam Movement and immediately afterwards through the ULFA's nationalist campaign. While the ULFA remained active with its separatist agenda, the rise of various tribal groups with their specific demands of greater autonomy, recognition and socio-economic development has slowly challenged the course of Assam's ethnic politics. The continuing armed insurgencies have an eroding effect on the overall Assamese identity as well.

## Can India accommodate Assamese nationalism?

As India celebrates its six decades of democratic rule, there is a looming question: can India be able to successfully accommodate the ethnic, separatist movements that have been on the rise along with its successful democratic stature? This section focuses on the possibility of accommodation with reference to the Assamese nationalism.

Unlike its neighbours, India's democracy is much celebrated as a success story despite its ethnic, religious, regional and linguistic diversity. Within its political boundary as a nation-state, India is rather a multi-ethnic, multi-religious, multi-lingual society where competition for power sharing takes place on the divided lines of ethnicity, race, region, religion, caste and creed (Kohli 2001; Ganguli *et al.* 2009). If India were to continue as a successful democratic state, it has to accommodate ethnic nationalism of Assamese or any other existing ethnic nationalist movements. As Donald Horowitz has explained 'Democracy is about inclusion and exclusion, about access to power, about the privileges' that go with inclusion and the penalties that accompany exclusion' (Horowitz 1994). Ethnic identities in divided societies serve as markers in the inclusion and exclusion practices. To accommodate ethnic identities is to share and safeguard the socio-cultural, economic

## 222  *Rubi Devi*

and political rights of those ethnic communities based on the democratic principles of rights and equality.

India has a strong central authority, a functioning judiciary and a parliamentary system which can be utilised for distribution of power and also safeguarding the democratic rights and practices. As Atul Kohli has discussed, a federal democratic policy needs to be devised in order to accommodate the multicultural diversity (Kohli 2001). The demand for power sharing and economic and political rights should not be seen as a challenge to democracy, but rather as elements that have contributed towards the deepening of Indian democracy. During the 1950s India under the leadership of Nehru successfully accommodated the ethnic demands of Tamil nationalists. Another example of successful accommodation was the redistribution of state territories based on the major linguistic divisions in 1956. Such language-based state reorganisation policy allowed space for preserving the language-based ethnic identity of various groups.

In the case of Northeast India, however, the breaking up of the greater Assam into smaller states of Nagaland, Mizoram, Meghalaya, Arunachal Pradesh and Assam was not based on the linguistic criteria. Rather it was a political strategy similar to the 'divide and rule' policy of the colonial masters, even though it was cited as a remedy to partly satisfy the ethnic demands of various groups, most notably the Nagas to divert their demand for a separate Naga nation. Mizoram was created to cater to the demands of the Mizo people. However, the continuation of ethnic tension and insurgencies in most of these states till date is a clear indication of the failure of such dividing strategy in Northeast India. Creating new states or granting autonomy in simplistic way will not solve the ethnic mobilisation of the groups in Northeast India as well as in Assam. Rather, it conveys a wrong signal to groups who are continuing their demand for statehood, as for example the Bodos. Unlike other parts of India, as James Manor has explained, the inherent heterogeneity of Northeast India would not allow such types of accommodation to last long (Manor 2001). It is also true for Assam.

At the heart of these ethnic crises lie the cry for socio-economic development and competition for power sharing to gain control of the resources. A reconsideration of India's federalism in terms of greater power sharing can be the key to address such demands. The centralised feature of India's institutional design does not allow states to have control over the financial resources; neither do the states have incentive towards resource mobilisation and hence to redress the socio-economic grievances at the state level (Baruah 1999:206). As a successful accommodative stand, the central authority can entrust the states with greater control of resources within their state boundary. In the case of Assam, if the state government were

*Accommodating differences* 223

entrusted with the responsibility to control its resources, most notably the oil, natural gas and tea industry, and share its benefits to steer the pace of socio-economic growth, perhaps the dynamics of political mobilisation would have been averted. Indian federal system during the beginning years has been built around the national unity of the nationalist movement (Kohli 2001). Over the years, this federal design has been modified through various constitutional amendments to incorporate the multicultural diversity. Therefore, modification or restructuring of federal system to incorporate ethnic nationalism should not be treated as 'out of question'. As Jyotirindra Dasgupta has explained, the evolutionary and resilient nature of the Indian federal system has helped to sustain India's democratic development (Dasgupta 2001:49). Therefore, reconsideration of a decentralised federal system with regard to power sharing will not hinder the democratic progression of the Indian state; rather, it will help to extinguish the separatist demand of the ULFA as well as many other groups. Alongside, the Indian state has to stop using undemocratic 'draconian' measures to forcefully suppress aspirations of ethnic nationalism. Such measures not only exacerbate the separatist ethno-nationalist feeling, but also result in erosion of democratic values and practices. As the citizens and groups take part in the democratic procession in developing democracies, dissident voices are bound to arise. India being a multi-ethnic, multi-lingual, multi-religious society increases the possibility of multiplicity of voices. India's success as a democratic country, therefore, depends on the inclusion of such voices within the broader institutional spectrum. This is a sign of democratic progression. In the case of Assam, even during the ULFA's campaign for nationalism, the state managed to hold elections; the elected representatives formed governments. In spite of their support for the ULFA, majority of the Assamese civil society groups have been actively participating in the political process. Unlike many of its neighbours, Assam has not encountered a situation of having parallel governments. This positively indicates deepening of democratic practices in Assam.

Accommodation strategy should also consider the ethnic-cultural aspect. An inclusive cultural policy – by promoting cultural icons and traits of specific ethnic groups at the national level – can create a sense of belongingness. The Universal Declaration of Human Rights (1948), the International Covenant on Civil and Political Rights (1966) and the International Covenant on Economic, Social and Cultural Rights (1966) all support the rights of indigenous people to assert their socio-cultural identity. India's claim for democracy will be at stake if it were to ignore the cultural rights of its ethnic groups. The recognition of *Xatriya* dance of Assam as a classical dance form is a commendable approach in this regard; however, similar steps should be taken for other ethnic groups of Assam and Northeast

224  *Rubi Devi*

India. The ethnic-cultural diversity should be promoted to create a sense of pride and social inclusion.

Another misleading peace strategy, which demands scrutiny, is the peace accord, most notably the Assam Accord. Setting up achievable targets is crucial for the success of such accords as failure of implementation breeds discontent.

## Question of sovereignty

The question of sovereignty becomes critical in the discussion of accommodations. The ULFA and other ethnic nationalist groups such as the NSCN base their claims on a separate sovereign nation. On the other hand, such claims are interpreted as unconstitutional by the Indian government.

Sovereignty in simple terms is the fundamental idea of authority embodied in the states/nations. At domestic levels, sovereignty of a state or a nation rests on its rights and responsibility within its bordered territory, including the rights to exercise power, maintain control over its citizens, take decisions and execute the laws, and at the same time take responsibility towards its citizens and provide security and law and order. At the international level sovereignty of a state is based on the recognition by other states.

A close look at the ULFA's claim for a sovereign Assam exposes its inherent problem areas. First, it hinders the prospect of accommodation from the Indian state. Second, the future of a small sovereign Assam is rather grim. A sovereign state of Assam will instantly face the over-arching security threats from the neighbouring countries – Bangladesh, China, Myanmar and Bhutan. Moreover, the alleged connection of ULFA leaders with Pakistan's Inter-Services Intelligence and the Directorate General of Forces Intelligence of Bangladesh also rules out the future prospect of a sovereign state of Assam. ULFA's base in Bangladesh, in reality, indicates an ideological shift in its stand on illegal immigration issue. On the other hand, Assam and the Northeast as a whole are vital to India's sovereign claim as a nation. This region shares international border with China, Bangladesh, Bhutan, Myanmar and Nepal; hence, it is strategically important to India's security. It is also vital to the future of India's cultural identity as a nation showcasing 'unity in diversity'. Therefore, the Indian government would not consider compromise on the sovereignty claim. The end of secessionist movement by the Sikh nationalists is an example. The Sikh nationalism was a strong and powerful movement during the 1980s and the movement gained strength from the civil society groups although their demands were varied – from greater power sharing to sovereignty. The Indian state used armed forces and strong repressive measures to suppress the militants, which resulted in greater violence and massive loss of civilian lives leading

Accommodating differences  225

to political turmoil and fragmentation of society at various levels. The civil society got tired and weary of violence and death. This minimised the support base of the insurgent groups and affected their morale. In the case of the Sikh nationalist movement, the demand for sovereign Khalistan slowly died out during the 1990s after the bloody decade of Operation Blue Star of 1984 and the assassination of Indira Gandhi and anti-Sikh riots. Similar is the case of Muslim nationalism in Jammu and Kashmir. The ULFA also faced the same challenge from the Assamese civil society after the Dhemaji blast on 15 August 2004 which took the lives of sixteen innocent schoolchildren (Talukdar and Kalita 2011). This caused statewide reaction against ULFA's activities and (ironically) the Assamese civil society questioned the validity of its claim for sovereignty.

The concept of sovereignty in terms of rights and responsibilities would allow scope for further negotiation between the government and the insurgent group. As Krasner has pointed out, a sovereign state has to incorporate citizens' individual, political and cultural rights to maintain its claim of domestic sovereignty (Krasner 1999; 2001). In this aspect, the Indian state can incorporate the sovereign claims made by the ULFA by making certain provisions such as political power sharing and accepting cultural and economic rights of the populace over its natural resources. Further autonomy for the state can also be a viable ground for peace talks between the ULFA and the Indian government. A serious consideration of greater autonomy on part of India's central authority would also widen the scope of peaceful negotiations between other secessionist groups such as the NSCN in Nagaland. Such arrangements will pave the way for conflict resolution and hence strengthen the democratic tradition. Most importantly, goodwill and commitment on part of the government as well as the ethno-nationalist militant groups is necessary towards peaceful resolution of the conflicts. Both sides have equal responsibility to let peace happen.

## References

Baruah, Sanjib. 1990. *India against Itself: Assam and the Politics of Nationality*. Pennsylvania: University of Pennsylvania Press.
Baruah, Sanjib. 2005. *Durable Disorder: Understanding the Politics of North East India*. New Delhi: Oxford University Press.
Dahl, Robert. 2000. *On Democracy*. New Haven: Yale University Press.
Dasgupta, Jyotirindra. 2001. 'India's Federal Design and Multicultural National Construction'. In Atul Kohli (ed.), *The Success of India's Democracy*, pp. 49–77. Cambridge: Cambridge University Press.
Diamond, Larry. 1999. *Developing Democracies*. Maryland: John Hopkins University Press.

## 226  *Rubi Devi*

Fukuyama, Francis 1992. *The End of History and the Last Man*. London: Avon Books Inc.

Ganguly, Sumit, Larry Diamond, and Marc F. Plattner, eds. 2009. *The State of India's Democracy*. New Delhi: Oxford University Press.

Gogoi, Dilip. 2007. 'Resurrection of a Sunset Dream: ULFA and the Role of the State'. In Jaideep Saikia (ed.), *Frontier in Flames: North East India in Turmoil*, pp. 116–34. New Delhi: Viking/Penguin.

Gurr, Ted and Barbara Harff. 2004. *Ethnic Conflict and World Politics*. San Francisco: West View Press.

Horowitz, Donald. 1985. *Ethnic Groups in Conflict*. Berkeley: University of California Press.

Horowitz, Donald. 1994. 'Democracy in Divided Societies'. In Larry Diamond and Marc F. Pattner (eds), *Nationalism, Ethnic Conflict, and Democracy*, pp. 35–55. Baltimore: John Hopkins University Press.

Huntington, Samuel. 1993. 'The Clash of Civilization', *Foreign Affairs*, 72: 3.

Hussein, Monirul. 1993. *The Assam Movement: Class, Ideology and Identity*. New Delhi: Konark Publications.

Khilnani, Sunil. 2004. *The Idea of India*. New Delhi: Penguin Books.

Kohli, Atul. 1991. *Democracy and Discontent: India's Growing Crisis of Governability*. New York: Cambridge University Press.

Kohli, Atul. 1993. 'Democracy amid Economic Orthodoxy: Trends in Developing Countries', *Third World Quarterly*, 14 (4): 671–89.

Kohli, Atul, ed. 2001. *The Success of India's Democracy*. Cambridge: Cambridge University Press.

Lijphart, Arend. 1977. *Democracy in Plural Societies*. New Haven: Yale University Press.

Manor, James. 2001. 'Center-State Relations'. In Atul Kohli (ed.), *The Success of India's Democracy*, pp. 78–102. Cambridge: Cambridge University Press.

Sen, Amartya. 2000. *Development as Freedom*. New York: Anchor Books.

Smith, Anthony D. 1986. *Ethnic Origins of Nations*. New York: Basil Blackwell.

Smith, Anthony D. 1993. 'Ethnic Sources of Nationalism'. In Michael E Brown (ed.), *Ethnic Conflict and International Security*. Princeton, NJ: Princeton University Press.

Talukdar, Mrinal and Kishor Kumar Kalita. 2011. *ULFA*. Guwahati: Nanda Talukdar Foundation.

Taras, Raymond C. and Rajat Ganguly. 2008. *Understanding Ethnic Conflict: The International Dimension*. New York: Longman Publication.

Varshney, Ashutosh. 2003. 'Nationalism, Ethnic Conflict and Rationality', *Perspectives on Politics*, 1(1): 85–99.

# 13 Postscript
## Ending the impasse and reintegrating Northeast India

*Dilip Gogoi*

There is an overlapping use of the concept of self-determination and right to claim sovereign states for the ethnic communities living in Northeast India. The claim of sovereign homeland initially had been made by the Nagas through armed movement, followed by the Mizos, Assamese, Manipuris and Bodos who put forward the incompatibility theory with the Indian nation-state. Several new demands have been raised by the other emerging nationalities, i.e. Karbi, Dimasa, Koshrajbanshi, Kuki, Garos and few others for territorial homeland to statehood on the basis of respective ethnic identities to realise self-determination of own ethnic people. In such a scenario, it is imperative to examine the interrelationship between self-determination and the right to have a sovereign state through secession. Neera Chandhoke argues that there is no essential link between self-determination and right to secession, but the link is of a contingent one (Chandhoke 2012:172). The United Nations legitimises the fact that 'all peoples have the right to self-determination. By virtue of that right they freely determine their political status and freely pursue their economic, social and cultural development'.[1] In Gandhi's view, a civic nation, in his word *praja* is 'a political community whose basic unit is the individual considered as a bearer of fundamental rights and a subject capable of *swaraj*, i.e. self-determination and self-development (Parel (ed.) 2009:xv). It is the responsibility of modern state to provide the ground for realisation of the right to self-determination and self-development of people by creating appropriate conditions and institutions. If a state does not allow these conditions, then aggrieved people might have a legitimate right to secede and determine their own future. The Indian nation-state can address and resolve the ethno-political conflicts in Assam and other north-eastern states by effectively redesigning the federal polity and establishing effective institutions. In this respect, an affirmative approach is required in the form of a constitutional rearrangement for the entire Northeast India. This would conceivably meet the aspirations of the ethnic communities of the

## 228  *Dilip Gogoi*

region if the Indian nation-state grants the people to exercise internal self-determination. This would be the most appropriate way to address the demand of secessionism raised by the ethno-political secessionist movements. Since self-determination is a constitutive aspect of democracy (Chandhoke 2012:158) and to realise substantive democracy, India needs to recognise the aspiration of the ethnic communities through internal self-determination. Granting internal self-determination by instituting appropriate institution for the north-eastern region would invariably strengthen Indian democracy. Democracy is not all about establishing majoritarian supremacy; at the same time, it is about safeguarding the rights of each individual irrespective of social status and cultural belonging. More considerably, democracy involves the establishment of institutions that protect rights of the citizens and the vulnerable groups within the state.

From these vantage-points, the concluding chapter attempts to address two central questions in the context of Northeast India: does self-determination of people justify the right to secede and claim a sovereign state in the light of history and practices of the principle of self-determination? Second it explores whether there is any scope for solving the ongoing multiple ethnic crises in the region within the framework of the principle of self-determination in an ethnically divided, territorially contested region called Northeast.

## A brief history of self-determination: continuity and changes

The principle of self-determination has never been articulated with any objective criterion. It has different forms and applications with changing meaning and context in the imagination of human history. It is well known that after the end of the First World War, President Woodrow Wilson of the USA espoused the cause of national self-determination on the eve of the breakdown of the gigantic multinational empires of the Austro-Hungarian and the Russian. In the wake of the collapse of these big empires, the international community encountered a particular question, i.e. on what principle the future of the constituent units of the large empires to be organised and whether they have the right to have an independent statehood. The link between nation and self-determination, or specifically the right of a nation to have a state of its own, appeared particularly significant at this phase of international history. However, ethno-national groups in Europe, caught up in the political and territorial grip of multinational empires, had raised demands for their own states. There was no single consensus on whether all nations had the right to determine their own form of state or had the right to self-determination. After the end of the First World War, the principle of national self-determination was used by the victorious

*Ending the impasse* 229

powers as a convenient tool for the reorganisation of Europe by splitting up the defeated territories in Eastern Europe, the Balkan and the Middle East to create new nations. At this stage, the application of the principle of self-determination had proved to be arbitrary, contradictory, and self-serving at the hands of big powers. The League of Nations rejected the principle of national self-determination, but it later came to capture the minds of the colonial world for national liberation. Thus, the birth of the principle of self-determination as a precept of international law has been rooted in ambivalence and in contradiction since its inception.

The end of the Second World War paved the way for the emergence of a new world order with the establishment of the UN. The UN took a stand for decolonising the world from the colonial powers through legitimisation of the principle of self-determination of people. It was extensively used in the context of colonial situation which recognised 'the people' instead of 'the nation' to have a right to exercise the principle of self-determination, resulting in emergence of several new independent states from the decolonised world. Article 1(2) of the Charter of the UN contains 'the self-determination of people as a defining goal of the organization'. Article 55 of the UN Charter further emphasises that 'the UN shall promote goals such as higher standards of living, full employment, and human rights with a view to the creation of conditions of stability and well being which are necessary for peaceful and friendly relations among nations based on respect for the principle of equal rights and self-determination of peoples'. Article 1(3) justifies the application of the principle of self-determination to all peoples without any restriction as to their status and obligation is on all states, including those having responsibility for the administration of (colonial) territories.[2] It states that all state parties to the covenant should take positive action to facilitate realisation and respect for the right to self-determination. Similarly, the African Charter of Human Rights has also applied this principle to both colonised and oppressed people.[3] However, a wider application of the principle outside the colonial practice cannot be overruled. The application of self-determination is also applied by different states with objectives to satisfy their own people within the respective territories. Such examples of application of self-determination can be drawn from the United Kingdom in respect of Ireland and Scotland, Quebec in Canada, Canton and Commune autonomy of Switzerland and Norway in respect of the 'Sami' people. The international community is also accepting the wider application of this principle for eradication of any form of oppression of the people and protection of human rights. Thus, self-determination principle applies to all people subjected to any form of oppression by subjugation, domination and exploitation by others, and it is

230　*Dilip Gogoi*

fundamental to maintenance of international peace and stability, and protection of national unity and integrity.

However, the right to exercise self-determination by people is often encountered with broadly two forms of demand, i.e. 'external' and 'internal' self-determination (McCorquodale 1994:863). The logic of seeking 'external' self-determination, which was frequently used during colonial times, implies its application to the territory of a country, its division, and enlargement of a state's external relations with other states or incorporation of new territories. The UN General Assembly also adhered to the three main methods for exercising the right to self-determination as emergence as a sovereign independent state, free association with an independent state and integration with an independent state.[4] The 'internal' aspect of the right to self-determination applies to the peoples to determine their position within a country, their participation in own political affairs including forming government without outside intervention, resource use and distribution, autonomy over formulating independent policies etc. In other words, application of such kind of principle affects the internal aspect of state sovereignty, which generally challenges the centralised structure of the state system.

However, a major debate has emerged whether the principle of self-determination would be applicable to the post-colonial situation with a right to exercise secession and external self-determination. The history of the UN shows that once attained independence and statehood by the people of former colonies, the UN is very much reluctant to recognise the fact that the sub-nationalist groups within an already liberated post-colonial state have right to have their own state and also the right to secede. In other words, the UN is in favour of territorial integrity of the member state which has reflected in the UN General Assembly Resolution. It has stated that 'all people have the right to self-determination', and also categorically stated that 'nothing in the foregoing paragraph should be constituted as authorising or encouraging any action which would dismember or impair totally or in part the territorial integrity or political unity of sovereign and independent states'.[5]

However, a few exceptions to it can be mentioned in the post-colonial period. In case of the secession of Bangladesh from Pakistan in 1971, the UN accorded the recognition after three years of its statehood. Earlier, the UN refused to recognise the two states of Katanga in the (Belgian) Congo and Biafra in Nigeria in the sub-Saharan Africa. The UN, through its Security Council Resolution of 169 of 24 November 1961, condemned the Secessionist Movement in Katanga and also stated that violation of Congo territorial integrity was not acceptable. However, the UN has recognised a few countries that acquired independent status as a result of unilateral

*Ending the impasse* 231

secession and armed conflicts such as Slovenia in 1991, Croatia in 1991 and Eritrea in 1993. The UN admitted the Baltic states – Lithuania, Latvia and Estonia – as members of the UN in 1991 after they were formally accorded recognition by the Soviet Union. Earlier these states were independent countries and members of the League of Nations. However the Soviet Union forcefully annexed these three states in 1940. Thus, these three countries emerged out of the principle of right to resolve their future status in free negotiation with the Soviet Union. In these three cases, it is seen that right to secede through self-determination was not exercised. Similarly after dissolution of the Soviet Union, all the states were recognised as independent states by the UN in 1992 after the formal recognition from Russia, but basis was not the principle of self-determination.

However, the history of the independence of East Timor was unique in the sense that it was subsequently recognised as a state on the principle of self-determination within the colonial context in the year 2002 by the UN. Earlier East Timor was a Portuguese colony. Indonesia invaded and made it a part of its territory in 1975. The region was declared by the UN as non-self-governing territory under the Portuguese supervision. The UN insisted the Indonesian authority to withdraw from the territory of East Timor and recognise the right of self-determination of its people. However, the Indonesian authority was reluctant to accept the proposal, which compelled the UN to support the independence cause of East Timorese. Accordingly, an interim administration was formed and a referendum on East Timor's future was held under the auspices of the UN Mission on East Timor. On 20 May 2002, East Timor was declared as an independent country and became a member of the world body.

The position of the international community and the UN on the right to secede and form state on the principle of self-determination outside the colonial context is comprehensible. The UN recognises that if a subnational group within a state demands a state of its own, the matter would fall within the jurisdiction of the respective government. It would be a matter of domestic concerns, and therefore, it is outside the jurisdiction of international law and the UN. However, in case of gross human rights violation, ethnic cleansing, genocide and other forms of crimes against humanity committed by any state, the world body reserves the right to intervene, including armed intervention, to secure the rights of the aggrieved people. Kosovo was such classic example where UN facilitated the people of Kosovo for getting independent statehood in contemporary time. Normally, the UN favours the continuity of the state and respect for territorial integrity of the member state, and therefore, it is not in favour of using the principle of self-determination outside the colonial context to create a new state. Although the UN ritually reiterates that right to self-determination

## 232 *Dilip Gogoi*

is a right that is possessed by all people, past experiences convince us that the world body is traditionally committed to the territorial integrity of its member states.

Despite the reservations of the international community on the issue of national self-determination, the idea continues to politically influence the emerging national groups of post-colonial states. Many post-colonial states have encountered this new challenge as the secessionist movements invoke the principle of national self-determination to justify the right to secede. Initially, the post-colonial states which emerged out of diverse population were believed to be the ultimate forms of political determination of the oppressed people of the colonial world. Subsequently, it is proved to be wrong, as many nationalities, within the post-colonial states, have been posing challenge to the states by claiming national self-determinations and sovereign homeland. The projects of nation-buildings of many post-colonial states have had a strike-back impact on the states. The lesson can be drawn from South Asia where minority and ethno-nationalist groups openly revolted against the states by expressing desire to secede through exercising national self-determination. Such cases are well evidenced from Baluchis in Pakistan; Tamils in Sri Lanka and Punjabis, Kashmiris, Nagas, Assamese and Manipuris in India. Similar challenges sprang out earlier in Canada, Spain, Sudan, Somalia and other regions around the world. These challenges are coming out from the minority groups which are subjected to suppression and injustice within the state.

Significantly a number of declarations and resolutions were adopted by the UN to protect the endangered rights of the minorities within nation-states. On 18 December 1992 the General Assembly adopted Declaration on *the Rights of Persons Belonging to National or Ethnic, Religious and Linguistic Minorities* which obliged the member states to protect the cultural diversity and identities of their own states. It states that persons belonging to minorities have the right to enjoy their own culture, to profess and practice their own religion and use their own language freely, and to exercise their individual and collective rights without discrimination. The UN also adopted the Declaration *on the Rights of Indigenous People, 2007* with a desire to achieve similar objectives to protect and promote the rights of indigenous peoples within the member states and around the world.

Similarly, the UN General Assembly, in its declaration in Commemoration of the Fiftieth Anniversary of the UN on 9 November 1995, reinstated the fact that 'the international community will not tolerate any violation of the principle of territorial integrity as long as the states conduct themselves in compliance with the principle of equal rights and self-determination, and as long as the government represents the entire people. The Vienna Declaration and Programme of Action, which was adopted at the World

*Ending the impasse* 233

Conference on Human Rights 25 June 1993 in Vienna, mentioned that 'the principle of territorial integrity applied (only) to governments representing the whole people belonging to the territory without distinction of any kind'. The position of the UN is that 'any attempt to partially or totally disrupt the national unity and the territorial integrity of a country is incompatible with the purposes and principles of the charter'. However, 'if the concerned government does not uphold the rights of all sections of society, particularly the minority and ethnic groups, the commitment of the UN to maintaining the territorial integrity of its member states might not hold'(Chandhoke 2012:171).

Thus, the commonly agreed point is that exercise of the right to self-determination doesn't essentially mean the right to secede. As the existence of the multinational empires and the process of decolonisation are formally over, the principle of self-determination needs to be rediscovered to suit the aspirations of the minorities and other ethno-national groups within the recognised states. The exercise of self-determination does not have to be engrossed with the formal break-up of the territory of a state except when the concerned state denies self-determination to the minority and other ethno-national groups. If the ethnic minorities have been subjected to institutionalise injustice and systematic discrimination in the larger socio-cultural and politico-economic milieu in the state, it is oblivious that the group rights will be suffered and their right to self-determination will be seriously jeopardised.

The question remains: how to remove the inequalities which are subjected to the ethnic minorities and have an equitable, non-discriminatory balance practice in an ethnically divided society? It is the most challenging task for the post-colonial states like India. To realise internal self-determination, the standard state practice suggests that minority ethnic groups which are at risk must be granted both universal (the right not to be discriminated against) and special group rights (Chandhoke 2012:178). Group rights are essential because individual members cannot exercise self-determination from a marginal and unequal position. In this respect, group rights are important for the meaningful exercise of individual rights in liberal democracy (Kymlicka 1995). Recognition of these two rights neutralises the secessionist demands of ethnic minorities. Group rights, which protect individual members of the vulnerable communities, constitute a precondition for the realisation of self-determination. It makes self-determination a constitutive part of democracy. The institutionalisation of this particular form of self-determination arguably would remove the tendencies of secessionism because it will allow the potential dissenters to transform into stakeholders of the system. In case of Northeast India, the multiple ethnic existences in an extremely contested territory with varied demands from

## 234 *Dilip Gogoi*

autonomy to secession by ethnic groups in the name of self-determination make the region one of the most unstable and politically explosive zones in the post-colonial world.

## Way forward: ending the impasse through a common ethnic house

Granting autonomy for realising self-determination of people to a region within a state is often puzzled with twin dichotomies: one view emphasises that granting autonomy will lead to secession, whereas the other view takes an opposite position by arguing that it will defuse secession and strengthen the democracy. 'Autonomy does not promote secession; on the contrary, true autonomy prevent secession.'[6] The democratic states have a good track record of settling conflict and defusing secession. Moreover, in well-established democracies such conflicts are witnessed less than in states in the democratising path. Liberal societies with the tradition of democracy and rule of law can preserve best the diversity and unity in a plural state. Many examples can be drawn on the techniques of managing diversity through granting regional autonomy around the world. Canada has adopted policies – both symmetrical for the most part of the country and asymmetrical for Quebec region and other aboriginals. China exercises 'one country two system' for the reunification of Hong Kong and Macau. Australia redefines its relationship with the Aboriginal peoples without territorial arrangement. Ethiopia grants the rights of its 'nations, nationalities and people' to seek wide-ranging powers as states within a federal arrangement and even recognises the right to secede. Relative stability through granting autonomy has been established in Nigeria, Spain, South Africa, Indonesia, Papua New Guinea and others. Considering the complexities of administering diverse states, autonomy through institutional innovation is found to be a viable option across the globe to minimise conflict and realise self-determination of people, in spite of its own difficulties.

Therefore, there is a call for granting self-determination of people through granting comprehensive federal autonomy and innovative common institution in India's Northeast for better governance and recognition of the region. At present, insufficient autonomy and *ad hoc* approach towards the region and its people provides neither true autonomy nor realisation of self-determination of ethnic people, resulting in multiple ethnic crises. The Indian state needs to realise its limitations of the existing arrangement and probe into the causes of such ongoing crises so that it can rightfully address the aspirations of ethnic people of the region. An imperative for a new initiative with an innovative arrangement for granting regional autonomy in the region is strongly felt. This process needs to be treated as a continuous

*Ending the impasse* 235

process of mutual communication, dialogue and accommodation between state and society within a liberal democratic and constructivist framework.

Here I would like to propose an alternative model of governance, encompassing the north-eastern region within the broad framework of consociational democracy[7] (Lijphart 1977:1) in India to overcome the present state of multiple crises. It is necessary on the part of the Government of India to realise the sensitivities underlying the crises and address the Northeast 'exceptionalism'[8] in the Indian Union through a comprehensive arrangement by inserting appropriate clauses in the constitution. The ethnic group–specific piecemeal approach within the present constitutional framework of India towards the crisis-ridden Northeast may engineer more conflicts instead of solving existing crises. The primary reason of such apprehension is that the Northeast is an ethnically divided and territorially contested region. It has also a different and wounded past in a cultural sense among the native ethnic minds which is often ignored by the mainstream-centric policymakers and representative institutions in the name of 'one nation, one identity'. Generally, ethnic groups are not prepared to give up their own small identities at the cost of one larger national identity. In a reasonable way, one has to agree that the Northeast is a unique zone of the Indian Union not only in geographical sense but also from ethno-political histories. All north-eastern states, although they are artificially created units, have organic linkages and mutual interdependence among themselves. Within this distinct zone, it is also equally true that the artificial ethnic territories and overlapping historical memories are common in the region; however, it is subjected to intense contestation. Instead of more segregation of the Northeast into small part one after another, time has come to visualise a common trans-ethnic space and form a trans-ethnic political community for better future of the people of the region, keeping in the mind equal recognition for multi-ethnicities. This logic justifies creating a trans-ethnic federating unit – a form of 'Common Ethnic House' on the line of liberal constructivist idea, as an inclusive alternative model of governance to ensure the group autonomy and promote collective well-being of the people of the Northeast. Selective policy interventions in case of Assam or Nagaland or Manipur may invite further complexities instead of solving the ongoing problem. It is difficult to have a consociational arrangement in an ethnically divided society, but it is not impossible to realise if ethnic communities have a collective will and desire to achieve the goals. The proposed model must recognise non-territorial basis of political arrangement and guarantee equal group autonomy and scope for sharing power among the communities. These recognitions may give more democratic space for dialogue and provide better scope for managing indigenous affairs by ruling out the probability of dominance by one

236   *Dilip Gogoi*

upon others. This would invariably provide the way for political stability, security and prosperity to the region. If we can agree that the present state of dismay in the Northeast is socially engineered and politically constructed, then possibilities of reversal of the situation is also equally greater under the proposed consociational democratic arrangement by incorporating all ethnic groups and democratising their group aspirations with greater degree of rationality and reality of life.

The idea of a Common Ethnic House – an inclusive institution for the Northeast – may give some degree of security to ethnic communities and also give an opportunity to manage their common properties through control over decentralised power and utilisation of own resources. The people of Northeast can draw a lesson from the US federalism, where regional units are more powerful in managing own affairs. Such arrangement is particularly relevant in respect of the Northeast in the Indian Union. Because geographically India is a large country, such arrangement will allow for the reconciliation of the national as well as regional principles with a greater degree of flexibility and cooperation. Devaluation of power and control over resources to regional body deepens democracy because local people have a greater access to regional body than a geographically distant centre. Moreover such arrangement ensures active participation, representation and greater degree of accountability in public institutions.

In this regard, the idea of a 'Common Ethnic House' – a form of non-territorial Ethnic Union of Northeast India – may not be inconsistent with the Indian democracy. Rather it would facilitate the greater strength of Indian democracy. The proposed regional body should meet the following objectives:

i    Recognise group autonomy and realise the internal self-determination of people of Northeast

ii   Recognise the diversity and at the same time unity for the region

iii  Protect the rights of every ethnic nationality and citizens of the region with an equitable principle.

iv   Neutralise the demands for right to secede from the Indian Union by democratising the aspirations of ethnic nationalities.

v    Empower the ethnic groups to resolve conflicts emerging from the region and in relation with the central government and manage common affairs democratically by themselves.

vi   Liberate the region from the geographical as well as economic trap of both the mainland India and neighbouring areas by building 'region-states'[9] and maximise the opportunity of liberal economic order for promoting regional economic development by connecting the greater Southeast Asian region through India's Look East Policy.

*Ending the impasse* 237

To organise a non-territorial federating unit for Common Ethnic House is a challenging task. Before initiating any move, it is necessary to have comprehensive dialogues among the ethnic groups of the region as well as with the stakeholders of state agencies for developing the 'common will' and functional modalities for the House. While doing so it has to be kept in mind that it should not affect the present Northeast states, organised under the Union of India. The existing states should remain as it were and would continue to perform the constitutional duties as essential structural units of the Indian Union and provide uniform basic services to the people. The proposed House is to be organised covering north-eastern region's ethnic and other reasonably identifiable social groups on the basis of non-territorial arrangement and principle of equal representation, based on adult franchise along with representation of women. The competitive party politics may be avoided at the initial stage. The principle of self-declaration – a form of volunteerism – is to be followed while recognising the membership of an individual of a particular ethnic or social group. The imposition of identity mark through census and other declarations by the state, which was inherited from the British colonial policy, should be discarded. The proportional representation on the basis of population size of the group is to be discouraged to give a sense of equality among all groups of the region to overcome the problem of social marginality of various groups arising out of the suppression of the dominant groups and the existing state structures. The proposed body can also give a sense of historic justice by incorporating the people of ethnic communities, living outside the region and country. Since it would be a non-territorial representative body of ethnic groups, it should give the opportunity to the divided communities living across the country and international borders to be a part of its own community affairs. The globalisation and changing practice of state sovereignty would make possible visualising such arrangement and integration of ethnic people with their own diasporas, living abroad. It can be one of the mediums of connecting the people not only with the rest of the world but also to the world's knowledge economy. One can draw inspiration in this context from the South Indian communities about how they maximise the economic benefits from Southeast Asia and Middle East. To achieve development the Northeast region cannot remain isolated. It is necessary to enlarge the geographic construct of the Northeast into a common economic region by recognising the trans-border inter- and intra-ethnic linkages of ethnic communities within and outside the region. It is also pertinent to mention that due to historical reasons and colonial interventions, for example, many tribes of the Nagas, the Mizos, Kukis and other small communities were divided between two sovereign countries – India and Myanmar – upsetting ethnic linkages and trade practices. Similarly,

238 *Dilip Gogoi*

the 1947 partition of British India caused the same harm to the Chakmas in Mizoram, the Khasis and Garos in Meghalaya, Tripuri, the Reang and other small tribes in Tripura. Koch-Rajbanshis in lower Assam, now scattered across Assam, West Bengal, Nepal and Bangladesh, are demanding a Kamatapur State. Here lesson can be drawn from the Nordic Sami Council,[10] where I witnessed in Sami areas about how they organised their own affairs and exercised autonomy since its establishment in 1956. It is a cooperative elected body, with a transnational character of Sami people, living across four sovereign states – Norway, Sweden, Finland and Russia. The aim of the Sami Council is to promote the interests of the Sami as an individual and as a people. The Council's responsibility is to ensure cultural, economic and social rights of the Sami people through appropriate legislations and agreements with the respective countries in the Sami-inhabited areas. Promotion of similar line of idea can benefit the Northeast, but we need to evolve the modality to suit the multi-ethnic character of the region so that apart from maintaining the specific group autonomy, it can also protect the collective interest of the people of the entire north-eastern region. Another cause of complexity of the region is internal mobility and changing habitation of ethnic groups across Northeast India – an internal dynamic which has caused a lot of ethnic conflicts and border tensions, making border areas violent, conflict-prone zones. Internal turf wars have already been witnessed several times in the borders of Manipur–Nagaland, Assam–Nagaland, Assam–Meghalaya and Assam–Arunachal, which caused death of innocent civilians, displacement of hundreds of people and destruction of properties. The present-day, inter-state boundary disputes are largely contributed by the colonial legacies of the practice of Inner Line[11] separating the hills from the plains of Assam. The creation of new states one after another on the basis of singular ethnic identity in the region by the central government further heightens the aggressive ethno-nationalist movements, ranging from autonomous territory to sovereign homeland. Therefore, the idea of a Common Ethic House in the context of the Northeast is quite logical and much needed to look after the common affairs and sort out the differences among ethnic groups through exchanges of dialogue and reconciliation among themselves instead of looking at the central government for unilateral solution at every time, when crisis arises.

In the functional sphere, the proposed House should act as a common deliberative body, but not a legislative one, at the initial period of its existence.[12] It should be in a position to supervise as well as recommend matters relating to the Northeast to the Union Government and the states concerned. Without the approval of this proposed House, no executive and legislative actions from the states of the region as well as the Union which affect the purely common interests and inter-state matters of the

*Ending the impasse* 239

region should be implemented. Besides, the body can deliberate and form opinions on the issues of internal self-determination of ethnic groups, protecting regional-level collective rights and group-specific cultural rights, trans-boundary issues, indigenous land rights, internal border management, trans-border migration issue, region's natural resource management, utilisation of common water resources and river basins, inter-state transport communications, sustainable regional economic development, region's diasporas issues, maximising transnational economic opportunity of India's Look East Policy and other subjects which relate to common interest of the region. Most importantly the House can act as a regional planning as well as dispute settlement body. The body should represent the collective will and perform collective responsibility for the people of Northeast. Any administrative and legislative matters, initiated by the Union and the state governments, affecting common interest and inter-state relations of the region must be tabled before the House. At present the Union Parliament by a simple legislation under Article 3 of the Constitution can create a new state without the formal approval of the affecting states as the subject matter directly comes under the jurisdiction of the Union Government. It affects the entire north-eastern region badly and also promotes ethnic divisive politics. Therefore, Common House is essential to overcome the existing shortcomings and solve the ongoing multi-ethnic crises. This exercise should be viewed as complementary to the existing structures of the states for better understanding and better governance, not an impediment to the state. A comprehensive constitutional design is required for the region in the form of separate constitutions like Jammu and Kashmir, which would be organically linked with the Indian Constitution. Here the existing Sixth Schedule of the Indian Constitution could be rearranged by enlarging its scope to cover the entire Northeast through constitutional reforms. None of these exercises shall mean to encourage centrifugal forces of the Indian nation-state. Rather, it means to strengthen Indian democracy by means of accommodating diversity in a suitable way for better governance. Since there is not a single Upper House – Legislative Council[13] – in any north-eastern state, the imperative is to build a Common House for promoting common interest with equal representation and recognition of ethnic communities by suitably arranging the Indian Constitution for a better solution to the problems affecting the region. It requires a holistic approach and constitutional amendment of Article 168 by using Article 368 in order to provide provision for such common house under the Indian Constitution, exclusively applicable to the north-eastern region.[14]

The time has come to rediscover the Northeast both by the people of the region and the Indian nation-state. The region has been grossly exploited and mismanaged by both the colonial power and the post-colonial Indian

240  *Dilip Gogoi*

state without considering much of the interests of local ethnic people, making the colonial thesis relevant till date. In other words, the political and economic destiny of the people of the Northeast since the days of the British is largely shaped by the people from outside the region. Past history tells us that history of the state formation in the region has never been uniform throughout the medieval period. Before colonial intervention, there were no group-specific ethnic boundaries. Even territorially identifiable distinct political boundaries in modern sense were absent among the ruling kingdoms in the region. Although they fought with each other occasionally, there was a shared past and exchange among them. The notion of modern territorial state, which is essentially a European origin, has been introduced to the region by the British. They divided the people by creating artificial territories for promoting colonial interest. In the process, age-old traditional linkages among the ethnic groups were disrupted. Further, during the British days a major demographic upheaval was witnessed in the region primarily due to the large-scale immigrant influx from the Bengal province of British India. British encouraged them to settle in Assam and work in colonial extractive economy like oil, coal and tea industries.[15] Identity consciousness among the ethnic groups in the region grew out of such demographic penetration and resource captures. The importance of land was subsequently realised by the native people with the introduction of colonial economy. At the same time, land became a scarce resource which was never felt before. Earlier native people of the region were not exposed to such development. For example the *Paik*[16] System of Ahom administration endorsed such claims and it revealed that land had never been a source of revenue of the state. It was primarily because of the British colonial intervention that the importance of land was realised and an ethnic consciousness in the territorial sense among the groups emerged. Similar practices have been legitimised subsequently by the Indian government in post-colonial period that culminated in the present state of ethnic obsession and territorial contestations among the ethnic groups. The British colonial administration also made it a point that sovereignty rested with the colonial power centre and they had a sovereign right to exercise sovereignty over its territory and its subjects. Same notion of 'colonial constitutionalism' (Baruah 2010:7) has been followed by the central government towards the region. However, with changing time and influences of democratic ideas, ethnic people are not prepared to see sovereignty to be exercised purely from the perspective of the central government. They see sovereignty rests with the people and it can be realised only through self-determination and self-development. In this context, considering the past shared history of the region, an idea of 'shared sovereignty'[17] though a non-territorial Common Ethnic House by the ethnic groups is deemed to be an appropriate step to

*Ending the impasse*  241

envisage the region's future. Although idea of 'shared sovereignty' is of a recent origin, similar form of practice well existed in Ahom monarchy in respect of organising the Ahom kingdom and also establishing relations with other neighbouring Kings of Chutias, Kacharis, Nagas, Bhutanese and so on by the Ahoms.[18] As nation-state continuously evolves with new ideas and experiments, India is not an exception to it. The present form of constitutional arrangement of India may not remain always as permanent system as history has witnessed multinational empires changing into nations and subsequently modern nation-states. A serious self-introspection and civic consciousness are required on such direction to shape the future of the region. It requires a comprehensive dialogue among all nationalities and with the state agencies so that a vibrant trans-ethnic political community and a Common Ethnic House can be established for realising greater democratic goals of ethnic nationalities and regional economic development. Without mutual recognition and interdependence, a dynamic region with dynamic communities and liberal institutions, with the guarantee of individual rights, human security and self-determination of people, cannot be realised.

## Notes

1 International Covenant on Economic, Social and Cultural Rights, and International Covenant on Civil and Political Rights adopted by UN General Assembly on 16 December 1966.
2 Article 1(3), International Covenant on Civil and Political Rights adopted by UN General Assembly on 16 December 1966.
3 Article 20(2), African Charter on Human and Peoples' Rights, adopted by OAU, 27 June 1981.
4 The UN General Assembly Resolution 1541(XV), Principle – VI, 15 December 1960.
5 The UN General Assembly Resolution, 2625 (XXV), 24 October 1970 on *Declaration of Principles of International Law on Friendly Relations and Co-operation among States in Accordance with the Charter of the United Nations.*
6 This is one of lessons that Yash Ghai draws by analysing the experience of autonomy through case studies. For further discussion see Ghai 2000. 'Ethnicity and Autonomy: A Framework for Analysis' in Yash Ghai. ed. *Autonomy and Ethnicity: Negotiating Competing Claims in Multi-Ethnic States.* Cambridge University Press.
7 According to Arend Lijphart consociational democracy consists of two important features: power sharing – which implies the participation of representative of all communities in political decision making; and group autonomy – which justifies the right of every group to have authority to run their own internal affairs.
8 'Northeast exceptionalism' the term is used by Samir Kumar Das in writing 'Governing the Ungovernable: India's Northeast', 2012, p. 33. He opines

242  *Dilip Gogoi*

that 'India's Northeast is viewed from so called mainland India is a part of India without really being a part'. Further he argues that Northeast exceptionalism constantly pulls it back from becoming a part of India.

9  The term is used by Kenichi Ohmae to refer to the natural economic zones, may be within a country or straddle the borders of two or more countries. The concept is quite relevant in the context of Northeast India. For more explanation see Ohmae, Kenichi. 1993. 'The Rise of the Region-state', *Foreign Affairs*, 172(2), pp. 78–87.

10  The Council is constituted with fifteen representatives: five from Norway, four from Sweden, four from Finland and two from Russia. The Sami people, approximately 40,000 in Norway, 20,000 in Sweden, 7,500 in Finland and 2,000 in Russia, are recorded in *The Sami People – A Handbook*, Karasjok 2006. I had an opportunity to visit the Sami areas particularly Karasjok, Alta and Kautokeino as a visiting scholar to the International Peace Research Institute (PRIO), Oslo, in 2009. After a long field trip and interactions with the local Sami leading personalities and common people, and visiting the Sami University College, Sami Parliament, Sami Radio and Television Centre, I am amazed to see how Sami people managed their own community affairs, revived their language and culture and subsequently became a champion for protection and promotion of the Rights of World's Indigenous People. I sincerely acknowledge Åshild Kolås, Research Fellow at PRIO for her effort to make me understand the Sami People's indigenous affairs which helped me relate with my study.

11  The colonial administration introduced the Inner Line under the Bengal Eastern Frontier Regulation of 1873 to demarcate the settled and unsettled areas of the British administration on the pretext of protecting the colonial interest in the region. It imposed restriction on British subjects' entry into beyond Inner Line. Accordingly, the plains districts of Assam fell within the Inner Line and the tribal areas of hills fell beyond the Inner Line. For more information see Gait, Edward 1926. (Reprint) *A History of Assam*. Guwahati: Lawyers Book Stall, pp. 316–17.

12  Till the consolidation of the idea of Common Ethnic House and functionally viable with political legitimacy from the entire region.

13  Assam had an Upper House for 10 years from 1937 to 1947 under the Government of India Act 1935. N. G. Mahanta argues in favour of an idea for formation of Ethnic Council in Assam along the line of Upper House of the state. However my opinion is that creating a state-specific non-territorial Ethnic Council will not serve the purpose and will follow the same constitutional procedure which will be neither helpful for solving the intra- and inter-ethnic problems nor will it allow the ethnic communities to exercise self-determination in true sense. Unless the Northeast is reunited under a common platform with a collective will, the problem of suppression-exclusive politics will remain and the ethnic people of the region will be subjected to more injuries in the near future. For Mahanta's view see his book *Confronting the States: ULFA's Quest for Sovereignty*. New Delhi: Sage, 2013. pp. 304–8.

14  Article 168 of the Indian Constitution contains a provision for creation or abolition of an Upper House-State Council in a state. Here, it is argued that the article should be amended suitably for creating a common house along the line of Upper House to look after the common affairs of the

*Ending the impasse* 243

entire north-eastern region. Article 368 provides provision for amendment of the Indian Constitution. Recently, the government of Assam has proposed to the Centre for creation of a Legislative Council for the state as per the provision of the Constitution to meet the aspiration of ethnic demand for statehood. However my opinion is that without suitably creating a provision and also enlarging its scope, exclusively applicable to the region to ensure that ethnic representation through constitutional amendment, creation of the Legislative Council, as proposed, for the state will not be able to solve the ongoing ethnic crises in the region.

15 Myron Weiner has given a detailed account on the migration trends and impact of plantation and Bengali Muslim migrants into Assam under the British rule in chapter three titled 'When migrants succeed and natives fail: Assam and its migrants'. pp. 75–138. For details see Weiner, Myron 1978. *Son of the Soil: Migration and Ethnic Conflict in India*. New Delhi: Oxford University Press.

16 The *Paik* system was a regular feature of Ahom's administration in order to render services to the state. No organised revenue system was in place. The *Paiks* were generally foot soldiers. Under this system, between the age group of fifteen and fifty, except nobles, priests and few others, the normal male population had to serve the state The *Paiks* were organised – twenty *paiks* commanded by a Borah, one hundred by a Saikia, one thousand by a Hazarika, three thousand by a Rajkhowa, and six thousand by a Phukan.

17 For reference and practice of 'shared sovereignty' see Williams, Paul R. and Pecci, Francesca Jannotti 2004. 'Earned Sovereignty: Bridging the Gap Between Sovereignty and Self-Determination', *Stanford Journal of International Law*, 40(1): 14–17.

18 The inter-community exchanges in Ahom days were known as *Posa* System. For details of Ahom's relations with other groups, see Devi, Lakshmi 1968. *Ahom-Tribal Relations: A Political Studies*. Guwahati: Lawyers Book Stall.

# References

Baruah, Sanjib. 2010. 'AFSPA: Legacy of Colonial Constitutionalism', *Seminar*, No. 615: 7–14.

Chandhoke, Neera. 2012. *Contested Secessions: Rights, Self-Determination, Democracy, and Kashmir*. New Delhi: Oxford University Press.

Das, Samir K. 2012. *Governing the Ungovernable: India's Northeast*. (Lecture series). Guwahati: Centre for Peace and Conflict Studies, Gauhati University.

Devi, Lakshmi. 1968. *Ahom-Tribal Relations: A Political Study*. Guwahati: Lawyers Book Stall.

Gait, Edward. 1926. (Reprint) *A History of Assam*. Guwahati: Lawyers Book Stall.

Ghai, Yash. 2000. 'Ethnicity and Autonomy: A Framework for Analysis'. In Yash Ghai (ed.), *Autonomy and Ethnicity: Negotiating Competing Claims in Multi-Ethnic States*. Cambridge: Cambridge University Press.

Kymlicka, Will. 1995. *Multicultural Citizenship: A Liberal Theory of Minority Rights*. Oxford: Clarendon Press.

244   *Dilip Gogoi*

Lijphart, Arend. 1977. *Democracy in Plural Societies.* New Heaven: Yale University Press.

Mahanta, Nani G. 2013. *Confronting the State: ULFA's Quest for Sovereignty.* New Delhi: Sage Publications.

McCorquodale, Robert. 1994. 'Self-Determination: A Human Rights Approach', *International and Comparative Law Quarterly*, 43: 857–85.

Ohmae, Kenichi. 1993. 'The Rise of the Region-State', *Foreign Affairs*, 172(2): 78–87.

Parel, Anthony J., ed. 2009. (Centenary edition) *'Hind Swaraj' and Other Writings.* New Delhi: Cambridge University Press.

Solbakk, John T. 2006. *The Sami People – A Handbook.* Karasjok: Davvi Girji OS.

The International Covenant on Civil and Political Rights adopted by UN General Assembly on 16 December 1966.

The African Charter on Human and Peoples' Rights, adopted by OAU, 1981.

The UN General Assembly Resolution 1541(XV), Principle – VI, 15 December, 1960.

The UN General Assembly Resolution, 2625(XXV), 24 October 1970 on *Declaration of Principles of International Law on Friendly Relations and Co-operation among States in Accordance with the Charter of the United Nations.*

The UN General Assembly Declaration on *the Rights of Persons Belonging to National or Ethnic, Religious and Linguistic Minorities*, 18 December 1992.

*The Vienna Declaration and Programme of Action*, 1993.

*The UN Declaration on the Rights of Indigenous Peoples*, 2007.

Weiner, Myron. 1978. *Son of the Soil: Migration and Ethnic Conflict in India.* New Delhi: Oxford University Press.

Williams, Paul R. and Francesca J. Pecci. 2004. 'Earned Sovereignty: Bridging the Gap Between Sovereignty and Self-Determination', *Stanford Journal of International Law*, 40(1): 1–40.

# Glossary

*Jati*  Nation
*Jatiyotabad*  Nationalism
*Mahajati*  Multi-nation or Great Nation
*Paradhinotar Duhswapna*  The Nightmare of Subjugation
*Sarbabhoumo Asom*  Sovereign Assam
*Satra*  Religious institution of Vaishnavite in Assam
*Swabalambita*  Self-reliance
*Swadhin Asom*  Independent Assam
*Swadhinatar Prastab*  The Proposal for Independence
*Swargadeu*  Royal address to the Ahom king, meaning descendent from Heaven in local language.
*Ulfocide*  It infers from the nature of some crimes committed with 'remote orchestration' and is used to describe the principle of 'kill and get killed'.

# Index

AASA *see* All Assam Students'
Association
agitation 97, 138–40, 142, 153;
anti-foreigners 97, 139–41
AGP government 64, 124, 192
All Assam Students' Association
(AASA) 138–9
All Assam Students' Union (AASU)
9, 17, 61–2, 97–8, 105, 120, 124,
133, 138–42, 152, 216, 218–19
All India United Democratic Front
(AIUDF) 99–100, 126–8
anti-foreigners agitation 97–8,
139–41; *see also* Assam movement
Armed Forces Special Powers Act
(AFSPA) 10, 18, 22–4, 168, 193
Asom Gana Parishad (AGP) 59, 65,
70, 98, 121, 124, 127–8, 141,
173, 181, 195, 220
*Asom ganatrantik nagarik sangstha*
(Assam Democratic Citizens'
Association) 192–6
Asom Jatiyatabadi Yuba Chatra Parishad
(AJYCP) 62, 181, 196, 203
aspirations 11, 79, 135, 137–8, 202,
206, 227–8, 233–4, 236
assailants 172, 174, 179–80
Assam: civil society in 73, 186–8,
200; culture of 42–4, 134; demand
of 41, 45; developments in 60,
147; ethnic communities of 65,
67; government 79, 84, 95, 98–9,
101, 105, 119, 136, 153–4, 179,
199, 201; human rights violation
in 165–83; independence 187–8,

190; indigenous communities of
52, 101; languages 53, 59–60, 96,
134, 138, 140, 144–51, 153–5,
157, 218; languages 36, 59–60,
96, 134, 138, 140, 144–51,
153–5, 157, 218; leadership 55,
61, 150, 152; literature 133–4;
middle class 62, 138, 141, 148,
158; multi-cultural existence of
144, 155–7; nation, distinct 41,
45; nationalism 6–10, 17, 30, 35,
40, 49, 59, 65, 80, 133–5, 138,
140, 209–10, 216–18, 220–1;
nationality question in 193; official
language of 36, 147, 154; people
of 40, 42–5, 52–3, 55, 59, 61, 63,
66–7, 133, 137, 142, 146, 149,
153, 216–18; politics 62, 119,
127, 150, 168; population of
218–19; resources of 43–4, 57,
60, 67; self-determination of 30–1,
35, 37, 41, 46; society of 38, 59,
82, 84, 100, 133, 140, 145–6,
156, 158, 188, 216–17, 220; state
language of 137, 148–9; student
movements in 139; students 134,
140; tea gardens of 43, 56–7, 60;
tribune 73–4, 76–8, 146, 206–7
Assam Accord 97–8, 102, 105, 116,
118–19, 126, 140–2, 172, 224
Assam Association 61, 134
Assam Democratic Citizens'
Association 191–2
Assamese elites 96, 134–6, 138, 140,
218

## 248 *Index*

Assamese identity 8, 10, 49–50, 59, 134, 138, 144–9, 151–3, 155, 157–9, 218, 221; composite 9, 65, 134; distinct 118, 219; ethnic 134, 216–17
Assamese language 148–52
Assamese nationalism 216–20; accommodation 221–4; disintegration of 220–1
Assamese nationhood 30–47; nation-making process 41
Assam Legislative Council 92, 136
Assam Movement 61, 63, 117–21, 124, 126, 128, 138–40, 153, 202–3, 209, 216, 218–21

Bangladesh, illegal immigrants 102, 106, 124
Barbora, P. K. 82
Barpujari, H. K. 108
Baruah, A. K. 138
Baruah, Sanjib 108
Bharatiya Janata Party (BJP) 64, 123–4, 126–8
Bhattacharjya, Kamalakanta 35
Bodo language 151, 153–5, 220
Bodo Sahitya Sabha (BSS) 151–6, 179
BSS *see* Bodo Sahitya Sabha

Cachar Political Conference 140
Chandra, Bipan 55
Charter of Demands 79–80, 205
Chatterjee, Partha 13
citizenship 4, 9, 22, 26, 90, 106–7, 109, 114–20, 122–3, 125, 127, 129; crisis of 118–21; and migrant in Assam 116–18; theoretical perspective on 115–16
civil society 9–10, 20–1, 82–3, 158, 166, 182, 186–8, 191, 194, 197, 207, 216, 220, 225; trans-ethnic 10, 186–7
Communist Party of India (CPI) 50, 65, 127, 172–3
counterclaims 8, 70–1, 83
counter-insurgency operations 168–71
cultural identity 39–40, 97, 117, 122, 145, 152, 157–8, 213, 218, 224

cultural interests 145, 157
cultural rights 165–6, 223, 225, 239

Das, Parag Kumar 51–8, 66–7
Deka, Kanaksen 58, 60, 61, 66
delineation 115–17
democracy 10, 39, 174, 205, 209–12, 214–15, 220–3, 228, 233–4; and ethnic nationalism 210–12; success or failure 214–16
demographic uniqueness 25
demonstration effect 33–4, 37
denial of rights 173–4
deportation 95, 97, 99, 105–6, 118, 120, 123, 126
Dima Halim Daoga (DHD) 74–5, 221
documentary citizenship 107, 108

environment, conducive 199, 201, 205–6
ethnic communities 3, 11, 46, 135, 140, 147, 154, 157–8, 187, 222, 227–8, 235–7, 239
ethnic conflict 128, 214, 238
ethnic demands 222
ethnic elites 23–4
ethnic groups 24–6, 36, 38, 100, 135, 140, 145–6, 149, 153–5, 157–8, 212–13, 216, 221, 223, 233–40
ethnic identity 7, 31, 82, 135, 148, 212–13, 216–17, 221
ethnic nationalism 3, 7, 10, 209–10, 214, 217–18, 221, 223; and democracy 210–12; and institutionalisation 212–14
ethnic people 227, 234, 237, 240
ethno-national groups 31, 38, 46, 213–14, 228, 232–3

Foreigners Act 95, 97, 119–21
freedom of expression 174–6

Gait, Edward 55
Gandhi, Mahatma 55
Gellner, Ernest 33
gender dimension 176–7
globalisation 7, 21–2, 237; frontiers of 20–2

*Index* 249

GoA *see* Government of Assam
GoI *see* Government of India
Gopinath Bordoloi government 136
Government of Assam (GoA) 84, 95,
    98–9, 101, 103, 105, 154, 179,
    199, 201
Government of India (GoI) 10, 18,
    77, 79–80, 84, 95, 97, 105, 186,
    188, 190–1, 195–207, 235
group identity 211, 213
group rights 26, 165, 233

hinterlands 22–5
Hobsbawm, Eric 4–5
human rights 22–3, 35, 165–70,
    173, 176, 180, 183, 223, 229,
    233; abuse of 10, 50, 167, 182;
    in Indian Constitution 166–8;
    violation of 9, 165–70, 179, 182

ICCPR *see* International Covenant
    on Civil and Political Rights
ICESCR *see* International Covenant
    on Economic, Social and Cultural
    Rights
identity consciousness 133–42
illegal immigrants 90, 95, 97–9,
    101–2, 105–7, 110, 125, 127
illegal immigration 97, 102, 105,
    106, 109, 110, 141
illegal migrants 97–8, 102, 105, 114,
    117–23, 126, 128
illegal migration 102, 114, 123–4, 128
Illegal Migration Determination by
    Tribunal (IMDT) Act 118–22,
    124, 126; implications of 118–21;
    judicial interpretation of 121–3
immigrant Muslims 65, 100, 102,
    104–5, 109–10
immigrants 9, 21, 71, 89–91, 93–6,
    98–100, 104–7, 110, 119, 136
immigration 8, 43, 71, 89–91, 93,
    95–7, 99–101, 103, 105, 107–9;
    from East Bengal 90–3
independent Assam 18, 30, 35,
    37–8, 46, 49–50, 57–8, 60, 66,
    71, 80, 167, 188, 190–1, 219
Independent Bodoland 3, 72, 83–4
Indian Constitution 19, 100, 109,
    117, 122, 166, 182, 201, 239

Indian democracy 10, 209–10, 214,
    216, 222, 236
indigeneity 89, 91, 93, 95, 97, 99,
    101, 103, 105, 107, 109
indigenous Assamese Muslims
    104, 109
indigenous discontent 102–5
indigenous people: of Assam 8, 141,
    192; rights of 21, 223, 232
indigenous rights 26
INGOs *see* international non-
    governmental organisations
innocent civilians, killing of 181–2
insurgency 63, 71, 81–2, 122–3,
    166–7, 176, 193, 198, 216, 222
insurgents 10, 165–7, 169, 171–3,
    175–7, 179, 181, 183, 193
Integrated Rural Development
    Programme (IRDP) 81
international community 8, 78,
    228–9, 231–2
International Covenant on Civil
    and Political Rights (ICCPR)
    182, 223
International Covenant on
    Economic, Social and Cultural
    Rights (ICESCR) 223
international market 56–7, 67
international non-governmental
    organisations (INGOs) 20–1
Inter-Services Intelligence (ISI) 74,
    77–8, 224

Jennings, Ivor 32

Keane, A. H. 52
kidnappings 177–9

language: minority 151, 154,
    156–7; official 137, 155, 209,
    216, 218; policy 151, 156; tribal
    148–9, 151
legitimacy 8, 23–5, 33, 36, 41–2, 45,
    67, 188–9, 192

multi-ethnic state 30–47
Muslims 44, 90–1, 100–1, 109,
    123–6, 128, 135; immigrants 96,
    99–100, 102
Myanmar 73–4, 77, 224, 237

250 *Index*

Nagaland 18–19, 71–3, 75–7, 79, 137, 189, 222, 225, 235
National Democratic Front of Bodoland (NDFB) 3, 8, 71–2, 74–6, 83, 195, 221
nationalism 4–6, 18, 133, 141, 223; civic 3, 7; pan-Indian 8, 35, 219
national self-determination 30–47
National Register of Citizens (NRC) 97–9, 126, 142; politics of 98–100
national self-determination 30, 32, 45, 228, 232; principle of 33, 45–6, 228–9, 232; theory 39–40
National Socialist Council of Nagaland (NSCN) 3, 8, 19, 71–7, 79, 168, 216, 225
Nehru, Jawaharlal 55

Official Language Bill 138–9
Operation Bajrang 168–9, 172, 192

PCPIA *see* People's Committee for Peace Initiatives in Assam
peace 10, 70, 72, 79, 83, 151, 157, 188, 191, 197, 199, 206–7, 225; process 10, 22, 26, 50, 79, 199–201, 206
People's Committee for Peace Initiatives in Assam (PCPIA) 73, 200
People's Consultative Group (PCG) 73, 79, 191, 196–201, 203
People's Liberation Army (PLA) 71, 75
PLA *see* People's Liberation Army
Plains Tribal Council of Assam (PTCA) 136, 153
plains tribal identity 152–5
Plamentaz 13
political parties 82, 98–9, 105, 107, 120, 157, 172, 204, 212
polity of Assam 124–6
post IMDT Act, electoral trends of 126–8
post-partition scenario 95–6
Prasad, Jyoti 59
PTCA *see* Plains Tribal Council of Assam
public discourse of Assam 49–50, 67

Roychoudhury, Ambikagiri 42, 49, 56, 92

Sahitya Sabhas 154–5
Sami People 238
Sangma, William A. 137
sanmilita jatiya abhibarttan 202–7
Scheduled Tribe (ST) 63, 136–7, 140
SCI *see* Supreme Court of India
secret killings 10, 50, 169, 179–81, 195
security forces 18, 22–4, 78, 80, 166, 169–70, 176, 179, 195, 200
selective policy intervention 11
self-determination 6–7, 17, 21, 26, 30–43, 45–7, 57–8, 64–6, 71, 73, 136, 189, 212–13, 227–34, 240; application of 229; of Assam 30–1, 35, 37, 41, 46; claims 8, 31, 37–40, 42; claims for 31, 34; demand for 31, 39–40, 42; demands 31–2, 35, 37–8, 40–1; ethnicity and 234–41; external 230; history of 228–34; internal 228, 230, 233, 236, 239; movements 8, 40, 58, 64, 66, 209, 214; nationalist theories 40–1; of people 229, 234, 241; realisation of 233–4; rights of 3, 192; status 35
self-government 7, 26
Sharma, Devabrata 8, 62, 64
Shillong 135
society, multinational 34, 38
'sovereign Assam' *(Swadhin Asom)* 6, 8, 52, 70–84
sovereignty 4–9, 17–26, 46–7, 49–50, 54–5, 57–8, 66–7, 82–3, 167, 190, 200, 203–4, 224–5, 230, 240; of Assam 3–4, 6, 8, 40, 45, 50–2, 56–60, 64, 66–7, 70, 72, 79, 84, 201, 224; concept of 224–5; contestations 20–2, 24–6; contests and contradictions 17–26; demand of 51, 60, 62, 83; and national identity 3–5, 7, 9, 11
state authority, central 214–16
state-building process 33–4
Sterling Capital 56
students' movements 133–42

## Index 251

Supreme Court of India (SCI) 98–9, 124, 166
surrendered ULFA (SULFA) 179–80, 183, 195
*Swadhin Asom* (independent Assam) 49–67
*Swadhinatar Prastab* 51

tea gardens, of Assam 43, 56–7, 60
territorial claims 38, 84
Tibeto-Burman influence 53
Tilly, Charles 24
Treaty of Yandabo 61
tribal peasantry 93
tribes 21, 26, 65, 75, 93, 135–6, 145–6, 149–50, 155–7, 220–1, 237–8; communities 93, 103, 135, 146, 149–51, 153, 155, 158, 218
tribunals 95, 98, 114, 118, 120–2, 124–5
turf wars 74

ULFA *see* United Liberation Front of Assam
ULFA–GOI conflict 187–8, 191, 196

United Liberation Front of Assam (ULFA) 3–4, 6–8, 49–51, 57–9, 61–5, 67, 70–84, 141, 167–9, 171–82, 186–8, 190–206, 209–10, 218–21, 223–5; cadres 62, 80, 171–2, 175–8, 181; and civil society 188–91; and Indian state 186–207; kangaroo courts of 171–3; leadership 83–4, 191, 194, 196, 200, 204–5; members 50, 83, 169; militants 50, 73–4, 76, 170, 173, 179; post-PCG developments 201–2; sovereignty demand 80, 190, 203–4
United People's Democratic Solidarity (UPDS) 74–5
United Revolution Movement Council of Assam (URMCA) 172, 192

Vajpeyi, Ananya 23
violence, legitimate use of 21, 23–4

Young, Iris Marion 46